D1566678

Trigger Warnings

Trigger Warnings

History, Theory, Context

Edited by Emily J. M. Knox

Rowman & Littlefield
Lanham • Boulder • New York • London

Published by Rowman & Littlefield
A wholly owned subsidiary of The Rowman & Littlefield Publishing Group, Inc.
4501 Forbes Boulevard, Suite 200, Lanham, Maryland 20706
www.rowman.com

Unit A, Whitacre Mews, 26-34 Stannary Street, London SE11 4AB

British Library Cataloguing in Publication Information Available

Library of Congress Cataloging-in-Publication Data Available

ISBN 9781442273719 (hardback: alk. paper) | ISBN 9781442273726 (electronic)

∞™ The paper used in this publication meets the minimum requirements of
American National Standard for Information Sciences—Permanence of Paper
for Printed Library Materials, ANSI/NISO Z39.48-1992.

Printed in the United States of America

CONTENTS

PREFACE

The use of trigger warnings—written or verbal statements that alert consumers to traumatic media content—is the subject of sometimes heated debates, and for the past three years, there has been a constant stream of articles and blog posts on the use of trigger warnings in academia. New opinion pieces and articles appear in blog posts, the *Chronicle of Higher Education*, and *Inside Higher Ed* at a regular clip. Are trigger warnings merely a courtesy? Are they an imposition on academic freedom? Should institutions regulate their use? Should individual instructors decide?

This book is not intended to settle the debate but rather to provide more in-depth context and theory, as well as a vocabulary for understanding the various arguments for and against using trigger warnings in the college and university classroom. The contributors come from a wide variety of disciplines and fields, which means that the theoretical foundations of each chapter vary widely. The first section of the volume focuses on the history and theory of trigger and content warnings. The chapters are intended to provide context for the use of trigger warnings in the classroom, particularly regarding how using a "heads-up" for traumatic material moved from the online feminist community to the academic classroom, as well as a theoretical analysis of the phenomenon. The second section consists of shorter case studies for using or not using trigger warnings. These range from an empirical study to one person's account of making a request for a trigger warning in a course.

Readers will find that there are arguments with which they strongly agree and others that they strongly oppose in the volume. This is simply the nature of the controversy at this point in time. No matter the reader's position, it is hoped that this book will add some depth of understanding to the trigger warning debate.

ACKNOWLEDGMENTS

First, I'd like to thank all of the contributors to this book. This is my first time editing, and I learned the importance of having clear directions and a spreadsheet. I cannot thank the contributors enough for their patience through all of my newbie mistakes. My editor at Rowman & Littlefield, Charles Harmon, suggested that I take up this topic, since it related to my work on intellectual freedom, and I deeply appreciate his support throughout the development of this volume. My colleagues at the University of Illinois School of Information Sciences, especially Nicole Cooke, are always there to lend an ear and talk through the stickier aspects of any controversial topic. A big shout-out to all my friends in Champaign and beyond! Thank you for listening to me through all of the ups and downs of editing. Finally, I would like to thank my parents, Jo Emily and Nathaniel Knox, for their constant support and love.

INTRODUCTION
On Trigger Warnings
Emily J. M. Knox

At the School of Information Sciences at the University of Illinois at Urbana-Champaign, I teach information policy. As a survey course, we spend each week covering topics such as intellectual property, the information economy, security and privacy, and digital labor. One of the articles that we read for the latter topic is "The Laborers Who Keep Dick Pics and Beheadings out of Your Facebook Feed."[1] The article, from a 2014 issue of *Wired*, is primarily about the invisible labor of people in developing countries who censor photographs on social media. However, it also includes graphic descriptions of some of the photos that the workers have to censor. The author notes that "staring into the heart of human darkness exacts a toll and many of the laborers suffer from PTSD from the trace memories of the images that they view on a daily basis."[2] When I assigned this reading the first time I taught the course, I did not offer a trigger warning or "heads-up" to my students. Was that the right decision? I am not sure. The article itself does not have a trigger warning, and the photos are not the focus of the writing. Would it have made a difference for one of my students if I had offered a warning? I do not know.

The Oxford English Dictionary defines trigger warnings as "a statement at the start of a piece of writing, video, etc. alerting the reader or viewer to the fact that it contains potentially distressing material." Trigger warnings are related to and sometimes contrasted with "content notes," which are statements that warn the reader that the material might contain information that is of a less traumatic nature.[3] Note that many people—including some of the authors in this volume—use these terms interchangeably.

My own ambivalence about trigger warnings and other labeling statements is related to my background in library and information science. The
field of librarianship has long been opposed to the labeling and rating of
materials. Labeling and rating systems are part of a larger issue of social classification and the "power to name," as Hope Olson writes, being given to a
certain few within society.[4] Labeling and classification of materials is never
free of politics and political implications. As Geoffrey Bowker and Susan
Leigh Star state in *Sorting Things Out*, the classification of things constructs
our life world, and all classification systems have a moral, political, and ethical agenda.[5] For example, the "Parental Advisory Explicit Content" stickers
on music with potentially offensive lyrics in many respects divides music into
"good" and "bad" music. There is an implication that music with the sticker
is in some fundamental way different from music without it. The latter is
"clean" while "explicit" music is "dirty." Also, note that an entire genre that
is associated with a minority community, rap and hip-hop, tends to receive
parental advisory labels on a regular basis. Ratings systems are also relevant
to trigger warnings; like other types of labels they are voluntary and seek to
inform the user regarding the content of the material. One of the most well-
known systems, the Motion Picture Association of America's voluntary film
ratings, affixes labels according to language, nudity, sexual content, substance
abuse, and violence. As demonstrated in the film *This Film Is Not Yet Rated*,
these ratings are arbitrary and merely imposed by a small board of ten people
who live in the Los Angeles area. In the field of library and information science, the simultaneously arbitrary and socially constructed nature of labeling
is among the reasons why labels are often met with suspicion.

Opposition to labeling in librarianship began in the 1950s when the
Sons of the American Revolution (SAR) of Montclair, New Jersey, objected to the appearance of communist materials in libraries. While the
SAR argued that such material should be clearly labeled as subversive,
librarians stated that such labeling was a limiting of the freedom to read.
Librarians felt that such labeling operated as a proscription against reading certain topics, since such labels might prejudice patrons toward certain
topics.[6] It would also be a reification of the material. That is, if the book or
magazine is labeled "communist," then it is a communist book or magazine. After some consideration, the statement on labeling—an interpretation of the Library Bill of Rights—was adopted by the American Library
Association in 1951. It stated that "libraries do not advocate the ideas

found in their collections" and "no person should take the responsibility of labeling publication."[7] Many libraries adopted the statement as policy over the following years. In 1971, it was revised to remove the specific paragraphs that referred to communism. The statement was further amended in 1981, 1990, 2005, 2009, and 2014. These subsequent amendments removed focus on legal actions and added information on viewpoint-neutral directional aids. The current interpretation states:

> Prejudicial labels are designed to restrict access, based on a value judgment that the content, language, or themes of the resource, or the background or views of the creator(s) of the resource, render it inappropriate or offensive for all or certain groups of users. The prejudicial label is used to warn, discourage, or prohibit users or certain groups of users from accessing the resource. Such labels sometimes are used to place materials in restricted locations where access depends on staff intervention.
>
> Viewpoint-neutral directional aids facilitate access by making it easier for users to locate resources. Users may choose to consult or ignore the directional aids at their own discretion.
>
> Directional aids can have the effect of prejudicial labels when their implementation becomes proscriptive rather than descriptive. When directional aids are used to forbid access or to suggest moral or doctrinal endorsement, the effect is the same as prejudicial labeling.[8]

I have argued elsewhere[9] that librarians' acceptance of reader-response theory has strengthened their support for intellectual freedom. This acceptance can also be seen in the interpretation above that warns against prejudicial labels. If, as reader-response theory posits, everyone comes to a text with their own baggage, then we cannot know what their response will be to it. A prejudicial label will color that response and may keep them from accessing certain information. It can be argued that trigger warnings are prejudicial labels, as they warn people from accessing a resource. The argument that trigger warnings are a form of censorship seems to be based in this understanding of labeling. However, as I noted above, although my field has taken a strong stance on labeling, like other instructors, I also have moral obligations to more than just my field. I am also concerned about the welfare of my students.

It cannot be denied that some media can be harmful. In my own work,[10] I study why people attempt to ban books in public institutions.

Challengers (those who try to remove, relocate, redact, and restrict material) give many different reasons for their actions: the books are inappropriate for a certain age group, they contain references to drug use, they have stereotypical characterizations of marginalized peoples. However, what all challengers have in common is a belief in the power of reading to change an individual's life. Reading is never a benign or neutral activity— we assign readings in coursework and say things like "this book changed my life" for a reason.

My research centers on what I call "commonsense" interpretations of text wherein the text "means what it says, and says what it means." Challengers from many different political viewpoints argue that texts can only be understood in one way and that this understanding will have a direct effect on the reader. This argument is somewhat similar to the argument made by supporters of trigger warnings. However, the latter would also argue that not everyone would have the same interpretation of a text or be subject to certain traumatic effects but that we must always be aware of those who are vulnerable to such reactions. This is one way in which trigger warnings can be seen as a different kind of tool than the practices of censorship such as restriction, redaction, relocation, and removal.

I remain ambivalent about trigger warnings in the classroom. I do not wish to cause my students harm, yet I am concerned that the materials most likely to have trigger warnings are those of marginalized communities. It is not a coincidence that, for example, the University of Kentucky issued a trigger warning (discussed in chapter 8 by Joe Martin and Brandi Frisby) for *Picking Cotton* or that Oberlin College's statement on the use of trigger warnings used *Things Fall Apart* as an example. The lives of members of marginalized communities tend to be traumatic. I wonder what it would it mean if we lived in a world where trigger warnings were primarily attached to the works of women, racial minorities, LGBTQ people, and other marginalized groups? I do not know the answer to this question, but I believe it is something to keep in mind as trigger and content warnings become more prevalent. In the end, trigger warnings are essentially about relationship: What is my relationship as instructor to my students? How do I embody this relationship in my teaching? What are my moral obligations to my students and to the ethics of my field? These are not always easy questions to answer, and it is hoped that this book will provide some context and vocabulary for thinking through these questions. In my own case, regardless of my ambivalence, I will use a trigger or content warning the next time I assign the *Wired* article.

On Trigger Warnings

In an unpublished article for the MIT Center for Civic Media, my fellow Mapping Information Access research team member, Chris Peterson, describes several themes that contextualize the debate over trigger and content warnings.[11] The first theme centers on medical jargon and metaphors. As Peterson notes, those who support the use of warnings focus on PTSD and relived trauma, while those against them discuss exposure therapy. The next theme is "informed consent," which compares trigger warnings to other labels and ratings such as those discussed above. Supporters tend to argue that such warnings are simply "more speech" and provide information about the material, while opponents argue that such labels are a form of censorship. The final theme, "Don't Be an Asshole," centers on power dynamics and "organizes warnings into the ethical sphere, where proponents see warning as an acknowledgement of actually-existing differences in experiences of social power,"[12] while those who oppose warnings state that there will always be material that makes people uncomfortable yet it is necessary to learn such material in order to become an educated person.

Peterson sees two causes for the controversy over trigger warnings. The first is the neoliberalization of higher education and the insecurity of instructors and students in such an organization. It is well known that graduate students are often at the mercy of the students in their classes, but Peterson points out that undergraduates are also concerned about the effect of grades on their future careers and the power that professors have over their education. The second cause relates to how power in general has been redistributed in society and the devaluation of expertise. As he notes, "The evident disruption in higher education regarding who is qualified to know and what is appropriate to teach, is another symptom of the same underlying skepticism regarding the 'establishment,' whether that establishment is an economic or academic elite."[13] In the end, Peterson argues that the way forward is to have respect for and treat students as adults.

The readers of this book may or may not agree with Peterson's conclusion and should note that volume is not intended to provide a definitive statement regarding trigger warnings in higher education. The contributors come from a wide variety of fields and viewpoints. Some of the chapters directly contradict each other. These contradictions and conflicting viewpoints reflect the current mood in higher education regarding trigger warnings as well as the contributing authors' research fields. Rather than detracting from the authors' arguments, these competing narratives demonstrate how our understanding of a phenomenon is informed by our own context and histories. This is in no way a settled matter.

The book is divided into two parts. The first, History and Theory, is intended to provide both historical context and theoretical analysis for the use of trigger and content warnings in academia. As noted, the authors of these chapters come from many different fields and present rival histories of trigger warnings. In her chapter on the history of trigger warnings and PTSD, Sarah Colbert begins with the effects of war on soldiers in ancient Rome through today, as well as how PTSD is understood in civil society, in order to provide a long view on the intersection between trauma and trigger warnings. Holly Taylor's chapter centers on the Universal Declaration of Human Rights, the Canadian Human Rights Act, and the use of trigger warnings as a form of accommodation for those who have been through trauma. Before they were part of academic discourse or even used in feminist communities online, trigger warnings were used to mediate content related to eating disorders. Stephanie Grey traces this history in her chapter on "contagious speech." Like Taylor, Jordan Doll's chapter also focuses on trigger warnings as accommodations but employs the theories of constitutional law scholars to elucidate the construction of gender as it relates to the use of trigger warnings. Jane Gavin-Hebert's discussion of trigger warnings is rooted in the experience of trauma and its effects on the educational experiences of Indigenous peoples who were forced into residential schools in Canada as well as the subsequent embedded experience of academia in a society that is inherently unjust. Trigger warnings are inherently related to constructions of audience, and in her chapter on equal access, Bonnie Washick argues for trigger warnings as a counter-public practice. Finally, Barbara Jones presents an insider's history (along with her own reflections) of the development of the American Association of University Professors and the Association of College and Research Libraries statements on trigger warnings.

The second part, Case Studies, consists of short chapters that describe situations in which trigger warnings were or were not used or requested for course material. The first is an empirical study by Joe Martin and Brandi Frisby on the University of Kentucky's use of trigger warnings for the university's common reading selection in 2015. Jami McFarland describes her experience of asking for trigger warnings in a women's studies graduate course and how this led her to support institutional-wide trigger warning policies. In her chapter on gender and trigger warnings, Pinky Hota demonstrates how debates over free speech construct female students. By arguing for a trauma-informed pedagogy, Kari Storla discusses general guidelines for using trigger warnings and other techniques for creating spaces for learning in the classroom. The final chapters of the section all discuss trigger warnings in various courses. The first, by Elizabeth Tolman, offers examples of using trigger and content warnings for different types of course content in an introductory women's studies course. Next, Susan Sterns makes a case for not using trigger warnings in a senior capstone course on stigma. In their chapter on military veterans and trigger warnings, Gretchen Oltman and Kristine Leibhart discuss how the responses of veterans to literature have influenced their teaching philosophies and practices. Kristina Ruiz-Mesa, Julie Matos, and Gregory Langner focus on trigger warnings in public speaking courses. Finally, in her chapter on trigger warnings in a course on young adult literature, Davin Helkenberg links the precariousness of teaching in the neoliberal university to the choices instructors make in the classroom.

The two parts of the book are not meant to be mutually exclusive; and, as one reads through the volume, it becomes clear that some chapters include material that might be a better fit for the other part. In any case, it is hoped that the present volume provides fodder for discussion as well as context and vocabulary for the controversy over trigger warnings in academia. Readers will have to come to their own conclusions regarding the debate.

Notes

1. Adrian Chen, "The Laborers Who Keep Dick Pics and Beheadings out of Your Facebook Feed," *Wired*, October 2014, https://www.wired.com/2014/10/content-moderation/.

2. Ibid.

3. s. e. smith, "On the Difference between Trigger Warnings and Content Notes, and How Harm Reduction Is Getting Lost in the Confusion," *xoJane*, May 27, 2014, http://www.xojane.com/issues/trigger-warnings-content-notes-and-harm-reduction.

4. Hope A. Olson, "The Power to Name: Representation in Library Catalogs," *Signs* 26, no. 3 (2001): 639–68.

5. Geoffrey C. Bowker and Susan Leigh Star, *Sorting Things Out: Classification and Its Consequences* (Cambridge, MA: MIT Press, 1999).

6. Louise S. Robbins, "Segregating Propaganda in American Libraries: Ralph Ulveling Confronts the Intellectual Freedom Committee," *Library Quarterly* 63, no. 2 (April 1993): 146.

7. Trina J. Magi et al., *A History of ALA Policy on Intellectual Freedom: A Supplement to* The Intellectual Freedom Manual, Ninth Edition, 2015, 202, http://search.ebscohost.com/login.aspx?direct=true&scope=site&db=nlebk&db=nlabk&AN=1053710.

8. American Library Association, "Labeling and Rating Systems: An Interpretation of the Library Bill of Rights," 2014, http://www.ala.org/advocacy/intfreedom/librarybill/interpretations/labelingrating.

9. Emily J. M. Knox, "Intellectual Freedom and the Agnostic-Postmodern View of Reading Effects," *Library Trends* 63, no. 1 (2014): 11–26.

10. Ibid.; Emily J. M. Knox, *Book Banning in 21st-Century America*, Beta Phi Mu Scholars Series (Lanham, MD: Rowman & Littlefield, 2015).

11. Chris Peterson, "Mapping the Concepts of Content Warnings: Three Themes, Two Causes, One Possible Path Forward," 2016, unpublished manuscript.

12. Ibid.

13. Ibid.

Bibliography

American Library Association. "Labeling and Rating Systems: An Interpretation of the Library Bill of Rights." 2014. http://www.ala.org/advocacy/intfreedom/librarybill/interpretations/labelingrating.

Bowker, Geoffrey C., and Susan Leigh Star. *Sorting Things Out: Classification and Its Consequences*. Cambridge, MA: MIT Press, 1999.

Chen, Adrian. "The Laborers Who Keep Dick Pics and Beheadings out of Your Facebook Feed." *Wired*, October 2014. https://www.wired.com/2014/10/content-moderation/.

Knox, Emily J. M. *Book Banning in 21st-Century America*. Beta Phi Mu Scholars Series. Lanham, MD: Rowman & Littlefield, 2015.

———. "Intellectual Freedom and the Agnostic-Postmodern View of Reading Effects." *Library Trends* 63, no. 1 (2014): 11–26.

Magi, Trina J., and Martin Garnar, eds. American Library Association, Office for Intellectual Freedom. *A History of ALA Policy on Intellectual Freedom: A Supplement to* The Intellectual Freedom Manual, Ninth Edition, 2015. http://search.ebscohost.com/login.aspx?direct=true&scope=site&db=nlebk &db=nlabk&AN=1053710.

Olson, Hope A. "The Power to Name: Representation in Library Catalogs." *Signs* 26, no. 3 (2001): 639–68.

Peterson, Chris. "Mapping the Concepts of Content Warnings: Three Themes, Two Causes, One Possible Path Forward." 2016, unpublished manuscript.

Robbins, Louise S. "Segregating Propaganda in American Libraries: Ralph Ulveling Confronts the Intellectual Freedom Committee." *Library Quarterly* 63, no. 2 (April 1993): 143–65.

smith, s. e. "On the Difference between Trigger Warnings and Content Notes, and How Harm Reduction Is Getting Lost in the Confusion." *xoJane*, May 27, 2014. http://www.xojane.com/issues/trigger-warnings-content-notes-and -harm-reduction.

Part I
HISTORY AND THEORY

CHAPTER ONE

LIKE TRAPDOORS
A History of Posttraumatic Stress Disorder and the Trigger Warning
Sarah Colbert

I t is not uncommon to see news stories, blog posts, and even works of fan fiction online prefaced by a statement alerting readers to content that may be difficult to view. Late-night television host Jimmy Fallon even issued a warning statement to viewers, warning them to not google the term "ring avulsion" after a domestic accident that almost cost the comedian his left ring finger.[1] These statements, commonly referred to as "trigger warnings" or "content warnings," have lately entered into mainstream media and conversations, especially in recent months. However, these warnings are anything but new. From the study of posttraumatic stress disorder (PTSD), doctors and psychologists have found that individuals with PTSD might "see, hear, or smell something that causes [the individual] to relive the event," and this sensory input became known as a "trigger."[2]

These triggers can come from anything, anywhere, and any time. In the introduction to one of his latest books, aptly titled *Trigger Warning*, Neil Gaiman describes triggers as "things that upset us . . . images or words or ideas that drop like trapdoors . . . our hearts skip a ratatat drumbeat in our chests . . . and what we learn about ourselves in those moments, where the trigger has been squeezed, is this: . . . the monsters . . . in our minds . . . are always there in the darkness. "[3]

What often triggers one individual may not trigger another individual, and that is what makes these triggers concerning to so many. As with most controversial topics, to truly understand the concept of the modern-day debate over the utilization of trigger warnings, one must first understand the history of posttraumatic stress disorder, how the trigger warning entered into the modern vernacular, and what is happening with trigger warnings in recent history.

Through the examination of trigger warnings in light of the historical perspective, there emerges a potential greater understanding behind the necessity of the warning, as well as the realization that trigger warnings could become "as common and useless as adult content warnings on HBO"[4] if appropriated by individuals simply seeking to shield themselves from content that they deem unpleasant. Perhaps through education individuals will come to understand what is best for their mental health and well-being and allow other individuals to decide for themselves as well.

A History of Posttraumatic Stress Disorder

As early as 490 BCE, we see historians describing symptoms eerily similar to those of modern-day PTSD in soldiers. After the famous battle of Marathon, Herodotus wrote of one soldier, "Cuphagoras, while fighting in the medley, and behaving valiantly, was deprived of his sight, though wounded in no part of his body, nor struck from a distance; and continued to be blind from that time for the remainder of his life."[5]

It also bears pointing out that in ancient Roman armies, the bravest soldiers in each legion were given the honor of bearing the army's insignia, the eagle. However, a soldier's "personal valor" offered little protection against what came to be known as "war neurosis." It was not uncommon for the Eagle Bearer to suffer some sort of breakdown on the battlefield. This type of behavior continues throughout history, and in the early seventeenth century, European physicians studied the strange malady that affected soldiers, which caused the soldiers to "sink into a state of deep despair."[6] This condition seemed especially prevalent among Spanish soldiers conscripted for service by the Netherlands during the Thirty Years War. Swiss medical student Johannes Hofer wrote of the condition in his 1678 *Dissertatio Medica de Nostalgia, oder Heimweh* (Medical Dissertation on Nostalgia, or Heimweh).[7] In his dissertation, Hofer coined the term *nostalgia* to name the condition in which the individual suffers because he is not in his native land or fears that he will never see it again. He goes on to discuss symptoms ranging from "continuing melancholy" to "cardiac palpitations." As for treatment, Hofer prescribed purgatives and narcotics to help restlessness or insomnia.[8]

4

PTSD-type conditions continued to be studied and written about by military surgeons and other physicians. Dominique Larrey, a surgeon in Napoleon's army, argued that nostalgia was a form of insanity, and in 1836, Hector Gavin published *Feigned and Fictitious Diseases*, claiming that a great number of soldiers who suffered from "nostalgia" were simply pretending to have the condition in hopes of being sent home due to insanity. Other physicians described a condition they referred to as "soldier's heart" or "the irritable heart of a soldier," in which soldiers suffered from exhaustion, angina, and other symptoms, typically after periods of intense stress.[9]

During the American Civil War, doctors attempted to treat nostalgia, claiming that soldiers simply needed more to occupy their time between battles, noting that patients who were sent to hospitals near their own homes were more likely to contract nostalgia than patients who were sent elsewhere to convalesce. Numerous soldiers were diagnosed with soldier's heart, but most seemed to recover after they were sent to the hospital for a few months. There were also many soldiers sent home after being determined to be insane. At this time, soldiers who were declared insane were sent home immediately. However, due to such a high volume of soldiers being sent home, the War Department issued orders that no soldiers were to be discharged on reasons of insanity after 1863.[10]

During the First World War, doctors switched from calling the malady "nostalgia" to referring to it as "shell shock." While the term's origins may have come from the troops themselves, use of the term "shell shock" as a diagnosis is credited to Dr. Charles Myers. Myers's work on shell shock was published in *Shell Shock in France, 1914–1918: Based on a War Diary*. In this work he claimed that soldiers who were in the immediate vicinity of exploding shells were at risk of "shell concussion," a physical ailment, or "shell shock," a mental ailment.[11] "Barbed Wire Disease" was also a common diagnosis in prisoners of war as a result of "confinement and monotony of life in a prison camp accentuated by sexual deprivation and lack of privacy."[12] Looking back, it becomes apparent that the symptoms of "Barbed Wire Disease"—irritability, restlessness, and difficulty concentrating—all mirror symptoms of PTSD, which would not be a stretch to diagnose in soldiers who had been confined to prison camps during their time abroad. While doctors were now aware of and studying shell shock (also called "combat fatigue"), they were not terribly sympathetic to the plight of the individuals who were afflicted. The soldiers were blamed for their condition. Dr. Arthur F. Hurst, a British neurologist, wrote in his 1918 book *Medical Diseases of the War* that "a man with a good family history, who has never suffered from any nervous disability, only develops war neuroses, including shell-shock, under exceptional circumstances."[13]

After the First World War, the Fifth International Psycho-analytical Congress held a symposium in Budapest in which four doctors spoke on the subject of "Psycho-analysis and War Neuroses."[14] In their discussion they laid out information on what would become known as "posttraumatic stress disorder" after Vietnam. Prior to the Vietnam conflict, doctors began studying stress reactions in soldiers after World War I. As a result, military psychologists found that, according to some studies, up to "80 percent of American fighting men that succumbed to acute stress reaction were returned to some kind of duty within the week [of their diagnoses]. Thirty percent returned to combat units."[15]

While studies on PTSD were being conducted, large-scale examinations into trauma reactions were not implemented until the post-Vietnam era. After Vietnam, doctors who treated individuals with PTSD were deeply divided for some time, much as they had been during previous wars: Hawkish psychiatrists were adamant that concepts like combat fatigue had no diagnostic value. As a Veterans Affairs psychiatrist told the *Los Angeles Times* in 1975, there was "no evidence that Vietnam had produced a disproportionate share of people who are maladjusted to society and no evidence that the primary contributor to that maladjustment was military service." In an essay published in *Strangers at Home: Vietnam Veterans since the War,* psychologist Charles R. Figley noted, "In the mid-1970s the mental health profession barely recognized the plight of the emotionally disabled Vietnam veteran."[16]

As opposed to soldiers from previous wars and conflicts who often suffered in silence, these soldiers chose to depend on one another, and they chose to speak out against the horrors they had witnessed. Prior to this time, admitting they were troubled was seen as a sign of weakness, as is still the case in some circles today. Soldiers who had been jaded and traumatized by the conflict had formed what they called "Rap Groups," in which they met and discussed what they had lived while deployed. These groups served a few purposes, not the least of which was to give soldiers an outlet to discuss their trauma with other soldiers, all while refusing to hide behind a stigma of shame. Michael Norman, a former marine, said of his experience after returning from Vietnam:

> Family and friends wondered why we were so angry. What are you crying about? they would ask. Why are you so ill-tempered and disaffected? Our fathers and grandfathers had gone off to war, done their duty, come home and got on with it. What made our generation so different? As it turns out, nothing. No difference at all. When old soldiers from "good" wars are dragged from behind the curtain of myth and sentiment and brought into the light, they too seem to smolder with choler and alienation. . . . So we were angry. Our anger was old, atavistic. We were angry as all civilized men who have ever been sent to make murder in the name of virtue were angry.[17]

Norman was not alone in his experience. Family and friends of returning soldiers had no idea of the atrocities witnessed and could offer no explanation for the changes in their loved ones. In response, numerous groups popped up around the country catering to the needs of returning soldiers. Through pressure from these soldiers, various other veterans' groups, and psychologists who were not invested in government interests, the government eventually created a program called Operation Outreach, which involved mandated psychological treatment. And finally, in 1980, the American Psychiatric Association added PTSD into the *Diagnostic and Statistical Manual of Mental Disorders* (*DSM*) for the first time. The symptoms included in the manual were very similar to symptoms that had been outlined forty years earlier by psychologist Abram Kardiner, a pioneer in studying war neurosis.[18]

In more recent years, there has been a jump in numbers of diagnosed cases of PTSD. "In 2003, there were 190,000 veterans seeking care for PTSD. By 2014, the number had nearly tripled to 540,000."[19] In fact, according to a study conducted by the RAND Corporation, "evidence suggests that the psychological toll of these deployments [in Operation Enduring Freedom and Iraqi Freedom]—many involving prolonged exposure to combat-related stress over multiple rotations—may be disproportionately high compared with the physical injuries of combat."[20] With continuing military action taking place around the world, it is not a far leap to conclude that the numbers of soldiers afflicted with PTSD will continue to rise. With the rise in individuals with PTSD, the number of individuals affected by triggers will also increase. This could account, in part, for the current demand for trigger warnings on college campuses, the Internet, and in other types of media.

It is important to remember that soldiers are not the only individuals who are afflicted by posttraumatic stress disorder. The key word in determining who may be diagnosed with PTSD comes from the word *trauma*. Susan Bryson identifies trauma as "an experience of being helpless in the face of an overwhelming, life threatening force."[21] By Bryson's definition, that includes anyone who has experienced a severely traumatic experience, extending to the civilian population as well.

PTSD in the Civilian World

PTSD in Women

As previously stated, PTSD can exist in any individual that has been through a severely traumatic experience. In fact, psychologist Judith Herman argues that the medical condition "hysteria" was a form of PTSD in women who had been sexually assaulted or molested as young children. Hysteria became a catch-all diagnosis for women, some doctors believing it was a real physical ailment originating in the uterus. Others felt that the condition was "a dramatic metaphor for everything that men found mysterious or unmanageable in the opposite sex."[22] Jean-Martin Charcot, a French neurologist, was the father of the study of hysteria. He took female hysteria patients from Salpêtrière, an asylum, and paraded them in front of audiences while lecturing on his findings as a result of treating these women. Before Charcot's studies and lectures, women with hysteria were considered "malingerers" and were often only able to seek treatment from hypnotists and other "popular healers."[23] Sigmund Freud, one of Charcot's disciples, spent hours in meetings with female patients. He and others came to the similar belief that hysteria was indeed caused by psychological trauma. By the 1890s, investigators had discovered that recovering and discussing the feelings that the traumatic memories were tied to could alleviate the symptoms of the condition; this treatment became the precursor to modern psychotherapy.[24]

In 1896, Freud published *The Aetiology of Hysteria* and claimed, "I therefore put forward the thesis that at the bottom of every case of hysteria there are *one or more occurrences of premature sexual experience.* . . . I believe that this is an important finding."[25] However, less than a year later, Freud had come to the decision that the numbers of women presenting with symptoms of hysteria were so high that he would have had to conclude that "what he called 'perverted acts against children' were endemic, not only among the proletariat of Paris, where he had first studied hysteria, but also among the respectable bourgeois families of Vienna. . . . This idea was simply unacceptable."[26] Thus, Freud ceased to study and treat hysteria and others soon followed until the condition fell into obscurity.

It was not until the women's liberation movement of the 1970s that doctors discovered the "most common post-traumatic stress disorders are not those of men at war, but of women in civilian life."[27] The majority of women with PTSD have been victims of sexual violence, but it was not until 1972 when Ann Burgess, with the help of Lynda Holmstrom, conducted research into "rape trauma syndrome." Out of the study came the realization that "[t]he early conceptualizations of the stress response patterns of rape victims are consistent with the diagnostic criteria of Post-Traumatic Stress Disorder (PTSD) of the DSM-III within the major category of Anxiety Disorders."[28] If one out of every six American women has been the victim of attempted or completed rape in her lifetime,[29] is it any wonder that PTSD is more common in women? And, if PTSD is more prevalent in the female population, should anyone be surprised that one of the most frequent trigger warnings requested is for rape or violence against women?

PTSD by the Numbers

While the numbers of individuals afflicted with PTSD are dispro-portionately high for people who serve in the military, the numbers of civilians living with PTSD as a result of any number of traumatic events is by no means a small number. A study conducted by the U.S. National Comorbidity Survey Replication (NCS-R) interviewed a nationally representative sample of 9,282 Americans over the age of eighteen to assess for signs of PTSD. What the NCS-R found was that of those 9,282 individuals, using *DSM-IV* criteria, 5,692 were assessed to have or have had PTSD. The lifetime prevalence of PTSD among adult men was 3.6 percent, while the lifetime prevalence for adult women was 9.7 percent.[30]

While there have been no comprehensive population-based studies conducted on the prevalence of PTSD in children and adolescents, studies have been conducted on the prevalence of PTSD in high-risk juvenile populations. These studies found, using *DSM-IV* criteria, similar numbers of PTSD in males when compared to adults (3.7 percent) and slightly lower numbers in adolescent females when compared to their adult counterparts (6.3 percent).[31]

As far as international studies go, the World Health Organization began collecting data in the late 1990s. By 2008, data from twenty-seven countries and nearly two hundred thousand people had been collected. Estimated results from seventeen of these countries have been published, and the numbers for lifetime prevalence of PTSD range from 0.3 percent in China to 6.1 percent in New Zealand. Statistics reported from these countries should not be compared, however, as the methodology in sample selection and survey administration varied.[32]

With the increasing numbers of individuals afflicted with PTSD, it stands to reason that the number of individuals who could be triggered by seemingly innocuous events, stories, or pictures has also increased. All of these factors working together have created the desire for some sort of warning system. Out of this desire sprung the concept of a "trigger warning."

Trigger Warnings Enter the Modern Vernacular

As a result of all of the studies conducted on PTSD, doctors began to understand the concept of outside stimuli that could "trigger" episodes in individuals with PTSD. Again, triggers are those "small, seemingly insignificant reminders" that can bring to life memories of the traumatic event, causing the traumatized individual to relive the trauma "with all the vividness and emotional force of the original event. Thus, even normally safe environments may come to feel dangerous."[33] Out of this consideration, the concept of the "trigger warning" began to emerge in medical circles. While movies, video games, and television shows all come with a ratings system, it wasn't until the rise of the Internet as a method of communication and information dissemination that the trigger warning entered into the modern vernacular.

According to Ali Vingiano, it is impossible to trace the first appearance of the term *triggering* or *trigger warning* on the Internet, but prior to using those exact terms, it was not uncommon to see bloggers preface entries with warnings for readers who might be sensitive to topics like eating disorders or sexual assault.[34] Message boards and online communities like Tumblr, a social networking website that allows users to re-blog and tag entries shared by other users; Ao3 (Archive of Our Own), an online repository of fan fiction; and *LiveJournal*, a blogging and networking site, are frequent locations for these warnings to appear. According to *LiveJournal*'s public archives, the first versions of trigger warnings were seen in 2002 with a user warning readers that her blog was "pro-ana," or contained information about eating disorders. The user explained in a comment that the "pro-ana" tag was meant to inform readers that the discussion and entries to her blog could be triggering to individuals recovering from anorexia or bulimia.[35]

It is not at all uncommon to see tags on social media platforms like Twitter and Tumblr prefaced by "TW." The "TW" (standing for trigger warning) serves to notify users that something another individual has shared, written, or posted contains material that could potentially be triggering, meaning that it could set off someone who has been through a traumatic event. When both Twitter and Tumblr were created in the mid-2000s, users who had previously added trigger warnings to their own blogs began using them when sharing links and posts on both platforms, even when the original post did not contain a warning.

On Tumblr, the tag serves a dual purpose. It informs readers of potentially triggering content, but it also serves to allow individuals who utilize browser extensions like Tumblr Savior to "black list" certain keywords in order to prevent them from appearing on their page as they browse. On Ao3, writers can often be found tagging their stories with "Graphic Depictions of Violence," "Rape/Non-Con" (Non-Consensual), or "Major Character Death" in order to clue readers in on potentially problematic content that could trigger a response or negative reaction. Similar tagging can still be found on *LiveJournal* as well.

Other websites have created their own system of warnings. *Shakesville*, a feminist blog, uses trigger warnings, which they prefer to call "content notes." Almost every post coming from the site contains a warning of some sort. Melissa McEwan, the founder of *Shakesville*, even labels pictures of her dogs if they are shown with their teeth bared in a manner that could be considered menacing. McEwan believes that "no harm comes from telling readers what content to expect in a post."[36]

In a somewhat ironic twist, the very thing that was invented to protect individuals from content that could be offensive or harmful has itself become offensive in some circles. In 2010, a writer named Susannah Breslin wrote a scathing piece on the trigger warning for *True/Slant*. According to Breslin:

> [F]eminists are all over their TRIGGER WARNINGS, applying them like a Southern cook applies Pam cooking spray to an overused nonstick frying pan. It's almost impressive really. I guess the idea is that blog posts are TOTALLY SCARY, and if you are EASILY UPSET, if you see a TRIGGER WARNING coming, you can look away REALLY FAST.[37]

In some circles, even the word *trigger* can be considered triggering. Websites like *Everyday Feminism* prefer to use the term *content warning* rather than *trigger warning* as "the word 'trigger' relies on and invokes violent weaponry imagery. This could be re-traumatizing for folks who have suffered military, police, and other forms of violence."[38] The logic behind this statement being that even the mention of the word *trigger* could conjure up images of the trigger of a gun, thus reminding the individual of the trauma sustained as a result of gun violence.

Trigger Warnings and Academia

Even more recently, the fight over trigger warnings has come to colleges and universities across the United States. The *New York Times* published an article in 2014 speaking out about the surge in student demand for trigger warnings. The article points out that the University of California–Santa Barbara has seen the strongest demand, with the student government association going so far as to pass a resolution demanding that professors incorporate the warnings into the course content. Schools like Oberlin, Rutgers, and George Washington University have also seen similar requests from the student body.[39] An article in *The Atlantic* mentions that law students at Harvard requested that professors not teach rape law, or even use the word "violate (as in 'that violates the law') lest it cause students distress."[40]

Oberlin College found itself in the middle of some controversy in 2014. An online guide was published in hopes of educating professors as well as protecting students who may suffer from PTSD. The guide asked professors to "understand that sexual misconduct is inextricably tied to issues of privilege and oppression." It went on to ask professors to consider topics like "racism, sexism, heterosexism, cissexism, ableism, and other issues of oppression" and how those topics could affect their students.[41] Carlo Davis, a reporter for *New Republic*, spoke to a faculty member, Marc Blecher, at Oberlin who had never actually heard of these guidelines until he had read about them online. Blecher went on to discuss that numerous other faculty were unhappy with the guidelines and Oberlin quickly shelved the proposed guidelines until further research could be conducted.[42]

In 2016, the University of Chicago incited a firestorm of attention from the media and the public by sending a letter to all of their incoming students. In this letter, John "Jay" Ellison, Dean of Students, informs students that the University is committed to the idea of academic freedom. A portion of the letter reads:

> Members of our community are encouraged to speak, write, listen, challenge, and learn, without fear of censorship. Civility and mutual respect are vital to all of us, and freedom of expression does not mean the freedom to harass or threaten others. You will find that we expect members of our community to be engaged in rigorous debate, discussion, and even disagreement. At times, this may challenge you and even cause discomfort.[43]

Ellison goes on to inform students that the best way to encourage "debate, discussion, and even disagreement" is by eliminating the idea of "trigger warnings" and "safe spaces" on the University's campus.[44] While defending the idea of academic and intellectual freedom, Ellison is also creating an atmosphere that could potentially isolate or disenfranchise students who have a legitimate need to discuss potentially triggering information with their professors due to a PTSD diagnosis. This is not to say that professors and teachers should be required to label content in classrooms as potentially triggering, but the professors, and by extension the university or school, should create an environment that allows students the freedom to discuss concerns in a face-to-face setting.

Problems Arising out of Trigger Warnings

Professors at colleges and universities around the country have become concerned about the potential effects of mandated warning labels on course content. In an opinion piece for *Vox*, a professor using the pseudonym "Schlosser" writes about changing his or her course content as "political winds have shifted" and about making sure that any dissenting opinions are hidden behind anonymity or pseudonyms. Schlosser also mentions that many colleagues have done the same because they have seen what happens to other adjunct professors, including one who did "not get his contract renewed after students complained that he exposed them to 'offensive texts.'"[45] The texts over which contracts were terminated? Stories and books written by authors like Mark Twain and Edward Said.[46]

In *Freedom from Speech*, Greg Lukianoff, a constitutional attorney, writes about Oberlin's rejected policy and says:

> What colleges like Oberlin describe as PTSD bears little resemblance to its original meaning, which focused on the results of exposure to severe and often prolonged physical violence, atrocities or other life-threatening or terrifying events. Survivors of sexual assault have experienced the type of trauma that fits this definition, but it is hard to see how people who have merely been exposed to "classism"—something that virtually anyone can claim to have encountered in some way at some point—can be put in the same category.[47]

Lukianoff's statements about the trigger warnings proposed at Oberlin could be applied to any college or university. The statement then creates a whole new array of questions. Does utilizing trigger warnings become insensitive to sufferers of PTSD? Where does a professor draw the line at what could be triggering? Does a professor in an art history class have to warn against graphic depictions of violence before showcasing *Judith Slaying Holofernes* by Artemisia Gentileschi? What about warning students before showing pictures of dogs, like *Shakesville*'s founder, because a student who was once bitten by a dog might be uncomfortable with dogs? These questions, and more, have become the norm when discussing the potential downfall of academic and intellectual freedom when debating trigger warnings for those who are not in favor of such disclaimers.

Advocating for Trigger Warnings

There are a number of individuals and organizations that find trigger warnings to be controversial and even harmful to the concept of intellectual freedom. However, there are just as many people who find trigger warnings necessary and helpful. Lindy West, in a piece for *The Guardian*, noted that Jimmy Fallon's aside about not googling his ring avulsion was simply a common courtesy and that it served as a way to let the audience know that searching for the injury online would return some very graphic images. "If Fallon were to actually show the images on TV a quick 'heads up. . .' would be basic human decency and no one would think twice" about his warning.[48] Proponents for trigger warnings would also argue that ratings on other forms of media serve to alert viewers to content that may be "inappropriate" for certain audiences, and trigger warnings act in much the same way. They serve to alert individuals that the content may be psychologically harmful. "The goal is not to keep challenging materials off syllabuses or allow students to meekly excuse themselves from huge swaths of the literary canon because bad words hurt their feelings."[49] Instead, advocates for the warnings believe that the content warning would give students who do have PTSD or traumatic histories the opportunity to manage their mental health and better prepare to engage with the potentially triggering materials.

Maddy Myers, a writer who identifies as someone with PTSD, goes so far as to say that these warnings do not keep her from engaging in the content. These warnings instead "help [her] prepare for what [she] might endure."[50] It has already been established that individuals with PTSD cannot always prepare for what may trigger their condition, so it becomes impossible to determine what they should and should not avoid. These warnings, according to people who are pro-warning, simply give the individual the ability to mentally prepare themselves. Many therapists who treat PTSD often use exposure therapy to treat their patients. Through controlled exposure to triggers and situations that could potentially be triggering, the patient learns to continue to "enjoy and interact with media *in spite of* triggers."[51]

In Summation

Posttraumatic stress disorder is a long-reaching illness. From the earliest days where it had no name to becoming nostalgia, then war neuroses and battle fatigue in soldiers, and hysteria in women, for centuries this condition and individuals with it have been misunderstood, misdiagnosed, and maligned. It has only been since the end of the Vietnam conflict that doctors and society have begun to understand the seriousness of the condition and begun to treat both soldiers and civilians alike in a manner befitting their illness. With medical progress came understanding, and out of that understanding came the concept of the trigger, and later the trigger warning.

A vast part of the history of the trigger warning has become the modern debate over the warning itself. From the creation of the trigger warning and its first appearance online, this label has been a hotly contested one. It seems that in recent months and years, not a week goes by that the trigger warning is not in the news. Whether it be due to a university trying to require that professors include trigger warnings in their syllabi for "racism, classism, sexism . . . and other issues of oppression"[52] or because a university refuses to "cancel invited speakers because their topics might prove controversial,"[53] it seems that trigger warnings have become the newly contested topic to discuss in intellectual freedom circles, academia, and the media.

Knowledge of these triggers has become part of daily life for many people who suffer from PTSD and as a result has entered into daily discussions in higher education. These warnings are going to continue to exist in all of their controversial glory. It is time that individuals and academia begin to understand the concept and come to their own conclusions about the use of these warnings.

Notes

1. Amanda Michelle Steiner, "Jimmy Fallon's Finger Injury: *Tonight Show* Host Explains," *Entertainment Weekly*, July 14, 2015, http://www.ew.com/article/2015/07/14/jimmy-fallon-finger-injury-tonight-show.

2. U.S. Department of Veterans Affairs, "Symptoms of PTSD," August 13, 2015, http://www.ptsd.va.gov/public/PTSD-overview/basics/symptoms_of_ptsd.asp.

3. Neil Gaiman, *Trigger Warning: Short Fictions and Disturbances* (New York: HarperCollins, 2015), xv.

4. Conor Friedersdorf, "What HBO Can Teach Colleges about Trigger Warnings," *The Atlantic*, May 20, 2014, http://www.theatlantic.com/education/archive/

2014/05/what-trigger-warning-activists-and-critics-can-learn-from-hbo/371137/.

5. Anthony Babington, *Shell-Shock: A History of the Changing Attitudes to War Neurosis* (London: Leo Cooper, 1997), 7.

6. Ibid.

7. Maiken Umbach and Bernd-Rüdiger Hüppauf, *Vernacular Modernism: Heimat, Globalization, and the Built Environment* (Stanford, CA: Stanford University Press, 2005).

8. Babington, *Shell-Shock*, 8.

9. Ibid., 8–12.

10. Ibid., 16–17.

11. Charles S. Myers, *Shell Shock in France, 1914–1918: Based on a War Diary* (Cambridge: Cambridge University Press, 1940).

12. Emanuel Miller, ed., *The Neuroses in War* (New York: Macmillan, 1940), 15.

13. Jeet Heer, "Generation PTSD: What the 'Trigger Warning' Debate Is Really About," *New Republic*, May 20, 2015, https://newrepublic.com/article/121866/history-ptsd-and-evolution-trigger-warnings.

14. Sándor Ferenczi, *Psycho-analysis and the War Neuroses: Issue 2 of International Psycho-analytical Library*, edited by Ernest Jones (London: International Psychoanalytical Press, 1921).

15. Judith L. Herman, *Trauma and Recovery: The Aftermath of Violence—from Domestic Abuse to Political Terror* (New York: Basic Books, 2015), 26.

16. Heer, "Generation PTSD."

17. Herman, *Trauma and Recovery*, 27.

18. Ibid., 26–27.

19. Heer, "Generation PTSD."

20. Terri Tanielian et al., *Invisible Wounds of War: Psychological and Cognitive Injuries, Their Consequences, and Services to Assist Recovery* (Santa Monica, CA: RAND Corporation, 2008), iii, http://www.rand.org/pubs/monographs/MG720.html.

21. Susan Bryson, "Personal Identity and Trauma," in *Encyclopedia of Philosophy and the Social Sciences*, edited by Byron Kaldis, 708–10 (Thousand Oaks, CA: Sage, 2013).

22. Herman, *Trauma and Recovery*, 10.

23. Ibid., 10.

24. Ibid., 12.

25. Ibid., 13.

26. Ibid., 13–14.

27. Ibid., 28.

28. Ann Wolbert Burgess, "Rape Trauma Syndrome," *Behavioral Sciences & the Law* 1, no. 3 (1983): 97–113.

29. RAINN, "Women and Girls Experience Sexual Violence at High Rates," *Victims of Sexual Violence: Statistics*, https://www.rainn.org/statistics/victims-sexual-violence.

30. Jamie L. Gradus, *Epidemiology of PTSD*, U.S. Department of Veterans Affairs, February 23, 2016, http://www.ptsd.va.gov/professional/PTSD-overview/epidemiological-facts-ptsd.asp.

31. Ibid.

32. Ibid.

33. Herman, *Trauma and Recovery*, 37.

34. Ali Vingiano, "How the 'Trigger Warning' Took Over the Internet," *BuzzFeedNews*, May 5, 2014, https://www.buzzfeed.com/alisonvingiano/how-the-trigger-warning-took-over-the-internet?utm_term=.ph5AGvMEw#.pn0ZJbnLX.

35. Ibid.

36. Ibid.

37. Susannah Breslin, "Trigger Warning: This Blog Post May Freak You the F*** Out," *True/Slant*, April 13, 2010, http://trueslant.com/susannahbreslin/2010/04/13/trigger-warning-this-blog-post-may-freak-you-the-f-out/.

38. Gillian Brown, "Not Sure What People Mean by 'Triggering'? This Article Is Your One-Stop 101," *Everyday Feminism*, June 7, 2015, http://everydayfeminism.com/2015/06/guide-to-triggering/.

39. Jennifer Medina, "Warning: The Literary Canon Could Make Students Squirm," *New York Times*, May 17, 2014, http://www.nytimes.com/2014/05/18/us/warning-the-literary-canon-could-make-students-squirm.html?_r=2.

40. Greg Lukianoff and Jonathan Haidt, "The Coddling of the American Mind," *The Atlantic*, September 2015, http://www.theatlantic.com/magazine/archive/2015/09/the-coddling-of-the-american-mind/399356/.

41. Greg Lukianoff, *Freedom from Speech* (New York: Encounter Books, 2014), Kindle edition.

42. Carlo Davis, "Oberlin Amends Its Trigger-Warning Policy," *New Republic*, April 9, 2014, https://newrepublic.com/article/117320/oberlin-amends-its-trigger-warning-policy.

43. John "Jay" Ellison, Letter to the Class of 2020, August 2016, http://www.intellectualtakeout.org/sites/ito/files/acceptance_letter.jpg.

44. *Time* IDEAS Desk, "University of Chicago: 'We Do Not Support So-Called Trigger Warnings,'" *Time Magazine Online*, August 25, 2016, http://time.com/4466021/uchicago-trigger-warnings/.

45. Edward Schlosser, "I'm a Liberal Professor, and My Liberal Students Terrify Me," *Vox*, June 3, 2015, http://www.vox.com/2015/6/3/8706323/college-professor-afraid.

46. Ibid.

47. Lukianoff, *Freedom from Speech*.

48. Lindy West, "Trigger Warnings Don't Hinder Freedom of Expression: They Expand It," *The Guardian*, August 18, 2015, https://www.theguardian.com/education/commentisfree/2015/aug/18/trigger-warnings-dont-hinder-freedom-expression.

49. Ibid.

50. Maddy Myers, "Saying Trigger Warnings 'Coddle the Mind' Completely Misses the Point," *The Mary Sue*, August 11, 2015, http://www.themarysue.com/trigger-warnings-arent-coddling/.

51. Ibid.

52. Oberlin College Office of Equity Concerns, "Support Resources for Faculty," *Sexual Offense Resource Guide*, web archive, http://web.archive.org/web/20131122144749/http://new.oberlin.edu/office/equity-concerns/sexual-offense-resource-guide/prevention-support-education/support-resources-for-faculty.dot.

53. *Time* IDEAS Desk, "University of Chicago: 'We Do Not Support.'"

Bibliography

Babington, Anthony. *Shell-Shock: A History of the Changing Attitudes to War Neurosis*. London: Leo Cooper, 1997.

Breslin, Susannah. "Trigger Warning: This Blog Post May Freak You the F*** Out." *True/Slant*, April 13, 2010. http://trueslant.com/susannahbreslin/2010/04/13/trigger-warning-this-blog-post-may-freak-you-the-f-out/.

Brown, Gillian. "Not Sure What People Mean by 'Triggering'? This Article Is Your One-Stop 101." *Everyday Feminism*, June 7, 2015. http://everydayfeminism.com/2015/06/guide-to-triggering/.

Bryson, Susan. "Personal Identity and Trauma." In *Encyclopedia of Philosophy and the Social Sciences*, edited by Byron Kaldis, 708–10. Thousand Oaks, CA: Sage, 2013.

Burgess, Ann Wolbert. "Rape Trauma Syndrome." *Behavioral Sciences & the Law* 1, no. 3 (1983): 97–113.

Davis, Carlo. "Oberlin Amends Its Trigger-Warning Policy." *New Republic*, April 9, 2014. https://newrepublic.com/article/117320/oberlin-amends-its-trigger-warning-policy.

Ellison, John "Jay." Letter to the Class of 2020. August 2016. http://www.intel lectualtakeout.org/sites/ito/files/acceptance_letter.jpg.

Ferenczi, Sándor. *Psycho-analysis and the War Neuroses: Issue 2 of International Psycho-analytical Library*, edited by Ernest Jones. London: International Psychoanalytical Press, 1921.

Friedersdorf, Conor. "What HBO Can Teach Colleges about Trigger Warnings." *The Atlantic*, May 20, 2014. http://www.theatlantic.com/education/archive/ 2014/05/what-trigger-warning-activists-and-critics-can-learn-from-hbo/ 371137/.

Gaiman, Neil. *Trigger Warning: Short Fictions and Disturbances*. New York: HarperCollins, 2015.

Gradus, Jamie L. *Epidemiology of PTSD*. U.S. Department of Veterans Affairs, February 23, 2016. http://www.ptsd.va.gov/professional/PTSD-overview/ epidemiological-facts-ptsd.asp.

Heer, Jeet. "Generation PTSD: What the 'Trigger Warning' Debate Is Really About." *New Republic*, May 20, 2015. https://newrepublic.com /article/121866/history-ptsd-and-evolution-trigger-warnings.

Herman, Judith L. *Trauma and Recovery: The Aftermath of Violence—from Domestic Abuse to Political Terror*. New York: Basic Books, 2015.

Lukianoff, Greg. *Freedom from Speech*. New York: Encounter Books, 2014. Kindle edition.

Lukianoff, Greg, and Jonathan Haidt. "The Coddling of the American Mind." *The Atlantic*, September 2015. http://www.theatlantic.com/magazine/ archive/2015/09/the-coddling-of-the-american-mind/399356/.

Medina, Jennifer. "Warning: The Literary Canon Could Make Students Squirm." *New York Times*, May 17, 2014. http://www.nytimes.com/2014/05/18/us/ warning-the-literary-canon-could-make-students-squirm.html?_r=2.

Miller, Emanuel, ed. *The Neuroses in War*. New York: Macmillan, 1940.

Myers, Charles S. *Shell Shock in France, 1914–1918: Based on a War Diary*. Cambridge: Cambridge University Press, 1940.

Myers, Maddy. "Saying Trigger Warnings 'Coddle the Mind' Completely Misses the Point." *The Mary Sue*, August 11, 2015. http://www.themarysue .com/trigger-warnings-arent-coddling/.

Oberlin College Office of Equity Concerns. "Support Resources for Faculty." *Sexual Offense Resource Guide*. Web archive. http://web.archive .org/web/20131122144749/http://new.oberlin.edu/office/equity-concerns/ sexual-offense-resource-guide/prevention-support-education/support -resources-for-faculty.dot.

RAINN. "Women and Girls Experience Sexual Violence at High Rates." *Victims of Sexual Violence: Statistics.* https://www.rainn.org/statistics/victims-sexual -violence.

Schlosser, Edward. "I'm a Liberal Professor, and My Liberal Students Terrify Me." *Vox*, June 3, 2015. http://www.vox.com/2015/6/3/8706323/college -professor-afraid.

Steiner, Amanda Michelle. "Jimmy Fallon's Finger Injury: *Tonight Show* Host Explains." *Entertainment Weekly*, July 14, 2015. http://www.ew.com/ar-ticle/2015/07/14/jimmy-fallon-finger-injury-tonight-show.

Tanielian, Terri, Lisa H. Jaycox, David M. Adamson, M. Audrey Burnam, Ra-chel M. Burns, Leah B. Caldarone, Robert A. Cox, Elizabeth J. D'Amico, Claudia Diaz, Christine Eibner, Gail Fisher, Todd C. Helmus, Benjamin R. Karney, Beau Kilmer, Grant N. Marshall, Laurie T. Martin, Lisa S. Mer-edith, Karen N. Metscher, Karen Chan Osilla, Rosalie Liccardo Pacula, Ra-jeev Ramchand, Jeanne S. Ringel, Terry L. Schell, Jerry M. Sollinger, Mary E. Vaiana, Kayla M. Williams, and Michael R. Yochelson. *Invisible Wounds of War: Psychological and Cognitive Injuries, Their Consequences, and Services to Assist Recovery.* Santa Monica, CA: RAND Corporation, 2008. http://www .rand.org/pubs/monographs/MG720.html.

Time IDEAS Desk. "University of Chicago: 'We Do Not Support So-Called Trigger Warnings.'" *Time Magazine Online*, August 25, 2016. http://time. com/4466021/uchicago-trigger-warnings/.

Umbach, Maiken, and Bernd-Rüdiger Hüppauf. *Vernacular Modernism: Heimat, Globalization, and the Built Environment.* Stanford, CA: Stanford University Press, 2005.

U.S. Department of Veterans Affairs. "Symptoms of PTSD." August 13, 2015. http://www.ptsd.va.gov/public/PTSD-overview/basics/symptoms_of_ptsd .asp.

Vingiano, Ali. "How the 'Trigger Warning' Took Over the Internet." *BuzzFeed-News*, May 5, 2014. https://www.buzzfeed.com/alisonvingiano/how-the -trigger-warning-took-over-the-internet?utm_term=.ph5AGvMEw#. pn0ZJbnLX.

West, Lindy. "Trigger Warnings Don't Hinder Freedom of Expression: They Expand It." *The Guardian*, August 18, 2015. https://www.theguardian.com/ education/commentisfree/2015/aug/18/trigger-warnings-dont-hinder-free dom-expression.

CHAPTER TWO

ACCESSIBILITY ON CAMPUS
Posttraumatic Stress Disorder, Duty to Accommodate, and Trigger Warnings
Holly Taylor

Trigger warnings and their function in the university classroom have become a contentious issue for many students, professors, and administrators alike. Proponents of their application may liken their use to content warnings, which are standard practice within contemporary Western society, used to preface material that may be deemed offensive within film, music, theatre, video games, and other spaces. On the other hand, opponents of trigger warnings may indicate that the academy is a unique exception to this rule, suggesting that higher education should not be subjected to the same regulations that other institutions abide by in order to preserve the intellectual exploration offered through such academic liberties. In this chapter, I illustrate how trigger warnings can provide a compromise between conflicts that surface when the right to freely express ideas collides with the basic human right for individuals to be safe and free from harm within the university classroom. I do this by envisioning trigger warnings as one tool that can be used to mitigate ongoing experiences of harm that individuals who have experienced trauma may face on a daily basis. In doing so, I endeavor to broaden the scope of existing conversations by raising considerations of what individuals living with posttraumatic stress disorder (PTSD) experience and by examining the relevance of trigger warnings as accessibility criteria for those who are impacted by PTSD.

I begin by contemplating victimization and trauma as concerns disproportionately impacting marginalized and minoritized groups, and I reference statistics on violent crimes to assess patterns of violence through an intersectional lens in order to recognize populations most likely to be affected by trauma and, consequently, PTSD. By clearly outlining causes and impacts associated with PTSD, the benefits of trigger warnings can be recognized in terms of accessibility and harm-reduction strategies as opposed to coddling and censorship. I offer this analysis from a trauma-informed, human rights–based perspective and consider legal provisions designed to protect individuals and groups from discrimination and injury. In particular, I deconstruct the classification of PTSD as a mental illness and consider the unique implications of human rights legislation designed to protect the rights of individuals living with disabilities in terms of access to equal opportunities in a postsecondary educational context.

I ultimately make a case for the application of trigger warnings as appropriate accessibility accommodations for students living with PTSD within guidelines of human rights legislation, including the Universal Declaration of Human Rights and the Canadian Human Rights Act. I argue that trigger warnings pose little to no harm when applied within a group of students who do not require them, yet offer significant benefits to students who find particular material triggering. In other words, trigger warnings may indeed be more beneficial for certain (marginalized) demographics than for privileged populations. Thus, while they may not benefit everyone directly, it is in essence a privilege simply to *not require* trigger warnings. It is therefore not only ethical, but *equitable* practice to provide accommodations such as trigger warnings in a university classroom in order to abide by universal human rights standards and reduce the volume of harm that is committed when requests for trigger warnings are disrespected, scoffed at, criticized, or ignored. Universities are obligated by law to provide accessible opportunities for students with disabilities, and trigger warnings offer an effective compromise in these circumstances. When an individual or group's right to be safe collides with inclusion of challenging or traumatic subject matter, trigger warnings deliver an alternative to the omission or censorship of triggering content while integrating safety provisions for students living with disabilities caused by exposure to trauma.

Patterns of Victimization and Trauma

Experiences of trauma and victimization are much more likely to affect particular demographics. Everyone has different experiences of privilege, oppression, and trauma that shape their position in the world and in any given space, such as the classroom. Most notably, individuals and groups who are members of marginalized, racialized, and other minoritized groups are statistically more likely to be abused, assaulted, under-resourced, and unsupported, all factors that correlate strongly with higher instances of posttraumatic stress disorder among these populations. By providing statistics around violent crimes, I demonstrate how some demographics are at higher risk for violence, and hence trauma, as a result of their respective sex, gender, sexuality, ethnicity, socioeconomic class, ability, or other factor. In order to rationalize the merit of trigger warnings within academia, it is important to understand the implications of trauma and PTSD as these issues are experienced within particular populations. To illustrate the dramatic differences in patterns of victimization among marginalized demographics, I use intimate-partner abuse as a point of reference from which to compare incidences of violence among defined groups.

The General Social Survey (GSS), which is conducted every five years, is the most comprehensive source of information on patterns of criminal victimization in Canada and contains the widest range of data that is cross-referenced within a single source. Some examples of demographics that are most likely to be impacted by criminal violence as indicated within the 2014 GSS are first and foremost women, who were found to be "twice as likely as men to experience being sexually assaulted, beaten, choked or threatened with a gun or a knife."[1]

Results from the same survey indicated that individuals who self-identified as "gay, lesbian, or bisexual" were victimized within intimate partnerships at rates that were double those reported within heterosexual relationships.[2] Indigenous women (classified as "Aboriginal" within government statistics) were more than three times more likely to experience abuse at the hands of their current or former intimate partners as compared to non-Indigenous-identified Canadian women, and their abuse also tends to include the most severe forms of violence reportable.[3] Activity limitations such as physical and mental impairment, disability, and health problems were also significant factors contributing to vulnerability to violence, with rates of spousal abuse doubling among this population.[4] Significantly, mental health was cited as "the second most influential factor associated with the risk of violent victimization in 2014," and individuals who reported concerns about their mental wellness experienced rates of violence that were more than four times higher than those who evaluated their mental health as "excellent or very good."[5] Notably, individuals who reported a history of homelessness were victimized at rates five times higher than those who consistently maintained stable housing.[6] These statistics represent only a sample of the data that exist in support of the knowledge that marginalized demographics are significantly more vulnerable to violent crimes, with members of black, poor, and immigrant communities, transsexual persons, and individuals living with HIV or addictions or engaged in sex work all experiencing elevated rates of violence and, consequently, trauma. It is also important to note that intersecting identities further increase vulnerability among individuals who are members of multiple marginalized groups. For example, female Indigenous sex workers who are addicted to substances have been victimized in unspeakable numbers, as demonstrated in the 2014 Royal Canadian Mounted Police (RCMP) Report *"Missing and Murdered Aboriginal Women: A National Operational Overview."*[7]

To be clear, inclusion within one or multiple marginalized groups is not itself a risk factor for victimization. Rather, corresponding social structures such as racism, sexism, homophobia, transphobia, ableism, and classism enable heightened rates of violence, and offenders perpetrate with the conscious intention of selecting victims with reduced social power. Not only does membership in specific identity groups increase vulnerability to violence; it also decreases the likelihood that a report of violence will be believed if disclosed. Intersections between marginalization and poverty also indicate that members of the populations in question are frequently underresourced and undersupported—factors that have been closely linked to the development of PTSD among those who experience violence and trauma.[8] Consequently, the difference between a "natural" recovery and manifestation of PTSD is closely linked to the level and quality of social supports in place for each individual. This understanding helps to contextualize the difference between experiences of trauma and manifestation of PTSD, since not everyone processes trauma in the same way, and individual responses depend on several factors, including personal history (which may or may not include abuse or trauma), belief systems, resources, relationships, stability, supports, abilities, and mental health. The nature of a traumatic event is therefore not the sole or even the most significant factor in determining an individual's response, both immediately as well as on an ongoing basis. In other words, an individual's unique experience and interpretation of a traumatic event is more indicative of the outcome than the details of the event itself.

Approximately 75 percent of the general population will experience an incident broadly defined as "traumatic" over the course of their lifetime.[9] As demonstrated in the statistics around intimate partner violence, victimization is not random, and specific groups are much more likely to be among that 75 percent. However, even within those populations, only a small percentage will develop symptoms of or be diagnosed with PTSD. In approximately 25 percent of cases, exposure to trauma will result in posttraumatic stress disorder, which is determined based on the persistence of intrusive symptoms, including flashbacks, anxiety, and panic attacks, often activated by exposure to material that triggers memories of an initial trauma, such as visual imagery.[10] The classification of PTSD as a disorder, illness, or disability is problematic for a number of reasons. The pathologization of human response to unnatural traumatic stressors does not account for the disproportionate victimization of vulnerable sectors, which is itself the most significant determinant of "risk" for PTSD. That said, in the context of current medical paradigms, PTSD remains categorized as such. It is not my position that a medicalized approach is the most appropriate or accurate method to respond to this framework of trauma reconciliation. However, this chapter is written within the parameters of the current model in order to draw attention to the legislative obligations of public institutions, such as universities, often acting as authorities in the absence of ethical considerations.

Posttraumatic Stress Disorder

The *Diagnostic and Statistical Manual of Mental Disorders-5* (*DSM-5*) specifies which criteria determine the presence of PTSD in an individual who has experienced trauma. The first factor is exposure to a traumatic stressor, which includes "exposure to actual or threatened death, serious injury or sexual violation" in relation to one or more of the following scenarios: An individual may experience a traumatic event directly or witness it in person; may learn that a traumatic event has been threatened or happened to a close friend or family member; or may experience "first-hand repeated or extreme exposure to aversive details of the traumatic event [that is] not through media, pictures, television or movies unless work-related."[11] The impact of such exposure remains the same regardless of whether the event is accidental or of a deliberately violent nature.

There is a wide range of potential human responses to trauma, and resilience is the most widespread outcome. Challenging consequences may also include depression, substance use, eating problems, and changes in personality function.[12] However, the presence of such behaviors does not always constitute a manifestation of PTSD. In fact, among those who experience trauma, including those who initially exhibit symptoms associated with PTSD, the majority will experience a reduction in symptoms within one to three months in the absence of any interventions,[13] although approximately 9 percent will go on to experience symptoms that are characteristic of PTSD. Significantly, women comprise 12.8 percent of this cohort, whereas men represent only 5.3 percent.[14] There are many factors contributing to the vast difference between these groups, including the nature of trauma affecting women, who are much more likely to experience sexualized violence as well as intimate partner abuse. The type, severity, and rate of violence are clear factors in determining correlations between intimate partner violence and the onset of PTSD. For example, survivors of violence that was classified as being of the "most severe" type, including "sexual assault, beating, choking, or being threatened with a gun or knife," as well as those who reported multiple incidents as opposed to a single assault, were much more likely to experience symptoms related to PTSD.[15]

In addition to exposure to a traumatic stressor, the criteria for PTSD includes four distinct categories, each encompassing clusters of symptoms used to determine the presence of PTSD. These categories are "re-experiencing, avoidance, negative cognitions and mood, and arousal." Re-experiencing includes flashbacks, "spontaneous memories," and recurring dreams, whereas avoidance refers to "distressing memories, thoughts, feelings or external reminders of the traumatic event." Negative cognitions and mood may indicate "a persistent and distorted sense of blame of self or others," memory loss around key aspects of the event, and social detachment and lack of engagement with others. Arousal symptoms include hypervigilance, sleep disturbances, and engagement with "fight, flight, or freeze" responses in the absence of an actual threat.[16] Arousal symptoms are normative in the presence of an active threat and signify the human body's natural inclination to remain safe by reverting to primitive, instinctual protective mechanisms as an intrinsic form of self-defense. However, the same responses persist for individuals with PTSD on an ongoing basis, which is the differentiating factor. Indications of PTSD relate to persistence of symptoms beyond a defined period of time (generally three months), and impairment of function that is associated with symptoms of the traumatic event and unrelated to preexisting issues connected to mental health or substance use.[17] While these conditions often present in the aftermath of a significant encounter with trauma, the most prominent indicator of PTSD is the inability to recover. Thus, the brain of an individual who is impacted by PTSD may remain in "trauma mode" when that person is exposed to triggers of the traumatic event, even when the individual is physically safe, and the same reactions that everyone experiences in response to a traumatic event can occur as a result of exposure to memories of the initial trauma.

It is important to understand PTSD in order to truly comprehend the all-encompassing effects that may be experienced by individuals living with PTSD who are exposed to triggers of their traumatic event. As indicated in the *DSM-5*, this condition is the result of trauma and not the consequence of a co-occurring disorder. Trauma responses are a natural human reaction to violence, which impacts particular groups of people at rates that are much higher than others. The "arousal" category highlights the very real physical manifestations of fear that can accompany experiences of PTSD and may be triggered by anything that provokes memories of an individual's experience of trauma. This includes smells, sounds, tastes, words, images, and more; it is unique to each individual and dependent on what one's own memory retained in relation to the trauma. Thus, "triggers" can be anything that serves as a reminder of the initial traumatic event. For example, a woman who was sexually assaulted may recall details such as the smell of a deodorant, cologne, gum, cigarettes, or alcohol or be triggered by a song or film that was playing at the time of the incident. She may even react to a specific article of clothing, season, or type of furniture. While it is not feasible to predict the unique elements that may be associated with individual experiences of trauma, it is quite reasonable to expect that sexual assault and rape as overarching themes are reasonable sources of trauma and therefore triggering to those who have been impacted by sexual violence. This fact remains consistent regardless of the unique details surrounding individual circumstances. Thus, while it is not always reasonable to offer trigger warnings for content pertaining to specific personal items (such as gum or deodorant), it is entirely feasible to let a class know that course content will be dealing with the broader topic of sexual abuse. Since women are disproportionally affected by sexual violence—a risk that is increased through intersections of marginalized identities—it is women and marginalized demographics who are most likely to be triggered by exposure to images and material related to sexual violence. The same comparisons can be made in relation to engagement with graphic or violent content related to racism, colonialism, homophobia, transphobia, ableism, classism, war, disordered eating and body-shaming, suicide, and other broad themes connected to structural oppressions impacting marginalized communities and individuals.

Support, Management, and Recovery

Therapies and strategies that promote effective healing in the aftermath of trauma are based on the restoration of control, which is an element that is generally absent during an initial traumatic event. Thus, by offering trigger warnings, safety and healing are promoted by allowing opportunities to engage with triggering content in an environment that is safe and controlled. Treatment for PTSD varies, and many people living with the condition routinely employ techniques that permit them to maintain control in response to distress provoked by "triggers." Such strategies provide valuable resources for persons who have experienced trauma, as they are self-directed; may be confidentially practiced in silence, in any space, at any time; and can restore control in situations where a trauma survivor is physically safe, yet emotionally triggered. Trigger warnings therefore offer opportunities for trauma survivors to prepare for exposure to traumatic material by deliberately engaging in strategies that reduce or prevent the loss of control, which may otherwise be experienced in such circumstances. Certain techniques have been particularly successful in mitigating the impacts of PTSD for those who are affected by trauma in their day-to-day lives, especially in regard to meaningful engagement within academic institutions. Trigger warnings provide opportunities for individuals to practice self-care strategies such as grounding prior to and

29

throughout exposure to triggering content, thus alleviating the potential for harm that arises when exposure to traumatic content occurs in the absence of ability to prepare for exposure.

Grounding techniques are an example of strategies communicated in counseling and widely practiced as a coping mechanism in order to manage PTSD symptoms. They work by incorporating actions that emphasize safety through "grounding" oneself in the present moment, thus reducing the loss of control that may arise when one is triggered. Grounding techniques provoke engagement with one's present surroundings and often employ various senses in order to reinforce physical safety. Grounding is a particularly effective strategy as it encourages the brain to focus on the safety of one's current physical environment rather than being overcome by anxiety or panic as a result of intrusions that have been triggered by content associated with a historical traumatic event. This approach allows the individual an opportunity to differentiate between an intrusion (which feels very real in that moment) and an actual present physical threat. Trigger warnings are especially helpful for trauma survivors who need to practice grounding strategies in order to avoid being overwhelmed by trauma symptoms, including anxiety, flashbacks, or panic attacks, in response to exposure to triggering content.

Exposure therapy is another method that is frequently employed by trauma therapists in order to redirect arousal symptoms that do not serve a functional purpose in the current context. The successful application of exposure therapy is controlled and guided by the individual who is impacted by PTSD, ideally with the support of someone who is practiced and knowledgeable in the field of trauma and recovery. The guiding philosophies behind exposure therapy are based on safe and coordinated engagement with triggering material in order to reinforce security in the absence of active physical threats. Trigger warnings may therefore be applied as one element of exposure therapy by providing measured opportunities to engage with traumatic themes within a context of safety and support.

As demonstrated above, PTSD has the capacity to significantly impair function in those impacted by trauma, yet these approaches offer realistic alternatives to avoidance behaviors. This perspective differs from arguments that suggest that trigger warnings maintain avoidance and instead demonstrates the function of trigger warnings as a tool to support meaningful opportunities for engagement among PTSD-impacted individuals in academic pursuits that involve triggering themes. Therefore, as I have previously stated, the use of trigger warnings does not work to censor content that may provoke associations with trauma. Rather, trigger warnings offer a practical compromise for educators and students in circumstances where traumatic themes are applicable for educational purposes. In such instances, the triggering content may be contextualized in terms of its relevance to the course objectives, and problematic themes can ideally be deconstructed and analyzed in a safe and productive environment. Not only do these approaches benefit trauma survivors by providing opportunities to mentally prepare for exposure to the triggering themes, they enrich the educational experience by incorporating meaningful conversations about the implications of trauma and violence on community members whom we encounter and engage with it on an everyday basis. Furthermore, acknowledgment of the disproportionate violence, abuse, oppression, and trauma consistently affecting members of marginalized communities sensitizes privileged students to issues that impact others in significant and relevant ways.

Disability and Human Rights

Thus far, I have made a case for the application of trigger warnings primarily based on the need for equitable approaches to classroom design. These recommendations have been grounded in a recognition of the contrasting experiences of privilege and oppression that exist across identity groups, and they incorporate numerous, complicated contributing factors. While it is my position that trigger warnings are ethical practice in general due to aforementioned considerations, I will now shift toward a legal perspective in order to substantiate the merit of trigger warnings from a human rights–based legislative standpoint. Being that disability is a protected ground under the Canadian Human Rights Act, Canadian universities are legally accountable as employers and service providers under "Duty to Accommodate" provisions to engage in deliberate measures to eliminate differential treatment and barriers to opportunities for individuals or groups of individuals identified under "prohibited grounds of discrimination."[18] Adverse impacts of rules and practices experienced as the result of institutional failure to take steps toward eliminating disadvantages apply to the *impact* on protected individuals and groups, rather than the *intentions* of the institution. Posttraumatic stress disorder is classified as mental illness within the *Diagnostic and Statistical Manual of Mental Disorders* and recognized as such by the Canadian Mental Health Association.[19] This fact adds an additional dimension to conversations about the applicability of trigger warnings in university classrooms due to institutional obligations to meet accessibility requirements for students living with disabilities as identified under protected grounds outlined in human rights legislation. In order to put this information into perspective, I offer a brief background on human rights law.

In 1948, the Universal Declaration of Human Rights was adopted by the UN General Assembly as a guiding document upon which member nations have based individual guidelines for human rights legislation in their respective countries. The Universal Declaration of Human Rights thus sets standards to which all member nations must comply, as is the case with the Canadian Human Rights Act, which came into effect in 1977.[20] Although specific wording and interpretations vary somewhat by member state, the human rights essential frameworks are structured in accordance with this central document. Human rights legislation is designed to secure fundamental rights, including the right to be free from harassment and discrimination, the right to safety and security, the right to education, and the right to human dignity.[21] The Canadian Human Rights Act is therefore committed to the following principles:

> [A]ll individuals should have an opportunity equal with other individuals to make for themselves the lives that they are able and wish to have and to have their needs accommodated, consistent with their duties and obligations as members of society, without being hindered in or prevented from doing so by discriminatory practices based on race, national or ethnic origin, color, religion, age, sex, sexual orientation, marital status, family status, disability or conviction for an offence for which a pardon has been granted or in respect of which a record suspension has been ordered.[22]

As such, discrimination, including exclusion from full participation in society based on any of the aforementioned "protected grounds," is strictly prohibited. The legislative authority of Parliament has actively embedded antidiscrimination policies within legislation that pertains to equal access to education and employment. Whereas disability constitutes a "prohibited grounds of discrimination" within this act, individuals are protected from any action deemed discriminatory by employers, governments, and private companies, including universities.[23] Canadian law recognizes the fact that "sometimes people need to be treated differently to prevent or reduce discrimination" and therefore stipulates an "obligation to take steps to eliminate different and negative treatment of individuals, or groups of individuals based on prohibited grounds of discrimination," which includes disability.[24] This is referred to as "Duty to Accommodate" and "may require that alternative arrangements be made to ensure full participation of a person or group."[25] The Canadian Human Rights Commission acknowledges that it may be necessary to "accommodate people's needs on an individual basis," but advises that the courts have "made it clear that federal organizations should build accommodation into the way they do business as much as possible."[26] As an example, the Human Rights Commission suggests instituting policies designed to be universally accessible, rather than making individual accommodations on an as-needed basis, because it is preferable to "prevent barriers to accessibility from occurring in the first place, rather than to remove them retroactively."[27] Applying this principle to the use of trigger warnings in university classrooms supports proactive efforts to reduce discrimination based on disability by ensuring accessibility for students affected by common triggers associated with PTSD. In acknowledging social issues that have been a source of trauma for significant numbers of people, affected individuals are given an opportunity to participate fully in the pursuit of education, free of the fear that stems from nonproductive exposure to traumatic material.

Conclusion

In this chapter, I have advocated for the application of trigger warnings in academia from a trauma-informed, human rights–based perspective. I have explored statistics pertaining to crime and victimization in relation to demographic status and in particular marginalization in order to demonstrate connections between vulnerability, victimization, and trauma. I then contemplated the symptoms and consequences of trauma and PTSD in order to illustrate the all-encompassing impacts of trauma within the lives of those who are affected. I discussed healing mechanisms that are widely successful in managing the loss of control that individuals living with PTSD may experience when exposed to triggering content in the absence of trigger warnings, establishing the value of trigger warnings for survivors of trauma and PTSD. I then identified human rights legislation that university institutions are accountable to and that justify the use of trigger warnings as accommodations for students living with PTSD. While it is my position that the use of trigger warnings is universally advantageous as ethical pedagogical practice, this legislation provides the means to support the relevance of trigger warnings that are requested by students impacted by PTSD. In summary, I encourage those who are threatened or challenged by this practice to consider the comprehensive implications of this pedagogical method and to evaluate the importance of safety mechanisms in contrast to risks posed for trauma survivors in the absence of access to such accommodations for students with disabilities. A compassionate approach demands equity, and trigger warnings are a powerful tool in the pursuit of this end goal.

Notes

1. Canadian Centre for Justice Statistics, "Family Violence in Canada: A Statistical Profile, 2014," *Juristat*, January 21, 2016: 7.

2. Ibid., 14.

3. Ibid., 5, 16.

4. Ibid., 15.

5. Ibid., 3.

6. Ibid., 15.

7. Royal Canadian Mounted Police, *Missing and Murdered Aboriginal Women: A National Operational Overview,* 2014, http://www.rcmp-grc.gc.ca/en/missing-and-murdered-aboriginal-women-national-operational-overview.

8. Canadian Centre for Justice Statistics, "Family Violence in Canada," 15.

9. Bruce J. Cohen, *Theory and Practice of Psychiatry* (New York: Oxford University Press, 2003), 275.

10. Ibid., 275.

11. U.S. Department of Veterans Affairs, "PTSD: National Center for PTSD Continuing Education—PTSD Overview," February 14, 2016, http://www.ptsd.va.gov/professional/continuing_ed/ptsd_overview.asp.

12. P. L. Farrugia, K. L. Mills, E. Barrett et al., "Childhood Trauma among Individuals with Co-Morbid Substance Use and Post Traumatic Stress Disorder," *Mental Health and Substance Use: Dual Diagnosis* 4, no. 4 (2011): 314.

13. Cohen, *Theory and Practice of Psychiatry*, 275.

14. Anne C. Wagner, "Foundations for Trauma Competent Care," workshop presented at Ontario Harm Reduction Conference, October 26–27, 2015.

15. Canadian Centre for Justice Statistics, "Family Violence in Canada," 9.

16. U.S. Department of Veterans Affairs, "PTSD."

17. Ibid.

18. Canadian Human Rights Commission, "Duty to Accommodate," last modified September 1, 2013, http://www.chrc-ccdp.gc.ca/eng/content/duty-accommodate.

19. Canadian Mental Health Association, "Post-Traumatic Stress Disorder," 2016, http://www.cmha.ca/mental_health/post-traumatic-stress-disorder/#.WIDJvlMrKUk.

20. Government of Canada, Canadian Human Rights Act (R.S.C. 1985, c. H-6), Justice Laws Website, http://laws-lois.justice.gc.ca/eng/acts/h-6/.

21. United Nations General Assembly, Universal Declaration of Human Rights (1948), http://www.un.org/en/universal-declaration-human-rights/.

22. Government of Canada, Canadian Human Rights Act.

23. Canadian Human Rights Commission, "How Are Human Rights Protected in Canada?" September 1, 2013, http://www.chrc-ccdp.gc.ca/eng/content/how-are-human-rights-protected-canada.

24. Canadian Human Rights Commission, "Duty to Accommodate."

25. Ibid.

26. Ibid.

27. Ibid.

Bibliography

American Psychiatric Association. *Diagnostic and Statistical Manual of Mental Disorders-5*. Washington, DC: American Psychiatric Association, 2013.

Canadian Centre for Justice Statistics. "Family Violence in Canada: A Statistical Profile, 2014." *Juristat*, January 21, 2016.

Canadian Human Rights Commission. "Duty to Accommodate." Last modified September 1, 2013. http://www.chrc-ccdp.gc.ca/eng/content/duty-accommodate.

———. "How Are Human Rights Protected in Canada?" Last modified September 1, 2013. http://www.chrc-ccdp.gc.ca/eng/content/how-are-human-rights-protected-canada.

Canadian Mental Health Association. "Post-Traumatic Stress Disorder." 2016. http://www.cmha.ca/mental_health/post-traumatic-stress-disorder/#.WIDJvlMrKUk.

Cohen, Bruce J. *Theory and Practice of Psychiatry*. New York: Oxford University Press, 2003.

Farrugia, P. L., K. L. Mills, E. Barrett et al. "Childhood Trauma among Individuals with Co-Morbid Substance Use and Post Traumatic Stress Disorder." *Mental Health and Substance Use: Dual Diagnosis* 4, no. 4 (2011): 314–26.

Government of Canada. Canadian Human Rights Act (R.S.C. 1985, c. H-6). Justice Laws Website. http://laws-lois.justice.gc.ca/eng/acts/h-6/.

Royal Canadian Mounted Police. *Missing and Murdered Aboriginal Women: A National Operational Overview*. 2014. http://www.rcmp-grc.gc.ca/en/missing-and-murdered-aboriginal-women-national-operational-overview.

United Nations General Assembly. Universal Declaration of Human Rights. 1948. http://www.un.org/en/universal-declaration-human-rights/.

U.S. Department of Veterans Affairs. "PTSD: National Center for PTSD Continuing Education—PTSD Overview." February 14, 2016. http://www.ptsd.va.gov/professional/continuing_ed/ptsd_overview.asp.

Wagner, Anne C. "Foundations for Trauma Competent Care." Workshop presented at Ontario Harm Reduction Conference, October 26–27, 2015.

CHAPTER THREE

CONTAGIOUS SPEECH
Mediating the Eating Disorder
Panic through Trigger Warnings
Stephanie Houston Grey

I n February of 2016 the Bias Response Team for Northern Colorado
University was called to action after concerns surfaced about a cooking
competition organized by residence halls that generated complaints
about strict dieting rules, promotion of unhealthy foods, and a competitive atmosphere that were triggering students with eating disorders. It can
be argued that no conversation about trigger warnings is complete without
a discussion of the role that eating disorders have played in shaping this
debate. As one surveys the medical cartography of mental illness, it becomes clear that no constellation of conditions has been more difficult to
define and treat for health care professionals than eating disorders. While
they have been recognized as medical conditions for close to two hundred
years, anorexia and bulimia erupted into both the professional and popular imagination in the late 1960s and early 1970s. During the past forty
years, these conditions have been the subjects of extensive research and
intensive clinical investigation and treatment. In one assessment of the
success rates of treatment programs and paradigms that came to dominate the eating disorder landscape during the latter part of the twentieth
century, researchers found that there had been no improvement in treatment outcomes and that the conditions seemed to be intensifying rather
than improving.[1] The way that anorexia and bulimia appear to spread at
an alarming rate has created frustration among those who have dedicated
themselves to treating them as they grapple with explanations for how
and why these conditions remain so difficult for modern medicine. Given
these concerns, the debate about trigger warnings has become central to
our understanding of eating disorders, and perhaps it is time to assess how

effective these strategies are in challenging these conditions given this lack of success.

Definitions of the modern eating disorder are heavily reliant on models of contagion to explain why they remain so prevalent, leading to the careful monitoring and containment of these conditions by policing triggering stimuli among vulnerable populations. Potentially triggering messages usually fall into one of two types: those that deal with strict dietary regimes and those featuring pictures of models that are perceived by the viewer as extremely thin. Over the past decade, the trigger warning has emerged as a controversial topic on college campuses in the United States and Europe, yet the practice of identifying certain types of speech or interactions as potentially harmful to the psychology of the listener actually extends back to the 1970s when therapists first began to confront eating disorders with a unified public health response. Often the debates surrounding trigger warnings in contemporary culture revolve around the idea that these attempts at monitoring trauma serve to limit the scope and depth of students' experience by disabling classroom debate.[2] This has led to a backlash against these forms of institutional control and self-regulation by scholars and commentators who are concerned that the practice of civil debate is threatened by these campaigns. Some commentators actually link the spread of trigger warnings to a form of cultural aggression, terming it "vindictive protectiveness," in which closed-minded thinkers place boundaries around themselves and others—leaving a generation of young people unable to cope with an inevitable set of social and political realities that will not respect their sensitivities.[3] Often these scholars will point to research that suggests that those individuals who make the trauma of past experiences central to their identity and fail to confront triggering stimuli in a direct fashion have a much lower rate of recovery.[4] Despite this ambivalence about trigger warnings and a lack of clarity in the research surrounding how effective they are in creating a safe environment, they continue to provoke dialogue as First Amendment advocates critique them as a first step toward using trauma as a means to limit public conversation. This chapter expands this conversation by exploring the eating disorder as one of the first areas where the trigger warning was deployed as a means to monitor behavior in the face of a public health crisis.

In an analysis of the ways that the language of trauma has influenced modern discourse, Kirby Farrell suggests that we have entered a uniquely posttraumatic era in which many differing types of discourse are often me-diated through the lens of traumatic experience.[5] Therefore, trauma dis-course often hovers beneath the surface of cultural consciousness, causing disruptions in indirect ways. Farrell also notes that trauma can be spread and amplified through a dialogue in which the idea of PTSD is symboli-cally connected to issues that might seem ancillary, such as cultural change or technological anxiety. While eating disorders have their roots in antiq-uity, their modern manifestation has been one marked by deep cultural anxieties surrounding consumption patterns and the size and shape of the human body. In this highly contested terrain, the eating disorder has become a symbolic container for a host of other cultural anxieties. By the late 1970s, these anxieties became so acute that containment strategies were deployed to contain the spread of these conditions—a campaign that was similar to a moral panic.

Stuart Hall defines the moral panic as a collection of events that gain widespread media attention by stimulating public concern and then provoking an emotional response, usually fear, that is disproportionate to the actual threat.[6] Thus, fear of an event, a group of individuals, or a set of ideas will stimulate a state-sponsored crackdown that is both unethical and ineffective. Historically, whenever contagion metaphors have been applied to public health crises, they can often lead to the criminalization and isolation of particular individuals and social groups.[7] When research-ers theorized that eating-disordered individuals, along with commercial culture, were "triggering" one another, the reaction from the therapeu-tic community was swift and forceful. As the following discussion will demonstrate, the result of these crackdowns was that eating-disordered individuals lost many basic civil rights in the effort to contain these ill-nesses. Yet these campaigns designed to contain triggering behaviors by limiting expression have thus far proven unsuccessful,[8] calling into ques-tion the capacity of any institutional body to limit the impacts of trauma by deploying barriers to expression.

The following analysis examines the ways that the eating disordered informed the history and theory of the trigger warning by exploring how these devices emerged as an uneasy détente between those with these conditions and the expert communities who seek to understand them. The first section surveys the emergence of the eating disorder as a mod-ern phenomenon, particularly the strategies employed by early therapists who sought to both treat these conditions and make sense of them to a larger public. A key component of the strategies deployed by this community was to define certain types of expression and symbolic action as triggering to individuals with eating disorders, warning the public that eating-disordered individuals had the capacity to spread their condition to an otherwise "healthy" individual. The second section then examines the politicizing of the eating disorder, which began to gain momentum in the 1980s, leading to a discourse that focused largely on the damaging consequences of certain body images used in the commercial culture, particularly among feminist scholars. While much of this body-image theorizing was designed as a tool of empowerment, the linkage of triggering events to the patriarchy inadvertently oversimplified the etiology of the eating disorder and led to an even more systematic discourse of criminalization. In her insightful essay on trigger warnings, Jill Filipovic notes that their very presence will often shape the auditor's response to what they are about to hear and see, preventing them from coming to the discourse with an open, critical mind.[9] For the history of eating disorders, the trigger warning, however well-intentioned, became an instrument of containment that shaped public perceptions about people with these conditions and may have inadvertently played a role in the lack of success that treatment programs have experienced.

Clinical Containment of Eating Disorders

Thinking of anorexia and bulimia as contagious illnesses like viruses, only spread via the channel of symbolic activity instead of a traditional biological route, has become a mainstay in clinical understandings of these conditions. This view was reinforced as early as 1978 in Steven Levenkron's *The Best Little Girl in the World*, a fictional account in which he dramatized his work with patients that he claimed to cure using methods that involved exercising strict control over communication with them and what they consumed.[10] This work became a significant component of the public health alerts surrounding anorexia and produced an after-school movie that launched the career of Jennifer Jason Leigh. Levenkron also gained some notoriety as the celebrity health counselor to pop star Karen Carpenter, who died of an ipecac overdose in 1983 after battling an eating disorder. The narrative surrounding

Carpenter was instructive to the public imagination about the ways that individuals were triggered to have eating disorders. As a pop icon, Carpenter was subjected to the commercial industry's demand for thinness, as well as criticism from family members when she began to gain weight. Carpenter would be the model for other therapists who viewed her as a naive young woman attempting to attain a false standard of perfection using these misguided practices.[11] The image that emerged of the eating-disordered individual was that of someone who was very strong-willed but at the same time highly vulnerable to the social triggers that provoke weight anxiety. This section explores how the emerging image of the eating-disordered individual led to widespread concern that discourse, cultural images, and language could trigger these psychological responses and subsequently generated anxiety that directly resulted in a new therapeutic regime in which language had to be policed to avoid these triggering effects. This anxiety would become one of the direct forerunners of the modern trigger warning.

Often, eating disorders are treated using an addiction model rather than traditional mental illness categories such schizophrenia. One of the key concepts within addiction treatment literature is that of social network triggers, the idea that once an individual exits a recovery program she or he should avoid people or organizations associated with the addictive behavior because these experiences will provoke a relapse.[12] This model has been extended and amplified in the eating disorder debate to suggest that individuals with these conditions tend to trigger one another's behaviors. In one study, researchers replicated analyses from the 1980s using geographical cluster methodologies that suggested that self-reports of eating-disordered behaviors tended to occur in specific populations, leading to the conclusion that these conditions were being spread from one person to the next.[13] Another recent investigation cautions clinicians against allowing both in-patient and out-patient eating-disordered individuals to participate in group therapy because the participants will intensify and spread their conditions to others in the group setting.[14] This concept would become a guiding principle in monitoring the wider eating disorder community. If individuals are capable of triggering one another's conditions, then it was recommended that communication between these persons should be monitored by a clinician who would regulate what could or could not be said in certain clinical settings. By suggesting that an individual who might express certain feelings or experiences could trigger another to engage in these behaviors reinforced the idea that not only was the commercial beauty culture to blame for these conditions, but that individuals identified with them became vectors for their spread. More specifically, eating disorders were not so much triggered by beauty culture, but by contact with other individuals who had already been triggered to engage in eating-disordered behavior. The resulting perspective was that eating-disordered behaviors spread in chain reactions from person to person.

Perhaps one of the areas where trigger warnings have some of their most controversial applications is the sharing of eating disorder experiences on the Internet. As online eating-disordered communities began to emerge in these digital spaces, including groups that were initially termed pro-ana (i.e., pro anorexia), websites were shut down by clinicians who warned Internet providers that the individuals who participated on them were triggering the spread of eating disorders. Researchers began to study these sites and quickly found that viewing them did have the result of heightening body anxiety and recommended shutting them down without First Amendment consideration.[15] The bulk of Internet providers agreed without protest, and unmonitored eating-disordered websites soon became an outlaw community. Just to clarify for a general audience, groups of websites in which no illegal activity was taking place were shut down with no due process and no consideration for freedom of speech. This action might represent the most extensive and underreported violation of the First Amendment in Internet history. Given that the eating disorder community was highly vulnerable due to social stigma, it had few resources to fight back. The extent of these censorship campaigns was most vividly evidenced at the international level when a conservative member of the French Parliament, Valérie Boyer, proposed legislation to criminalize any means of mass communication found to promote eating disorders and punish it with up to three years in prison and a €45,000, or $71,000, fine. "We have noticed," she said in a press interview, "that the sociocultural and media environment seems to favor the emergence of troubled nutritional behavior, and that is why I think it necessary to act."[16] From this standpoint, simply expressing the feelings or ideations that one experiences while in an eating-disordered phase could be viewed as triggering and could be subject to criminal scrutiny.

The problem with labeling eating disorder expression as triggering was that these policies were operating with certain misconceptions about the true scope of the problem they were facing as well as ignoring the impacts that these campaigns had on these communities. For example, further research revealed that visiting a sanctioned eating disorder site that provided health information about these conditions from a clinical perspective was just as triggering as visiting sites that were run by non-sanctioned eating-disordered individuals.[17] As noted above, trigger warnings will often shape perceptions about texts. This argument can be extended to suggest that they can also influence our perceptions about people or groups. As clinicians were labeling the experience of eating disorders as a primary trigger for the condition, there was a steady rise in the stigmatization of individuals associated with these conditions. Both the general public and health care workers share highly negative attitudes toward anorexia and bulimia, leading those who self-identify with these conditions to isolate themselves from others.[18] The general public and health care workers alike are more likely to blame those with eating disorders for their conditions.[19] Perhaps even more disturbing, anorexics and bulimics are much more heavily stigmatized than sufferers of other mental illnesses such as schizophrenia and depression.[20] As eating-disordered individuals were increasingly associated with the spread of the condition, the use of trigger arguments became a primary means for justifying certain attitudes about these conditions that served to silence and isolate these individuals.

Today, non-sanctioned eating-disordered websites can exist if they provide trigger warnings for those who might visit them. As a result, trigger warnings are abundant throughout this Internet community. Often these bloggers and commentators proceed with a high level of self-awareness about these ways that trigger warnings shape their lives. The key factor that may have been overlooked by early researchers who were searching for a specific cause for anorexia and bulimia was the fact that triggering stimuli are virtually everywhere in the individual's environment. For example, Marya Hornbacher's 1998 memoir *Wasted*, which is one of the most unflinching and accurate portrayals of the eating-disordered experience ever written, was quickly banned in clinical settings because it was deemed a potential trigger threat.[21] In one analysis of the controversy surrounding *Wasted*, a prominent eating disorder blogger known as Grey writes that "eating [d]isordered people, when not actively attempting to recover, are going to find a way to trigger themselves, ultimately. We will. We're looking for material and we'll find it. There's a definite trend in memoirs and books about eating disorders to censor the numerical material: ie [*sic*], BMI, lowest weight, calories eaten in a day. But that doesn't stop eating disordered individuals from compulsively seeking out material that feeds our obsession."[22] Given the fact that we live in a toxic food culture and that so many people suffer from some form of food neurosis, it is not surprising that these conditions are so widespread. From this standpoint, the eating disorder trigger warning is virtually useless simply because these conditions can be triggered by so many stimuli.

Going back to the case at Northern Colorado, we see a healthy cooking competition labeled as triggering. No doubt it was. The problem that the eating disorder poses for the larger trigger warning debate is that it is impossible to completely limit stimuli because there are potentially harmful messages deeply coded in all of our eating practices. Locating all of a culture's eating neuroses in one group and then effectively criminalizing it as the primary vector for the spread of these conditions demonstrates the power that trigger warning censorship has in limiting expression. By labeling those who expressed their eating disorder experience as triggering others, and following through with an extensive censorship campaign, eating-disordered individuals soon learned that the burgeoning trigger warning practice was a primary means for policing how they communicated with one another and what they were able to share about what they thought and felt.

Politicizing the Eating Disorder

As one moves into the 1980s and 1990s, the eating disorder would find itself at the heart of debates surrounding feminism, body image, and commercial culture. As scholars began to explore the potential political impacts of cultural enactments such as movies, music, and advertising, eating-disordered individuals would find themselves caught in an uneasy tension. Since eating-disordered individuals would be labeled as symptomatic of this dangerous commercial culture, they would soon begin to employ the trigger warning in their own discourse as a means to avoid attack from feminist critics. The trigger warning became a means for bracketing discourse—allowing the individual to speak about an experience while attempting to avoid being labeled an agent of the patriarchy. This marked the time period when many scholars began to investigate the relationship between gender, politics, and patriarchy in an attempt to come to terms with the ways that mass media impact the consciousness of young women. One of the primary symptoms of the ubiquitous tendrils of the beauty culture in America was the presence of eating disorders—conditions that were viewed as symptoms of patriarchal oppression. This would be reinforced by scholars such as media critic Jean Kilbourne, whose books and university lecture tours called *Killing Us Softly* outlined the ways that visual advertising promoted unhealthy self-concepts.[23] These lecture tours would draw linkages between visual imagery and eating disorders, suggesting that marketers were playing a key role in the subjugation of women by subtly attacking their self-concepts. This was reinforced by authors such as Naomi Wolf, who coined the phrase "beauty myth" as way to describe the complex cartography between media images and particular adolescent women.[24] In these accounts, young girls' experience with media becomes a form of trauma that causes them to engage in self-destructive practices as a way to manage their own pain and suffering. These works sought to provide young women with a defensive network against these images. One outgrowth of the body image debates was the idea that certain graphic depictions of the human body could be harmful to young women, leading to concerns over the ways these images should be mediated. Given the prevalence of body image debates on college campuses, one unintended consequence of this discourse was a dialogue of marginalization that marked the human body as itself a terrain that could trigger eating-disordered behavior.

To understand how this debate unfolded requires exploring how the eating disorder became a symbol in the current political climate of the academy. One of the earliest eating disorder therapists, Hilde Bruch, drew early correlations between women with eating disorders and the current political climate surrounding gender in America.[25] The prevalence of certain body images led to the conclusion that when eating-disordered patients came together they could use this media climate as a stimulus to trigger one another's behaviors. She wrote that "in order to avoid the most dreaded fate, that of becoming fat, they brainwash themselves (this expression is used by nearly everyone) to change their feelings."[26] This idea that people with eating disorders represented political refugees that had been subjected to a brainwashing campaign would dominate this debate. When combined with the assumption that those with eating disorders could trigger one another's behavior, it led to the logical conclusion that anorexics and bulimics could actually stimulate the growth of the illness in others simply by representing themselves in a particular way or possessing a certain body type. From this standpoint, something as simple as photography can be triggering. Taking a picture of one's own body and displaying it in a public forum might be viewed as a form of political oppression and provoke censure. The result of this connection became problematic because it began to criminalize those with eating disorders as potential traitors to their own gender by spreading patriarchal codes. This was vividly demonstrated in one of the best-selling eating disorder books in history, Susan Bordo's *Unbearable Weight*. Bordo writes that "the anoretic, of course, is unaware that she is making a political statement. She may, indeed, be hostile to feminism and any other critical perspectives that she views as disputing her own autonomy and control or questioning the cultural ideals around which her life is organized."[27] This would lay the groundwork for a campaign that would further isolate those with eating disorders as not only difficult to treat but also as gender oppressors. As brainwashed agents of the patriarchy, the experiences that these individuals shared could not be taken at face value. Because they were triggering and spreading patriarchal codes, their narratives had to be filtered through the political and ideological lens of gender politics.

Long before trigger warnings became a First Amendment concern in the academy, bloggers and commentators who host recovery sites had been toying with the language of triggers as a way to navigate their own emotions. This dance was necessitated by a political climate in which certain forms of expression, such as describing a particularly symptomatic day, became an act of political treachery rather than an attempt to come to terms with a difficult condition and seek the comfort of others. The prevalence of the idea of triggering stimuli was thus woven into the discourse surrounding eating disorders, with some participants describing their own triggers as either positive or negative. These are not value assessments, but polarities of triggers that can be used to describe the impacts of certain images. Positive triggers are usually thin models, while negative triggers are depicted on the larger side of the body size spectrum. Positive triggers are seen as ideals toward which the eating-disordered individual should strive. The negative trigger would depict larger women in poses designed to elicit disgust and thus represented a means for motivating the eating-disordered person to avoid the uncontrolled consumption associated with these bodies. The focus in eating disorder sites on visual imagery is, in part, a response to the academic debates over the politics of gender and trigger warnings revolving around eating disorders. Some commentators have begun to take note of this discourse in Internet communities, with one author suggesting that they came about in the feminist sections of Tumblr around 2007.[28] The trigger warning discourse within the eating disorder community itself is far older, as these individuals have been grappling with trigger campaigns since 1978. Today, scholars and commentators who use art to mediate their experience with these conditions exercise care to label their work, almost always providing detailed self-analysis. For example, Collen Clark writes, "I know that some of my body-focused work can be triggering or indicative of some disordered tendencies, thoughts, and feelings, but I am no expert in eating disorders. I want to offer my art, my blog, and my inbox as safe places for anyone who needs to vent to a listening ear."[29] This focus upon safety in the eating disorder community is often not the result of media campaigns but an attempt to find a safe haven from the discourse of trigger warnings itself.

In what may seem to be an interesting irony, the trigger warning has not served to free eating-disordered individuals from their condition, but actually serves as a type of cultural prison. As political dissidents, these individuals have a long history with the trigger warning culture and thus a very complicated relationship to it. Eating disorder expert and blogger Caroline Miller sums this up quite well in one of her recent posts:

Not long ago, I posted a hopeful note on an eating disorder website to someone who was struggling. I don't recall everything I wrote, but it was compassionate and directed at the topic. It wasn't long before I got a note from the moderator saying that my post had been removed because it was "triggering," but there was no explanation of why that was.

Baffled, I continued to watch the site to see what *wasn't* considered "triggering," and it included long, sad posts from people who weren't doing well, and who were complaining about their lack of progress, their unfortunate circumstances, and their relapses. I found the posts honest, but wondered why they weren't "triggering" to someone who was hoping to find a way to get better and stay better.[30] [emphasis in original]

This example is included not because it is unique, but because it reflects the long-term trend of those with eating disorders viewing trigger warning censorship in political rather than medical terms. They often express frustration with these efforts and view them as a means to silence them from voicing their experiences. As one begins to share an eating disorder experience with others, these comments will be deleted because they are deemed to be triggering to others. This larger campaign provokes the question as to how such decisions are made and whether or not they are productive. As eating disorders have become a symbol within academic debates over gender, power, and body image, those suffering from eating disorders have found their experiences filtered through a political lens that necessitates that they grapple with this discourse.

Conclusion

The idea that certain experiences or images can transmit trauma from individual to individual has been one of the key ideas that have informed the eating disorder debate in America. It is not surprising, then, that trigger warnings have been one of the key ideas that have been used to mediate this body panic. It is important to note that eating-disordered contagion has been described as a condition that does not need to be directed at a traumatized individual to cause harm. Otherwise healthy non-traumatized individuals have been described as vulnerable to the influence of this discourse. This is the primary reason why these conditions are so heavily contained and regulated within the mass media and Internet. What the preceding analysis reveals is that these panics surrounding trigger warnings may in fact have negative consequences for those with these conditions. Given the prevalence of triggering images in a culture that suffers from a wide array of food neuroses, it is almost impossible to avoid these triggers. This is demonstrated by the fact that many individuals are not triggered by images of thin models, but may in fact be triggered by other stimuli such as descriptions of restrictive dietary purity as in the Northern Colorado University case. What is needed is a more comprehensive and complex approach to this problem rather than simply labeling these images and individuals as triggering and attempting to contain or silence the discourse. It may be time to develop a more systematic method of talking about eating behaviors in America in a way that provides critical thinking tools and skill sets that allow consumers of this discourse to engage with it in a productive and healthy way. Until this is accomplished, trigger warnings and censorship programs will simply serve to repress this conversation and keep the experiences of these individuals in the closet. Given the failure of prior approaches to stem the spread of these conditions, a reexamination of clinical and cultural strategies might provide us with new avenues for talking about these eating disorders. Any strategy that seeks to limit access or silence dialogue can only be counterproductive, as it ignores the fundamental nature of conditions that thrive in isolation.

Notes

1. Hans-Christophe Steinhausen, "The Outcome of Anorexia Nervosa in the 20th Century," *American Journal of Psychiatry* 159 (2002): 1284–93.

2. Mick Hume, *Trigger Warning: Is the Fear of Being Offensive Killing Free Speech?* (New York: HarperCollins, 2015), 1–10.

3. Greg Lukianoff and Jonathan Haidt, "The Coddling of the American Mind," *The Atlantic*, September 2015.

4. Richard McNally, "Hazards Ahead," *Pacific Standard* 7 (2014): 16–17.

5. Kirby Farrell, *Post-Traumatic Culture: Injury and Interpretation in the Nineties* (Baltimore, MD: Johns Hopkins University Press, 1998), 10–12.

6. Stuart Hall, Chas Critcher, Tony Jefferson, John Clarke, and Brian Roberts, *Policing the Crisis: Mugging, the State, and Law and Order* (London: Macmillan, 1978), 5.

7. Martin Pernick, "Contagion and Culture," *American Literary History* 14 (2002): 858–65. See also: Michel Foucault, *Madness and Civilization: A History of Insanity in the Age of Reason*, translated by Richard Hurley (New York: Vintage Books, 1965).

8. Steinhausen, "The Outcome of Anorexia Nervosa," 1284.

9. Jill Filipovic, "We've Gone Too Far with 'Trigger Warnings,'" *The Guardian*, March 5, 2014, https://www.theguardian.com/commentisfree/2014/mar/05/trigger-warnings-can-be-counterproductive.

10. Steven Levenkron, *The Best Little Girl in the World* (Chicago: Contemporary Books, 1978).

11. See Kim Chernin, *The Obsession: Reflections on the Tyranny of Slenderness* (New York: Harper & Row, 1981) and *The Hungry Self: Women, Eating, and Identity* (New York: Times Books, 1985).

12. Elizabeth Epstein and Barbara McGrady, *Treatment That Works: A Cognitive Behavioral Treatment Program for Overcoming Alcohol Problems* (Oxford: Oxford University Press, 2009), 101.

13. Valerie Forman-Koffman and Cassie Cunningham, "Geographical Clustering of Eating Disorder Behaviors in U.S. High School Students," *International Journal of Eating Disorders* 41 (2008): 209–14.

14. Walter Vandereycken, "Can Eating Disorders Become 'Contagious' in Group Therapy and Specialized Inpatient Care?" *European Eating Disorders Review* 19 (2011): 289–95.

15. Anna Gwizdek, Kevin Gwizdek, and Anna Koszowska, "Pro-ana, Murderous Face of the Internet," *Progress in Health Science* 2 (2002): 158–61.

16. Doreen Carvujal, "French Law Makers Target Pro Anorexia Websites," *Boston Globe*, April 16, 2008.

17. Kelley Harper, Steffanie Sperry, and Kevin Thompson, "Viewership of Pro-eating Disorder Websites: Association with Body Image and Eating Disturbances," *International Journal of Eating Disorders* 41 (2008): 92–95.

18. See Michele Crisafulli, Ann Von Holle, and Cynthia Bulik, "Attitudes toward Anorexia Nervosa: The Impact of Framing on Blame and Stigma," *International Journal of Eating Disorders* 41 (2008): 333–39, and Emma Rich, "Anorexic Dis(connection): Managing Anorexia as an Illness and an Identity," *Sociology of Health and Illness* 28 (2006): 284–305.

19. Arthur Crisp, "Stigmatization of and Discrimination against People with Eating Disorders Including a Report of Two Nationwide Surveys," *European Eating Disorders Review* 13, no. 3 (2005): 147–52.

20. Maria-Christina Stewart, Pamela Keel, and Steven Schiavo, "Stigmatization of Anorexia Nervosa," *International Journal of Eating Disorders* 39 (2006): 320–25.

21. Marya Hornbacher, *Wasted: A Memoir of Anorexia and Bulimia* (New York: Harper Flamingo, 1998).

22. Grey, "In Defense of Marya Hornbacher's *Wasted*," *The Lightness of Being Grey*, https://greybird77.wordpress.com/2014/01/02/in-defense-of-marya -hornbachers-wasted/.

23. Jean Kilbourne, *Deadly Persuasion: Why Women and Girls Must Fight the Addictive Power of Advertising* (New York: Free Press, 1999).

24. Naomi Wolf, *The Beauty Myth: How Images of Beauty Are Used against Women* (New York: Harper, 2002).

25. Hilde Bruch, *Eating Disorders: Obesity, Anorexia and the Person Within* (New York: Basic Books, 1973).

26. Hilde Bruch, *The Golden Cage: The Enigma of Anorexia Nervosa* (Cambridge, MA: Harvard University Press, 1978), 4.

27. Susan Bordo, *Unbearable Weight: Feminism, Western Culture, and the Body.* (Berkeley: University of California Press, 1993), 176.

28. Joni Edelman, "Trigger Warnings: The Good, the Bad, the Pancakes," *Huffington Post*, October 5, 2015, http://www.huffingtonpost.com/joni -edelman/trigger-warnings-the-good-the-bad-the-pancakes_b_8332786. html.

29. Colleen Clark, "Trigger Warning: Eating Disorder Blogs," http://col leenclarkart.tumblr.com/post/100444043664/trigger-warning-eating-disorder-blogs.

30. Caroline Miller, "Trigger Warnings: Are They Hurting or Helping Your Recovery?" *Eating Disorder Blogs*, January 28, 2016, http://eatingdisordersblogs .com/trigger-warnings-are-they-helping-or-hurting-your-recovery/.

Bibliography

Bordo, Susan. *Unbearable Weight: Feminism, Western Culture, and the Body.* Berkeley: University of California Press, 1993.

Bruch, Hilde. *Eating Disorders: Obesity, Anorexia and the Person Within.* New York: Basic Books, 1973.

———. *The Golden Cage: The Enigma of Anorexia Nervosa.* Cambridge, MA: Harvard University Press, 1978.

Carvujal, Doreen. "French Law Makers Target Pro Anorexia Websites." *Boston Globe*, April 16, 2008.

Chernin, Kim. *The Obsession: Reflections on the Tyranny of Slenderness.* New York: Harper & Row, 1981.

———. *The Hungry Self: Women, Eating, and Identity.* New York: Times Books, 1985.

Clark, Colleen. "Trigger Warning: Eating Disorder Blogs." http://colleen-clarkart.tumblr.com/post/100444043664/trigger-warning-eating-disorder -blogs.

Crisafulli, Michele, Ann Von Holle, and Cynthia Bulik. "Attitudes toward Anorexia Nervosa: The Impact of Framing on Blame and Stigma." *International Journal of Eating Disorders* 41 (2008): 333–39.

Crisp, Arthur. "Stigmatization of and Discrimination against People with Eating Disorders Including a Report of Two Nationwide Surveys." *European Eating Disorders Review* 13, no. 3 (2005): 147–52.

Edelman, Joni. "Trigger Warnings: The Good, the Bad, the Pancakes." *Huffing-ton Post*, October 5, 2015. http://www.huffingtonpost.com/joni-edelman/trigger-warnings-the-good-the-bad-the-pancakes_b_8332786.html.

Epstein, Elizabeth, and Barbara McGrady. *Treatment That Works: A Cognitive Behavioral Treatment Program for Overcoming Alcohol Problems*. Oxford: Oxford University Press, 2009.

Farrell, Kirby. *Post-Traumatic Culture: Injury and Interpretation in the Nineties*. Baltimore, MD: Johns Hopkins University Press, 1998.

Filipovic, Jill. "We've Gone Too Far with 'Trigger Warnings.'" *The Guardian*, March 5, 2014. https://www.theguardian.com/commentisfree/2014/mar/05/trigger-warnings-can-be-counterproductive.

Forman-Koffman, Valerie, and Cassie Cunningham. "Geographical Clustering of Eating Disorder Behaviors in U.S. High School Students." *International Journal of Eating Disorders* 41 (2008): 209–14.

Foucault, Michel. *Madness and Civilization: A History of Insanity in the Age of Reason*, translated by Richard Hurley. New York: Vintage Books, 1965.

Grey. "In Defense of Marya Hornbacher's *Wasted*." *The Lightness of Being Grey*. https://greybird77.wordpress.com/2014/01/02/in-defense-of-marya-hornbachers-wasted/.

Gwizdek, Anna, Kevin Gwizdek, and Ann Koszowska. "Pro-ana, Murderous Face of the Internet." *Progress in Health Science* 2 (2012): 158–61.

Hall, Stuart, Chas Critcher, Tony Jefferson, John Clarke, and Brian Roberts. *Policing the Crisis: Mugging, the State, and Law and Order*. London: Macmillan, 1978.

Harper, Kelley, Steffanie Sperry, and Kevin Thompson. "Viewership of Pro-eating Disorder Websites: Association with Body Image and Eating Disturbances." *International Journal of Eating Disorders* 41 (2008): 92–95.

Hornbacher, Marya. *Wasted: A Memoir of Anorexia and Bulimia*. New York: Harper Flamingo, 1998.

Hume, Mick. *Trigger Warning: Is the Fear of Being Offensive Killing Free Speech?* New York: HarperCollins, 2015.

Kilbourne, Jean. *Deadly Persuasion: Why Women and Girls Must Fight the Addictive Power of Advertising*. New York: Free Press, 1999.

Levenkron, Steven. *The Best Little Girl in the World*. Chicago: Contemporary Books, 1978.

Lukianoff, Greg, and Jonathan Haidt. "The Coddling of the American Mind." *The Atlantic*, September 2015.

McNally, Richard. "Hazards Ahead." *Pacific Standard* 7 (2014): 16–17.

Miller, Caroline. "Trigger Warnings: Are They Hurting or Helping Your Recovery?" *Eating Disorder Blogs*, January 28, 2016. http://eatingdisordersblogs.com/trigger-warnings-are-they-helping-or-hurting-your-recovery/.

Pernick, Martin. "Contagion and Culture." *American Literary History* 14 (2002): 858–65.

Rich, Emma. "Anorexic Dis(connection): Managing Anorexia as an Illness and an Identity." *Sociology of Health and Illness* 28 (2006): 284–305.

Steinhausen, Hans-Christophe. "The Outcome of Anorexia Nervosa in the 20th Century." *American Journal of Psychiatry* 159 (2002): 1284–93.

Stewart, Maria-Christina, Pamela Keel, and Steven Schiavo. "Stigmatization of Anorexia Nervosa." *International Journal of Eating Disorders* 39 (2006): 320–25.

Vandereycken, Walter. "Can Eating Disorders Become 'Contagious' in Group Therapy and Specialized Inpatient Care?" *European Eating Disorders Review* 19 (2011): 289–95.

Wolf, Naomi. *The Beauty Myth: How Images of Beauty Are Used against Women.* New York: Harper, 2002.

CHAPTER FOUR

GENDER CONSTRUCTIONS AND TRAUMA
Trigger Warnings as an Accommodation for Female Students in Higher Education[1]
Jordan Doll

This chapter uses a constitutional framework to analyze trigger warnings, asking whether they can be seen as a permissible accommodation for women in higher education. I will apply the theories of two constitutional legal scholars, Elizabeth H. Wolgast and Wendy W. Williams, to analyze trigger warnings in terms of the United States Constitution's First Amendment and the Equal Protection Clauses. These scholars' distinct analyses of how the Equal Protection Clause should be applied to women demonstrate how the cultural and legal implications of trigger warnings are bound together.

Critics of trigger warnings frequently raise First Amendment concerns that trigger warnings and the atmosphere they may promote will limit professors' voices in the classroom, violating their First Amendment rights. These criticisms examine the constitutional question strictly on free speech grounds. In addition, looking through the lens of Wolgast's and Williams's legal theory, trigger warnings also raise questions about the Fourteenth Amendment's Equal Protection Clause. The clause guarantees equal protection of the law to all persons in similar conditions and circumstances.[2] However, equal protection does not always mean treating people not similarly situated—such as men and women—identically under the law. Sometimes, the law must treat genders differently to achieve a level of equality because of differing biological and societal factors. What if trigger warnings are leveling the playing field between men and women in the college classroom, even promoting the speech of women in higher education? In this case, one could argue small limits on professors' expression may be constitutionally permissible on Equal Protection grounds.

Wolgast and Williams both consider the constitutional question of leveling the playing field between genders. Wolgast's support of offering accommodation for women contrasted with Williams's caution about differentiating genders under the law illustrates the variety of gender constructions implied in trigger warnings. I argue Williams's more cautious perspective can act as the foundation of an essential criticism in the trigger warning debate. The debate can seem to imply that women are more in need of accommodation than men when it comes to trauma and psychological distress. This assumption relies on, and feeds into, cultural as well as legal constructions of women that may be problematic.

Trigger Warnings as Accommodations for Women

Trigger warnings, proponents argue, are leveling the playing field. Students can more fully engage in their education where these warnings operate because they remove, or at least lessen, the psychological distress triggers may cause. Since the Equal Protection Clause allows the law to treat people differently, students who have suffered trauma may not be treated identically to students who have not been traumatized. This equalizing of the playing field is a form of accommodation. In higher education, accommodations are adjustments to typical standards in the classrooms to help differently situated students learn. Common accommodations are extra time on tests or modified attendance policies.

The Supreme Court has recognized attempts to level the playing field between genders as constitutionally permissible. The Court, and the two legal scholars I analyze, agrees that women are distinctly situated both biologically and socially in society. It is impractical or ineffective to treat women the exact same way as men, including in societal realms like higher education. The playing field must, to an extent, be leveled so that dissimilarly situated persons can have an equal chance at educational success. But, who is the playing field being leveled for? Instead of the broad sweep of every student who has suffered trauma, the focal point of what is considered "triggering" in this debate has been content that is statistically more likely for women to have experienced than men. Trigger warnings are also historically tied to accommodating women with trauma, not men.

Trigger warnings first arose as a major phenomenon in the feminist blogosphere. In the blogosphere, these warnings attempted to create a space hospitable to a viewership that often had experienced sexual assault, eating disorders, or other traumas that disproportionately affect women. Trigger warnings acted as a "heads-up"; viewers were prepared for the content or could choose not to engage with it. If this content were presented without a trigger warning, bloggers reasoned, the suddenness and surprise of the content could trigger adverse psychological effects and/or distress. Proponents argue that, as in education, these warnings were acting as an accommodation that enabled women to engage in this online forum.

Trigger warnings did not lose their gendered nature in their move from the blogosphere to higher education in the 2010s. As in the blogosphere, the focal point of content considered triggering in educational settings is trauma that disproportionately impacts women. A movie scene of a graphic rape paved the way to the mandatory trigger warning policy passed by the student senate at the University of California at Santa Barbara. An Oberlin faculty guide recommended trigger warnings under the heading, *"How can I make my classroom more inclusive for survivors of sexualized violence?"*[3] Jeanne Suk became an influential voice in this debate when she raised concerns about the difficulty of teaching rape law at Harvard Law School. She argued that some law students feared or sought to regulate how rape law is taught because of its "triggering" nature.[4] Suk also connected the trigger warning debate to ongoing efforts to raise awareness of sexual assault on college campuses.

This focus on sexual violence exemplifies a larger trend where topics like rape and sexual assault are prioritized in the conversation. In the United States, one in five women, compared to one in seventy-one men, will be raped at some point in their life.[5] On American college campuses, one in five women, compared to one in sixteen men, are sexually assaulted during their college career.[6] In contrast, war and military combat, which often seems secondary in the trigger warning debate, have historically disproportionately affected men. Though the numbers are difficult to calculate, it's estimated that around nine hundred twenty-four thousand veterans are enrolled in higher education; only about 10 percent identify as female. After sexual assault and rape, trigger warnings are secondarily aimed at eating disorders, another example of lopsided gender dynamics. In the United States, anorexia nervosa will affect between 1 percent to 4 percent of women in their lifetime, but only around 0.3 percent of men.[7] Bulimia nervosa as well disproportionately affects women.[8]

As of 2014, there are about 9.8 million female students and 7.7 million male students enrolled in American degree-granting undergraduate institutions.[9] Based on these numbers, in the United States around two million students will have experiences with sexual assault during or before their college career as opposed to less than one million who will have experienced war and combat. But, does this numerical difference mean one trauma should be at the forefront of the debate? Women, intentionally or not, become the intended targets of trigger warnings in higher education. Men are constructed less as the benefactors. This implies that women are more in need of the protection a trigger warning can offer than men.

This skewed emphasis on protection can imply a double standard and a notion that trigger warnings are tools or accommodations specifically for women. This leads to the argument that trigger warnings are equalizing the playing field for women. That is, when so many women have traumatic experiences, accommodations like this can be provided to help them learn, even if they do raise First Amendment concerns. The Supreme Court and many legal theorists are open to treating the genders differently in society, as I discuss below. But, we must keep in mind the implications of treating women differently under the law.

The Fourteenth Amendment and Gender Discrimination

The Supreme Court has ruled that the Fourteenth Amendment's Equal Protection Clause can sometimes protect policies and laws that attempt to equalize the playing field between the genders in a world where men and women are differently situated both biologically and societally.[10]

These policies are based on what the Court calls "permissible gender classifications"—distinct treatments of gender to forward a compelling interest. However, I argue that Williams's caution against treating women differently under the law is an apt way to understand trigger warnings.

The disproportionate effect of using trigger warnings for women can be read in a number of ways in a constitutional context. One reading, which I analyze in this section, is that trigger warnings are a constitutionally permissible accommodation for women in higher education. When many women have experienced rape and sexual assault, trigger warnings act as a heads-up and a form of preparation. A second reading is that the unequal effects between genders are irrelevant to their constitutionality. This reading, I argue, ignores the constructions of gender an accommodation like this may be based on and the far-reaching effects such constructions can have. A third analysis, and one that is not irreconcilable with the first two, is that trigger warnings imply a delicacy of woman's psyche compared to those of men—a construction of women Williams cautions against. Since men do not suffer from traumas at the same rate as women, most men do not need the preparation and sense of control offered by trigger warnings to take advantage of their education. Building off of Williams's theories on gender and the law, I argue that informally prioritizing women's traumas over men's shapes how we construct gender both in the legal realm and outside of it. This understanding of trigger warnings relies on a construction of women that may be problematic.

Before moving on, I want to address why I am considering only binary gender, and not trigger warnings as an accommodation for students of color, transgender students, or students with intersecting social identities. Because trigger warnings are often used for colonialism, racism, and police brutality, they also disproportionately affect students of color over white students. Further, transgender women have a far higher rate of sexual assault than other demographics of women.[11] However, the Supreme Court tends to define gender as binary. It has a history of allowing gender classifications between men and women because of societal differences, but not for transgender people or people of color. For these reasons, my analysis focuses only on binary gender.

Feminist Theory and the Doctrine of Accommodation

The Supreme Court and legal theorists acknowledge that women and men are uniquely situated both biologically and societally. An example of a biological difference is the ability to become pregnant; an example of a societal difference between men and women is the pay gap. The Fourteenth Amendment's Equal Protection Clause requires no person be denied the equal protection of the law, or, said another way, that the law treats all persons equally. Equal does not necessarily mean identical. It is impractical or ineffective, the Court has consistently argued, to treat each gender the exact same way. To what extent the law should treat women and men differently is debated both among legal theorists and within the Court. For the purpose of this chapter, I define different rates of rape and sexual assault as a societal difference between genders.

The Court reviews gender-based laws with intermediate scrutiny. Under intermediate scrutiny, a law or policy that treats the genders differently must forward an important government interest and cannot be based on arbitrary legislative choices or gender stereotypes. *Reed v. Reed* was one of the first Supreme Court cases that struck down a state statute because it was based on "arbitrary" distinctions between the genders. In the case, the Court invalidated an Idaho statute that preferred males to females as administrators to the wills of persons who had died intestate—without a will. The Court found no "rational relationship to (forwarding) a state objective" by discriminating based on gender.[12] However, this intermediate scrutiny is a less rigorous scrutiny process than race-based classifications, where the government interest must not only be compelling but the policy or law must be narrowly tailored and use the least restrictive means to accomplish its goal. Laws that use gender classifications must only connect gender to the state interest without relying on arbitrary stereotypes. To do this, the Court considers the likelihood that gender will influence a situation. In *Kahn v. Shevin*,[13] the Court upheld a state statute that provided a property tax exemption to female widows, but not to male widowers. The Court's justification was that there are greater economic struggles for women in the job market compared to men. The real world implications of a "male-dominated culture [deprive women of any] but the lowest paid jobs."

JORDAN DOLL

By contrast, the Court ruled in *Craig v. Boren*[14] that a gender classification was unconstitutional. In *Craig*, an Oklahoma statute differentiated drinking ages between men (21) and women (18) for certain alcoholic beverages. Young men, the state rationalized, received more drunk driving traffic violations than women; the age distinction was a safety measure. The Court found the data that connected gender and age was not strong enough to justify the gender classification. However, the majority opinion did not disqualify any gender classification based on societal differences between men and women. The Court only argued that in this specific case the "predictive empirical" relationship was too "tenuous" to satisfy a gender-based classification. The data used did not represent "a legitimate, accurate proxy for the regulation of drinking and driving (based on gender)."[15] Said another way, the difference between a 0.18 percent (women) and 2 percent (men) DUI rate does not prove a causal relationship between drinking and gender. As in *Reed v. Reed*, the distinction was too arbitrary. However, the Court left open the door to gender classifications if a statute could prove a causal relationship between gender and achieving the state's interest. These above examples illustrate that the Court allows some, but not all gender classifications. A constitutional classification must have more than a "tenuous" connection to the important interest.

The Court's doctrine on permissible gender classifications is not cut-and-dried, and theorists disagree on the benefits and implications of treating genders differently. As trigger warnings accommodate women over men, the law must consider whether this is a permissible gender classification. Wendy Williams's and Elizabeth Wolgast's distinct approaches to gender classifications are an apt framework through which to do this. Williams argues for a more symmetrical approach to gender, while Wolgast argues for a more asymmetrical approach. A symmetrical approach to gender, in its purest form, treats both genders identically under the law. Any societal asymmetries between the genders are illusions, overbroad generalizations, or "temporary glitches that will disappear with a little behavior modification."[16] Williams argues that women cannot have it both ways under the law—a symmetrical approach to gender on some issues and an asymmetrical approach to gender on others. Women must consider carefully which way they want to have it. In contrast, Wolgast supports an asymmetrical treatment of gender under the law. Asymmetrical approach promoters argue that gender differences, whether biological or societal, are a reality that can't be ignored. Wolgast argues that women deserve special rights for their special needs under the law.[17] Under this logic, the law should support policies that cater to best serving women's special needs, perhaps allowing accommodations to promote gender equality in higher education. I want to challenge this construction.

Standardized accommodations in American colleges were borne from the 1990 Americans with Disabilities Act (ADA), which requires institutions of higher education to offer accommodations for students with disabilities.[18] Psychological disabilities such as depression, anxiety, and PTSD are covered by the ADA in almost all colleges' interpretations of the act. Proponents of trigger warnings argue that warnings for material that might trigger symptoms of the above mental illnesses can act as an effective accommodation. The negative side effects of exposure to trauma, or reminders of trauma, can be tempered by warnings aimed at susceptible students. Accommodations' purposes are to increase accessibility to education. Typical accommodations for psychological disabilities include extra time on tests and attendance modification policies. The definitions of *accommodation* and *disability* are always evolving. For example, psychological disabilities have only gained significant acceptance in the last fifteen years, where before they were distinguished as less important than disabilities related to physical mobility. Because schools' interpretation of the ADA continues to evolve, it is feasible that trigger warnings could become an accepted accommodation. Just as the ADA changed the way we think of disability and accommodation in American higher education in 1990, thinking on what a legitimate and helpful accommodation is continues to evolve. Trigger warnings, proponents argue, have a place in accommodating those who are not conventionally able bodied. By their nature, accommodations effect how a teacher instructs. Leveling the playing field for students with disability constricts a professor's absolute freedom in the classroom, such as how much time is allowed on tests or the rigidness of the attendance policy. This constriction is similar to what many worry trigger warnings create, leading to the suppression of a professor's speech and other ideas in the classroom. Still, today the 1990 ADA accommodations are common practice and stir comparatively little controversy. For the purpose of this argument, consider if trigger warnings become an accepted accommodation in higher education. Free speech concerns would be less of an issue. But what gender construction is this accommodation based on?

Prioritizing Accommodations over the Right to Absolute Free Expression

A Wolgast-centered analysis of trigger warnings as an accommodation is based on flawed gender assumptions, and I worry it promotes stereotypes and constructions of women that may reverberate outside the trigger warning debate. Wolgast believes it essential that the law acknowledge; react to; and, if necessary, accommodate women, even if this means infringing on free speech. Proponents of trigger warnings argue they are increasing the free flow of ideas; female students feel more willing to communicate when they are better prepared for potentially disturbing material. From Wolgast's perspective, trigger warnings can be seen as simply a respectful tool that increases the flow of ideas and helps preserve the moral obligations that, Wolgast argues, are implied in the Constitution.

For example, Wolgast argues pornography should be regulated because it implies the inferiority of women and supports disrespecting them. She asserts that respect for other individuals is part of the U.S. constitutional heritage and protection of expression should not automatically trump this value of respect. Wolgast goes on to say the First Amendment was designed to protect speech that argues, not speech that disrespects persons. Pornography, in her estimation, does not forward an argument, but degrades women for the sake of pleasure. She compares free speech as an "idol" in American law that can blind us to other constitutional protections, such the Equal Protection Clause.[19]

Despite the overlaps between First Amendment rights and gender accommodation, I do not think Wolgast's argument on pornography is appropriate for a legal discussion of trigger warnings. For one, pornography does not equate to the academic material that trigger warnings target. Academic content is protected as high-value speech, while pornography is not protected to the same extent.

Secondly, even if pornography were the equivalent of academic material, the value judgment Wolgast makes is flawed and may rely on constructions of women that are too general. Wolgast argues that free expression, in whatever form it takes, must consider what is respectful to listeners as well as the rights of the speaker. "[The] terms of the issue as I frame it require only the value of individual respect, which is part of [the United States'] moral heritage, and the perceptions by members of the community about how they are respected."[20] She goes on to say that the First Amendment is not supposed to protect any type of expression, but the free exchange of ideas.[21] Wolgast's argument is based on the assumption that she knows how all listeners of a certain demographic will react to a certain type of speech. Women are oppressed, exploited, and degraded by pornography. Female victims of trauma can only engage in their education if a teacher gives them a trigger warning. This assertion may be an inaccurate assumption of how all women will react to pornography; the assumption is even more imperfect when it comes to something as complex as trauma.

Whether the demographic is defined as women, female victims of trauma, or male and female victims of trauma, a blanket statement about how a group will react to certain material is impossible to predict. One cannot easily identify what material will trigger. Secondly, one cannot assume a trigger warning is a helpful and respectful tool that increases the flow of ideas. Trigger warnings' effectiveness is by no means certain; however, a student's exposure to trauma is certainly unpredictable. An accommodation that has the potential to infringe on First Amendment rights cannot be based on such a tenuous connection to helping female students learn. Wendy Williams, another legal scholar, has also considered the implications of gender discrimination, adding to the conversation a caution of how we construct women in this debate.

Accommodations Based on Gender Constructions

In contrast to Wolgast, Williams's analysis of gender and the equal protection clause raises an important criticism of trigger warnings. Williams argues of gender accommodations, "[Women] can't have it both ways, we need to think carefully about which way we want to have it."[22] Williams connects the law directly to the perception of women in society, and her argument can be applied in the trigger warning debate. She contends that if the law constructs women as in more need of accommodation than men in some situations, it becomes more difficult to argue that they are absolute equals of men in other situations. Trigger warnings may contribute to a view of women as psychologically fragile compared to men. Taking this idea to its extreme, trigger warnings support the image of women as less capable of handling trauma than men—women are overly sensitive and unable to handle their emotions.

Williams argues that court decisions reflect society's cultural views on gender. "The way courts define equality, within the limits of their sphere, does indeed matter in the real world. Court decisions are inseparably connected to cultural values."[23] The Supreme Court frequently upholds law that excludes women from traditionally masculine spheres, like the draft.[24] It relies on culturally accepted gender roles, enforcing and adding to our cultural understanding of what is masculine and what is feminine. For example, in *Rostker v. Goldberg*, domestic life and family were constructed as inseparable from women's role as mother. In the case, the Senate Armed Services Committee Report, which supported the exclusion of women from the draft, argued that sending women into combat places "unprecedented strains on family life." The report constructed women as inseparable from their family role. While the mother is tied to the feminist sphere of family, the father can prioritize combat over his family role. The report further maintained that enlisting women in combat roles would affect the national resolve to go to war. The inclination to protect women would override the country's desire to accomplish its military ends.[25] In this case, women were kept out of a traditionally masculine sphere—the army—because the law relied on the age-old cultural constructions of women as needed, first and foremost, at home taking care of their children. The decision also relied on a construction of women as needing greater protection than men, asserting that a desire to protect women overshadows any use they could have in military combat.

This case's construction of women based on cultural traditions is not a one-off. In *Michael M. v. Superior Court of Sonoma County* the Court relied on traditional cultural expectations of the genders during intercourse. In this case, men are constructed as the only perpetrators in statutory rape cases.[26] A seventeen-and-a-half-year-old male had sex with a female under the age of eighteen, violating a California state statute that criminalized underage sex for men, but not for women. The Court ruled the statute's gender distinction did not violate the Equal Protection Clause because women have a natural incentive to avoid sex (pregnancy) while men do not. Men initiate sex. Women, the Court suggested, do not. To Williams, the decision forwarded the idea of the man as the aggressor and the woman as sexually passive, as she is culturally expected to be. In both these cases, the Court and culture worked in a positive feedback cycle, one adding to the constructed image of gender relied on by the other. These constructions are not segregated to their individual cases and can have repercussions in other court cases and in American society.

Avoiding gender stereotypes cannot be the Court's priority. I mention the above cases to suggest, as many before me have, that the Court is not isolated from cultural constructions of gender, just as the outside world is not isolated from how gender is constructed inside the courtroom. While this is not a legal argument, the Court, and those who shape the law generally, should be wary that the precedent set in a legal analysis of trigger warnings adds to a legal and cultural perspective on women. Seeing trigger warnings as a constitutional accommodation of women's varied experiences may shape future decisions on gender differences. It may further what some call the "protective doctrine," where "women's perceived differences from men [operate] to exclude women from the 'public' or market sphere—to set them apart, outside of the main avenues of power and economic dependence."[27]

This brings us back to Wendy Williams's argument—"If we can't have it both ways, we need to think carefully about which way [women] want to have it." A new case on the draft could refer to a court decision finding, for example, a trigger warning policy of accommodation for female students as constitutional under the Fourteenth Amendment's Equal Protection Clause. The state and society have accepted women as more susceptible to trauma and upset. This gender difference could threaten the cohesion of an army unit. Men may be more capable of dealing with the psychological burden of on-the-ground combat. A legal and cultural concept of women as requiring more psychologically based accommodation would be a point against gender-neutralizing the draft.

A legal construction of women as psychologically fragile could also influence other cases, such as the legality of equal pay. One could argue pay inequality is not the result of internalized societal prejudices but the natural result of women being less qualified for certain high-stress positions than their male colleagues. The potential for societal gender differences to be seen as natural leads us down a dangerous cultural and legal path. The societal becomes the biological. Societal differences between men and women—the pay gap for example—stem from biological differences that cannot be changed and so are acceptable. This leads us back to accommodation theory. Some gender accommodations are based on a social gender construction that forwards the notion that women have a unique place from men in our society both inside and outside the courtroom. This is an essential criticism of the trigger warning debate. The conversation promotes a construction of women that has both legal and cultural implications. The assumption that women may be less capable of handling trauma is problematic.

Conclusion

The trigger warning, as a constitutionally permissible accommodation, is a tricky concept. To a great extent, the argument would rely on whether trigger warnings are effective—that is, if there is causality between using trigger warnings and helping students learn. Causality could not be proven in *Craig v. Boren*, but could be in *Kahn v. Shevin*. The trigger warning debate prioritizes content, such as rape, sexual assault, and eating disorders that disproportionately affect women. However, no significant research has been done that shows trigger warnings are an effective accommodation that supports women's speech in classrooms. In contrast, a wealth of research supports that extra time on tests—a common accommodation in college classrooms, or an adjustment to typical standards to help students learn—is an effective tool for students with learning disabilities.[28] Trigger warnings have no comparable research to stand on. Professors and even victims of trauma do not always know what is triggering. Even if there was an effective way to identify triggering material, there is still no guarantee trigger warnings will be effective to all or even some students. Further, despite the disproportional use of trigger warnings for rape and sexual assault, it is difficult to prove trigger warnings are more helpful to women than to men. It would be extremely challenging to prove a causal relationship between an effective accommodation strategy for women and any systematic use of trigger warnings in a classroom. In the case of this tenuous relationship, legal questions of free speech should be prioritized over efforts at accommodation. As a result, a professor's choice to use a trigger warning as a wish to accommodate female students in contrast to a professor's choice to use a trigger warning for experimental purposes does not matter to the law. What matters is that it was the professor's choice to use the warning. First Amendment concerns trump any Equal Protection arguments.

Elizabeth Wolgast may not be satisfied with my reasoning. As she argues, being a respectful human being, such as the courtesy of using trigger warnings, should not be abandoned to the idol of free speech. However, pornography cannot be equated to academic material, and Wolgast's assumptions about the effects of speech on a certain demographic are based on shaky value judgments and certainly cannot be extended to something as complex as trauma. On the other hand, Wendy Williams may support my conclusion. This legal framework promotes a professor's choice over a gender accommodation. This conclusion does not forward a construction of women as psychologically fragile or less capable of handling trauma than men and is a symmetrical approach to gender. I agree with Williams's caution about how we construct women; a conception of women as psychologically fragile can have both legal and cultural ramifications. The trigger warning debate, both on the legal and cultural side, may be unintentionally forwarding this conception of women.

Notes

1. The following work is an excerpt from a much longer thesis—"Trauma and Free Speech in Higher Education: Do Trigger Warnings Threaten First Amendment Rights?" The original thesis, which was written as my honors project for the Oberlin College Politics Department, considered two constitutional frameworks through which to consider trigger warnings—the one given here and a second that considered a mandatory trigger warning policy at a public university. The original thesis also involved my own independent, institutional review board–approved research where I interviewed about forty professors and students about their opinions and experiences with trigger warnings in the college classroom. A foundation of the piece as it appears in this chapter is that trigger warnings are more frequently used for traumas that are statistically more likely to affect women than men. My individual research in my original thesis established and strongly supported this foundation.

2. U.S. Constitution Amendment XIV.

3. Oberlin College's Office of Equity Concerns, "Faculty Rules, Pedagogical Issues and Sexual Misconduct," *Support Resources for Faculty*, accessed November 2014, http://new.oberlin.edu/office/equity-concerns/sexual-offense-resource -guide/prevention-support-education/support-resources-for-faculty.dot.

4. Jeanne Suk, "The Trouble with Teaching Rape Law," *The New Yorker*, December 15, 2014, accessed January 6, 2015, http://www.newyorker.com/news/ news-desk/trouble-teaching-rape-law.

5. M. C. Black, K. C. Basile, M. J. Breiding, S. G. Smith, M. L. Walters, M. T. Merrick, J. Chen, and M. R. Stevens, *The National Intimate Partner and Sexual Violence Survey: 2010 Summary Report*, National Center for Injury Prevention and Control, Centers for Disease Control and Prevention, 2011, accessed October 2015, https://www.cdc.gov/violenceprevention/pdf/nisvs_report2010-a.pdf.

6. C. P. Krebs, C. Lindquist, T. Warner, B. Fisher, and S. Martin, *The Campus Sexual Assault (CSA) Study: Final Report*, The National Criminal Justice Reference Service, 2007, accessed October 2015, http://www.ncjrs.gov/pdf files1/nij/grants/221153.pdf.

7. F. R. Smink, D. van Hoeken, and H. W. Hoek, "Epidemiology of Eating Disorders: Incidence, Prevalence and Mortality Rates," *Current Psychiatry Reports* 14, no. 4 (2012): 406–14.

8. A. R. Pemberton, S. W. Vernon, and E. S. Lee, "Prevalence and Correlates of Bulimia Nervosa and Bulimic Behaviors in a Racially Diverse Sample of Undergraduate Students in Two Universities in Southeast Texas," *American Journal of Epidemiology* 144, no. 5 (1996): 450–55.

9. U. S. Department of Education, National Center for Education Statistics, Digest of Education Statistics, Table 303.70, https://nces.ed.gov/programs/digest/d13/tables/dt13_303.70.asp.

10. Geoffery R. Stone, "Heightened Scrutiny and the Problem of Gender," in *The First Amendment* (1st ed.) by Geoffrey R. Stone et al., 629–73 (Gaithersburg, MD: Aspen, 1999).

11. R. Stotzer, "Violence against Transgender People: A Review of United States Data," *Aggression and Violent Behavior* (2009): 170–79.

12. *Reed v. Reed*, 404 U.S. 71 (1971).

13. *Kahn v. Shevin*, 416 U.S. 351 (1974).

14. *Craig v. Boren*, 429 U.S. 190 (1976).

15. Ibid.

16. Diana T. Meyers, *Feminist Social Thought: A Reader* (New York: Routledge, 1997), 715.

17. Elizabeth H. Wolgast, *Equality and the Rights of Women* (Ithaca, NY: Cornell University Press, 1980).

18. ADA: Americans with Disabilities Act of 1990, Public Law No. 101–336, Section 1, 104 Stat. 328 (1990).

19. Elizabeth Wolgast, "Pornography and the Tyranny of the Majority," in *Feminist Jurisprudence*, edited by Patricia Smith, 433 (New York: Oxford University Press, 1993).

20. Ibid., 442.

21. Ibid., 434.

22. Wendy W. Williams, "The Equality Crisis: Some Reflections on Culture, Courts, and Feminism," in *Feminist Legal Theory: Readings in Law and Gender*, edited by Katharine T. Bartlett and Rosanne Kennedy, 18 (Boulder, CO: Westview Press 1991).

23. Ibid., 15.

24. *Rostker v. Goldberg*, 453 U.S. 57 (1981).

25. Ibid., 19.

26. *Michael M. v. Superior Court of Sonoma County*, 450 U.S. 464 (1981).

27. Williams, "Equality Crisis," 20.

28. N. S. Ofiesh and J. K. McAfee, "Evaluation Practices for College Students with LD," *Journal of Learning Disabilities* 33, no. 1 (2000): 14–25; L. C. Bell and C. A. Perfetti, "Reading Skill: Some Adult Comparisons," *Journal of Educational Psychology* 86 (1994): 244–55; E. Benedetto-Nash and R. Tannock, "Math Computation Performance and Error Patterns of Children with Attention-Deficit Hyperactivity Disorder," *Journal of Attention Disorders* 3 (1999): 121–34.

Bibliography

ADA: Americans with Disabilities Act of 1990, Public Law No. 101–336, Section 1, 104 Stat. 328 (1990).

Bell, L. C., and C. A. Perfetti. "Reading Skill: Some Adult Comparisons." *Journal of Educational Psychology* 86 (1994): 244–55.

Benedetto-Nash, E., and R. Tannock. "Math Computation Performance and Error Patterns of Children with Attention-Deficit Hyperactivity Disorder." *Journal of Attention Disorders* 3 (1999): 121–34.

Black, M. C., K. C. Basile, M. J. Breiding, S. G. Smith, M. L. Walters, M. T. Merrick, J. Chen, and M. R. Stevens. *The National Intimate Partner and Sexual Violence Survey (NISVS): 2010 Summary Report*. National Center for Injury Prevention and Control, Centers for Disease Control and Prevention (Atlanta, GA: 2011). Accessed October 2015. https://www.cdc.gov/violenceprevention/pdf/nisvs_report2010-a.pdf.

Craig v. Boren, 429 U.S. 190 (1976).

Kahn v. Shevin, 416 U.S. 351 (1974).

Krebs, C. P., C. Lindquist, T. Warner, B. Fisher, and S. Martin. *The Campus Sexual Assault (CSA) Study: Final Report*. The National Criminal Justice Reference Service (2007). Accessed October 2015. http://www.ncjrs.gov/pdffiles1/nij/grants/221153.pdf.

Meyers, Diana T. *Feminist Social Thought: A Reader*. New York: Routledge, 1997.

Michael M. v. Superior Court of Sonoma County, 450 U.S. 464 (1981).

Oberlin College's Office of Equity Concerns. "Faculty Rules, Pedagogical Issues and Sexual Misconduct." *Support Resources for Faculty*. Accessed November 2014. http://new.oberlin.edu/office/equity-concerns/sexual-offense-resource-guide/prevention-support-education/support-resources-for-faculty.dot.

Ofiesh, N. S., and J. K. McAfee. "Evaluation Practices for College Students with LD." *Journal of Learning Disabilities* 33, no. 1 (2000): 14–25.

Pemberton, A. R., S. W. Vernon, and E. S. Lee. "Prevalence and Correlates of Bulimia Nervosa and Bulimic Behaviors in a Racially Diverse Sample of Undergraduate Students in Two Universities in Southeast Texas." *American Journal of Epidemiology* 144, no. 5 (1996): 450–55.

Reed v. Reed, 404 U.S. 71 (1971).

Rostker v. Goldberg, 453 U.S. 57 (1981).

Smink, F. R., D. van Hoeken, and H. W. Hoek. "Epidemiology of Eating Disorders: Incidence, Prevalence and Mortality Rates." *Current Psychiatry Reports* 14, no. 4 (2012): 406–14.

Stone, Geoffery R. "Heightened Scrutiny and the Problem of Gender." In *The First Amendment* (1st ed.) by Geoffrey R. Stone et al., 629–73. Gaithersburg, MD: Aspen, 1999.

Stotzer, R. "Violence against Transgender People: A Review of United States Data." *Aggression and Violent Behavior* (2009): 170–79.

Suk, Jeanne. "The Trouble with Teaching Rape Law." *The New Yorker*, December 15, 2014. Accessed January 6, 2015. http://www.newyorker.com/news/news-desk/trouble-teaching-rape-law.

U.S. Department of Education, National Center for Education Statistics. Digest of Education Statistics, Table 303.70. https://nces.ed.gov/programs/digest/d13/tables/dt13_303.70.asp.

Williams, Wendy W. "The Equality Crisis: Some Reflections on Culture, Courts, and Feminism." In *Feminist Legal Theory: Readings in Law and Gender*, edited by Katharine T. Bartlett and Rosanne Kennedy. Boulder, CO: Westview Press, 1991.

Wolgast, Elizabeth. "Pornography and the Tyranny of the Majority." In *Feminist Jurisprudence*, edited by Patricia Smith, 431–48. New York: Oxford University Press, 1993.

Wolgast, Elizabeth H. *Equality and the Rights of Women*. Ithaca, NY: Cornell University Press, 1980.

CHAPTER FIVE

WALKING ON THE SHARDS
OF THE GLASS CEILING

Jane Gavin-Hebert

This chapter focuses on current debates about the use of "trigger warnings" to examine the historical institutional context that has prompted these linguistic and affective interventions in our cultural, academic, and political landscape. Interconnected with past and present pandemic perpetration of sexualized violence in patriarchal knowledge production institutions, the genocidal impact of the Canadian residential school system, and the colonial phenomenon of missing and murdered Indigenous women are foundational examples of how complex trauma is systematically denied by those invested in ongoing inequity in classrooms and courtrooms in order to maintain a façade of integrity traded by both the academic and judicial apparatus. Rituals of ideological and physical repression range from institutionalized resistance to substantive inclusion of diverse women and gender-variant peoples to the colonial curricula and pedagogy that antagonize and deny the embodied experience of students and staff subject to invasive colonial and sexualized trauma.

To mitigate some of the harm in advancing difficult pedagogy, professors can take practical measures to create trauma-informed environments that acknowledge and honor the struggles of survivors of violence. In line with regressive patterns of backlash against women and other marginalized peoples, trigger warnings as a feminist trauma-informed pedagogical tool have served as a debate flashpoint—which at its most reactionary rehashes the conflation of trauma-informed feminist anticolonial pedagogy with an attack on academic freedom and the dissolution of historically dominant masculinist disciplinary practices.

The emergence of trigger warnings as an aspect of autonomous feminist pedagogy seems to activate discomfort for those with a stake in the stratified status quo. Some professors may view their trigger warnings as merely a commonsense consideration of the diverse lived experiences of their students, while others also emphasize the political and anticolonial significance of negotiating free, prior, and informed consent in knowledge production on occupied territory. Regardless, antagonistic backlash to these efforts—in the form of predictable rhetoric scapegoating feminists and critical race scholars for their alleged undermining of academic freedom—speaks volumes about the regressive cultural flows that fear giving voice or agency to survivors.

"The glass ceiling" as a metaphor referring to the invisibility of the mechanisms of systemic marginalization faced by women and racialized, gender-variant, and differently abled people in the academy continues to be relevant. Even after the glass ceiling is occasionally broken by the rarified ascension of isolated individuals who are not part of the white, able-bodied, Anglophone, hetero-patriarchal male academic demographic, there is still the question of the broken glass. Who is cut by the fallout from reluctant or regressive institutional change? Who is receiving care and respect for their wounds? Who is validated when addressing the conflicts that emerge as institutions founded on invasion, elitism, and nepotism attempt to transform into something truly meritocratic? This chapter problematizes the notion of the modern Canadian academy as inherently or emergently progressive by contrasting commentary from institutional and political leaders with conditions faced by current and prospective students.

Walking on the shards of the glass ceiling symbolizes the ongoing wounding experienced by those who know that a campus, a class, or curriculum will label them deficient, uncompetitive, and inferior should they disclose their right and need to not be re-traumatized. Students can be unsettled by their own lived subjectivity as they are exposed to first-person narratives while studying topics that may trigger trauma responses. Trigger warnings are one cursory method of acknowledging entrenched formal and informal marginalization—and a method that seeks to form an alternative learning and dialogue environment, a counter-classroom to the stigma imposed by the privileged objectivity of invading institutions that tell the violated to settle down or leave. The American Association of University

Professors (AAUP) highlights in its report *On Trigger Warnings*[1] the pervasive function of the academic industrial complex on Turtle Island:

> The presumption that students need to be protected rather than challenged in a classroom is at once infantilizing and anti-intellectual. It makes comfort a higher priority than intellectual engagement and—as the Oberlin list demonstrates—it singles out politically controversial topics like sex, race, class, capitalism, and colonialism for attention. Indeed, if such topics are associated with triggers, correctly or not, they are likely to be marginalized if not avoided altogether by faculty who fear complaints for offending or discomforting some of their students. Although all faculty are affected by potential charges of this kind, non-tenured and contingent faculty are particularly at risk. In this way the demand for trigger warnings creates a repressive, "chilly climate" for critical thinking in the classroom.[2]

While expressing patronizing predictions about what will result from intentional preparation for triggering interactions in the classroom, the above quote from the American Association of University Professors feigns affinity with the plight of sessional instructors. However, it states that feminist pedagogical developments addressing the dearth of trauma-informed pedagogies are to blame for professors' precarious working conditions, not neoliberal capitalism. They say *our* demands create this "'chilly climate' for critical thinking in the classroom." This supposedly threatened academic tradition is predicated on the occupation of Indigenous territories, as well as the appropriation of Indigenous knowledge. This dichotomy of "trigger warnings vs. academic freedom" can be transformed through a trauma-informed feminist pedagogy of relationality and care. Scholar and visual artist Antonia Darder reflects on the role of humanizing love in the classroom inspired by Paulo Freire as a pedagogical practice. This intent sharply contrasts with the modular and clientized role of the student in the colonial neoliberal classroom. Darder writes:

> In the tradition of Antonio Gramsci, Paulo exposed how even well-meaning teachers, through their lack of critical moral leadership, actually participate in disabling the heart, minds, and bodies of their students—an act that disconnects these students from the personal and social motivation required to transform their world and themselves.[3]

This pedagogical pitfall of postsecondary education is conflated with efforts to represent pan-institutional trauma and used to obscure and dismiss movements advocating for trauma-informed classrooms. Settler sophistry is not only used to scapegoat workers for their working conditions but also to accuse students and teachers of failing an implicit toughness test seeking to normalize "objective" attitudes that obligate survivors to accept and maintain their own marginality within curricula and classroom discourse.

In her article in *The Guardian* titled "We've Gone Too Far with 'Trigger Warnings,'" Jill Filipovic highlights the suspected overuse and intellectual debility that would result from the controlling, spoiling, and ineffective function that trigger warnings may cause. A trigger warning is summarized by Filipovic as such: "It skews students' perceptions. It highlights particular issues as necessarily more upsetting than others, and directs students to focus on particular themes that have been singled out by the professor as traumatic." She continues:

> College isn't exactly the real world either, but it's a space for kinda-sorta adults to wade neck-deep into art, literature, philosophy, and the sciences, to explore new ideas, to expand their knowledge of the cultural canon, to interrogate power and to learn how to make an argument and to read a text. It is, hopefully, a space where the student's world expands and pushes them to reach the outer edges—not a place that contracts to meet the student exactly where they are.[4]

Filipovic's claim that colleges do not or should not "contract to meet the students exactly where they are" is patently false. Entrenched misogyny on campus ensures that predatory men are met where they are at, extracurricular rituals and core content caters to their conquest and comfort while their status is sacrosanct. The 2015 documentary film *The Hunting Ground* exposes sexism permeating university campuses across the United States that ignore, deny, and cover up sexualized violence.[5] The campus incidents examined later in this article prompted media investigations at universities across Canada with the following results from the Canadian Broadcasting Corporation about the conditions faced by the more than two million postsecondary students in Canada[6]:

> An investigation by CBC revealed that over 700 sexual assaults were reported between 2009 to 2013 at Canadian colleges and universities.

> That number is incredibly low when statistics illustrate that one in five
> women will experience sexual assault while attending a post-secondary
> institution and one in three women will experience some form of sexual
> assault in her lifetime. This is especially important since up until March
> 2015, colleges and universities did not have to publicly report on inci-
> dences of sexual violence on campuses.[7]

A one-in-five ratio applied to 1.1 million female students is two hundred
twenty thousand. In the wake of conservative estimates that more than six
thousand children were killed within the Canadian genocidal project of
residential schools, which began in 1883, there is a sense of continuity in
the targeted violence within these settler organizations as the last residential school closed but two decades ago in 1996.[8]

Indigenous knowledge, with methods of dissemination long predat-
ing settler campuses, is applied in realms advocating for Indigenous sov-
ereignty—promoting protocols of "free, prior, and informed consent."[9]
Free, prior, and informed consent has historically been an element of
sustaining ethical relations between different Indigenous nations across
Turtle Island. Currently, these traditional diplomatic protocols are applied as legal protections on extractive industries such as mining, forestry,
pipeline development, and fracking. Additionally, there is transformative
and sustaining benefit to applying decolonizing practices of free, prior,
and informed consent to sites of knowledge production.

Mi'kmaw educational scholar Marie Battiste's concept of "cognitive
imperialism" can provide context to the potential for trigger warnings to
be reframed: from a pathologizing and debilitating accommodation to an
anti-imperialist feminist method of trauma-informed relationality in the
spirit of free, prior, and informed consent. Battiste writes: "The Eurocentric teaching method instills the modern idea that the environment can
and should be manipulated. Eurocentric thought envisions water, earth,
sun, moon as inanimate—without life. But in the Mi'kmaw language,
some things are close to us because we build alliances with their spirits."[10]
Trigger warnings in the classrooms demonstrate an attunement with the
environment, an acknowledgment that sexualized violence occurs more
frequently on campus and that widespread institutional silencing and
repression of victims causes irrevocable harm, secondary wounding, and
trauma. Professors who use trigger warnings are politicized enough to

understand the individual and collective trauma histories that students embody, and, like picking up the shards of a glass ceiling, classroom encounters and content cut these wounds open over and over again. Trigger warnings can be understood as a way to build alliances with students, to truly see them, relationally facilitating genuine dialogical learning.

Battiste's relationality resonates with Donna Haraway describing, in 1985, a set of scientific and political relations that can be used to view the modern history of education systems in Canada, identifying the manipulative capitalist expansion targeting territories of production, reproduction, and imagination. Haraway writes,

> In the tradition of "Western" science and politics—the tradition of racist, male dominant capitalism; the tradition of progress; the tradition of the appropriation of nature as resource for the productions of culture; the tradition of reproduction of the self from the reflections of the other—the relation between organism and machine has been a border war. The stakes in the border war have been the territories of production, reproduction, and imagination.[11]

Eurocentric academic traditions rely on the binary social imaginary, creating divisiveness and opposition in place of unity and harmonious synchronization. In the book *Protecting Indigenous Knowledge and Heritage: A Global Challenge*, published in 2000, Battiste draws on her Mi'kmaw heritage and gives examples of Indigenous epistemologies that represent holistic relationality amid the border wars. An Indigenous approach of alliance is incompatible with the positivistic settler state goals of colonial industries, including education. The linear assembly-line approach of Taylorism in state-run schools under capitalism is at the core of reactionary resistance to trigger warnings; nonlinear remembered experiences and identities are fragmented by traumatic acts of invasion and denial, complicating the pedagogical machinery of cognitive imperialism and linear patriarchal curricula. Battiste also connects a lack of accountability to Eurocentic curricula:

> Eurocentric curricula isolate the known self; instead of creating communities, they reinforce specialized interests among students. These curricula teach that knowers are manipulators who have no reciprocal responsibilities to the things they manipulate. Thus students may know

a body of transmitted knowledge or set of skills but they do not know how to live in freedom. Often, these students have no inner sense of truth or justice.[12]

This critical profile of abstracted "Eurocentric curricula" also applies to the conduct of individual manipulators on campus, be they administrators and/or sexual predators. In the case of Canada, curricular traditions require the rationalization of an apartheid settler state and its subsequent invasion-based gender relations, which inform contemporary male entitlement to subjugating women's and other bodies transgressing dominant norms. With the prevalence of and public discourse related to sexualized violence and femicide, even emergent levels of honesty refocusing on male violence cause the façade of democratic meritocracy to crack. Academics in the colonial academy face a public relations crisis/opportunity, often addressed by synthesizing misogynist capitalist curricular ethics in three realms: the past, present, and future. This is a practiced institutional method of telling those on the margins to cease with the hysterics, pay attention to the teacher, and settle down.

A sharp example is revealed by comparing the discourse of both the official residential schools apology by Prime Minister Stephen Harper in 2008 and the 2015 bystander response of Dalhousie University president Richard Florizone to graduating male dentistry students who were sharing online surveys with each other about which of their female classmates they would rape. These discourses of power demonstrate repeating patterns of unaccountable pacification—the type of stifling discourse that feminist praxis and pedagogy seek to overthrow. In moments where the academy is under scrutiny by the public and potential investors, evasive rhetoric is used to diffuse the reproduction of rape culture as a "community" issue, de-emphasizing the role that colonial knowledge production plays in legitimizing male entitlement to sexualized violence. Catherine Martin, a Mi'kmaw filmmaker and educator, describes how the production of ideas that conflate racialized sexualization with deserved victimization of Indigenous women is situated "in the mind of mainstream society":

> Our women were raped. They weren't just raped back in the cowboy and Indian days, they are still raped. But that myth or misconception about our women (of being easy) is in the minds of the mainstream society, which is why our women end up being attacked and raped. The fact that

we have been raped makes them tend to think that we are easy. It is a way to excuse the rapist, or ignore the race issue.[13]

To set the national context for classroom-based trauma and to notice a template for pacifying resistance to a mass-scale violation of people in educational institutions proclaiming a higher purpose, the following apologetics of the prime minister can be closely read:

> A cornerstone of the Settlement Agreement is the Indian Residential Schools Truth and Reconciliation Commission. This Commission presents a unique opportunity to educate all Canadians on the Indian Residential Schools system. It will be a positive step in forging a new relationship between Aboriginal peoples and other Canadians, a relationship based on the knowledge of our shared history, a respect for each other and a desire to move forward together with a renewed understanding that strong families, strong communities and vibrant cultures and traditions will contribute to a stronger Canada for all of us.[14]

Stratifying political rhetoric attributes anthropomorphic personalities to patriarchal apparatuses as they operate for the purposes they were designed. While branded as humanized public entities, ideological apparatuses such as residential schools and postsecondary institutions present themselves in their time as progressive and responsive "learning" communities. Providing narrow and seemingly apologetic responses to concerns about their fundamental purpose (namely indentured labor, genocide, and femicide), schools conceal epistemic and repressive institutional violence, refocusing instead on legitimizing the organization and its need to "do better."[15]

This bait-and-switch tactic is a standard method to rebrand corruption in interdisciplinary pan-institutional contexts—such as the closure of the residential school system concurrent with the rise of the colonial child welfare system, which has fragmented more families than the residential school system,[16] or the means by which the Royal Canadian Mounted Police, facing internal charges of entrenched abuse and misogyny from nearly four hundred female members and staff,[17] secured $4 million of $10 million announced by the government to address the intentional neglect of missing and murdered Indigenous women brought to light by grassroots activists.[18] In a context of ongoing exploitation to frame delayed justice as a *"unique opportunity to educate all Canadians"* and in the eyes of the capitalist settler state, what could educational opportunities lead to other than economic development, not only for primary extractive industries but also for schools—the incubators of patriarchal nationalism and gendered public knowledge?

Trauma-informed methods could be implemented in postsecondary classrooms yet must be considered in the historical and contemporary experiences of students in the cultural context of settler patriarchy. Viewed in an appreciative light, trigger warnings represent a demand from students and teachers for social justice pedagogies in the classroom. Current revelations about the rates of campus sexual assault are one critical avenue to consider affect in the classroom for demographics of students who remain outside the streams of privilege, security, and consideration afforded to most male students. While trigger warnings often focus on prefacing course content with the acknowledgment that upcoming topics could be re-traumatizing for some students, additionally the history of genocidal curricula and the crisis of campus sexualized violence are significant aspects to the teaching and learning context as implicit and explicit lessons are taught about white and male privilege and impunity. The silencing of victims echoes in the absence of voices in the trigger warning debate critiquing cultural appropriation and survivor exploitation frequently used to advance difficult pedagogy, a pattern commonly traced in Eurocentric and male-dominated curricula. Often, the added layers of harmful teaching methodologies impede traumatized students' safety and learning in the classroom. A trigger warning can provide a buffering layer of protection by offering nominal notice and fostering empathy.

Trigger warnings are singled out as a flashpoint of antagonism toward feminist pedagogy. The logic behind Harper's use of "educate all Canadians" and "Aboriginal peoples and other Canadians" is to validate a hegemonic model of education. Similar patronizing expressions in backlash to the suggestion of trigger warnings in academia highlight a gendered element in recurring themes implying "you need to be taught what real education is" and "real scholarship has a masculinist style and doesn't have time for needs which are feminized, pathologized, and dismissed." To conflate trigger warnings with "treating PTSD" is a reactionary exaggeration that further stigmatizes requests for inclusive consideration of survivors and equates responsive relational teaching with "exposure to all manner of discipline and punishment." For example, the AAUP contends:

> The classroom is not the appropriate venue to treat PTSD, which is a medical condition that requires serious medical treatment. Trigger warnings are an inadequate and diversionary response. . . . The range of any student's sensitivity is thus impossible to anticipate. But if trigger warnings are required or expected, anything in a classroom that elicits a traumatic response could potentially expose teachers to all manner of discipline and punishment.[19]

There is irony in this type of rhetoric, which proves the point about punitive human resources practices instilling fear in patriarchal institutions, yet survivor advocates and academics in favor of trauma-informed teaching are blamed for inciting these punitive and regulatory aspects of institutional culture.

Closely reading the similarities in this denial and distraction can assist in developing a critical lens with which to analyze the antifeminist colonial backlash prompted by the suggestion that trigger warnings be recommended or obligatory in courses. In the discourse analysis of federal and corporate educational authorities, both invoke a mythologized tradition of gender equity and concluded colonization, apologizing for the presently exposed atrocity of that tradition, and then proceed in "moving forward" by identifying future markets for labor and capital extraction.

The following example of official response to campus men threatening rape in Halifax, Nova Scotia, follows this pattern closely: "I believe we can work together to exemplify equality, inclusivity and respect. Moments of crisis make us stronger. They are an opportunity to test our principles and examine our values. I believe in Dalhousie, and I believe we can do better."[20]

The progression of survivor-led movements demanding transformation, yet met with tepid apology and rebranding, is demonstrated in this high-profile example of appropriating paternalism as the president of Dalhousie University responds to threats exposing a normalized rape culture on campus.[21] Again, similar to the Canadian federal government, to retain brand integrity in a patriarchal knowledge economy, trauma precipitates a unique opportunity to *test* and *examine* students, further asserting a colonial monopoly on knowledge production, evaluation, and an imposed patriarchal definition of moral strength in the face of corruption and human rights violation.

This institutionally simulated sentiment is required by a corporate brand facing repeated existential crises as the chasms between its stated functions and its actual operation are described by the raised voices of people resisting victimization and invasion. Under pressure from the cultural and economic consequences for failing to maintain white male privilege, Dalhousie's Florizone was compelled not to expel male students using an online student group to survey each other about which of their female classmates they would "*sportfuck* or *hatefuck*." Instead, Dalhousie implemented a remedial class especially for twelve male, fourth-year dentistry students complicit in threatening sexual violence against their female classmates on social media. A semester later, they graduated to practice dentistry.

This crisis of legitimacy in the university's capacity to uphold its code of conduct and grant credentials to professionals suitable to work in the field[22] informed Florizone's vocabulary as he used the verbs "exemplify, test, and examine" and framed crisis as opportunity. These themes are consistent with the school's brand image as an imagined site for international ministries of education to invest in, as administrators and perpetrators repeat statements of feigned accountability and Dalhousie continues to market the reputability of its curriculum and credentials with admission that "a lot of progress has been made, and we believe we can be an example for diversity and inclusiveness." This hypocritical mix of humility and self-promotion reads with a sentiment similar to the "punished" students who returned from sensitivity training empowered with the ability to transform from uttering rapist threats to being role model practitioners administering general anesthesia to the public and supported by the extra credit of customized ethical remediation.[23]

Similar to the events at Dalhousie in early 2015, in the fall of 2013, St. Mary's University in Halifax, Canada, applied the same apologetic formula, attempting to pacify an outraged public, after students were recorded being initiated to their campus with annually recited pro-rape chants by paid student executives.[24] Reports of similar rape chants at esteemed schools across North America, as well as the ritualization of male sexualized violence against women, has made the excuses of administrators sound as strategic as they are inadequate. "Hate-fuck" and "No consent" as utterances included in rapist rituals in Nova Scotia and beyond demonstrate explicit admission of intent. In cases ranging from verbal sexual harassment to promoting and perpetrating rape, male character is beyond refute—benign "locker room banter," feigned confusion about consent, and rape myth repetition are normalized justifications repeated in classrooms and courtrooms. Convictions are rare and sentences are light as racist and rapist redemption trumps survivor justice.

As educational institutions respond to male-led collective sexualized violence, the negative press generated is only one factor schools negotiate. Additionally, there is the more pressing influence of the possibility that men, held accountable, would have to face limited social mobility based on their participation in ritualized sexualized violence. In these institutions, the implications of accountability for perpetrators of sexualized violence are untenable to authorities invested in their current priorities and structure.

Despite temporal dissociation inherent in the rigid grammar of English past/present/future, the violence of colonization is not dispelled or contained by the linear progress of synthesized regret, apology, or reconciliation. Furthermore, through media that generally accept policy developments uncritically, this type of public relations incident management leaves institutions "cleansed" and reborn with a competitive advantage on the international market of commodified knowledge transfer. These are examples of academic corporations, corporate states, and privileged castes of students having public access to a spectrum of human experiences not offered to individual survivors attending university. The university, the nation state, and the good old boys are upset. They are upset by the exposure of invasive trauma (in which they are complicit); they are permitted to act erratically; they can contradict themselves without losing significant power or legitimacy, can make commitments to sweeping changes, and are entitled to beneficence and believability when they claim to need public support, patience, trust, and investment. These are the affective needs that power is entitled to. Meanwhile, survivors pursuing legal justice are labeled vindictive, inconsistent, and culpable in their victimization, as students seeking dignity and security are labeled coddled, lazy, entitled millennials. How dare survivors seek advance notice and support should course content require abstracted group discussions about rape, torture, and other outcomes of marginality and oppression! To the extent that violence endured at the neglect or intent of an institution is less abstract than the secondary trauma sensitivity addressed by the promotion of trigger warnings, it is relevant to compare the degree of recognition of campus sexual violence by universities when discussing trauma-informed pedagogies.

The imposition and simultaneous denial of trauma, from residential schools to the modern university where we invest our intellectual labor, embodies in the colonial and misogynist curricula and pedagogy re-traumatizing survivors attempting to support their own and others' feminist and antiracist consciousness. The depth of denial, the prevalence of strategies of avoidance, and invasive cognitive imperialism requires a general trigger warning: The colonial education system refuses to provide adequate "free, prior, and informed consent."

Notes

1. American Association of University Professors, Committee A on Academic Freedom and Tenure, *On Trigger Warnings*, August 2014, http://www.aaup .org/report/trigger-warnings.

2. Ibid.

3. Antonia Darder, *Teaching as an Act of Love: Reflections on Paulo Freire and His Contributions to Our Lives and Our Work* (Covina: California Association for Bilingual Education, 1998).

4. Jill Filipovic, "We've Gone Too Far with 'Trigger Warnings,'" *The Guardian*, March 5, 2014.

5. Kirby Dick, *The Hunting Ground* (Beverly Hills, CA: Anchor Bay Entertainment, 2015), DVD.

6. Statistics Canada, "Postsecondary Enrollments by Institution Type, Registration Status, Province and Sex," CANSIM, table 477-0019, 2016, last modified November 23, 2016, http://www.statcan.gc.ca/tables-tableaux/sum-som/l01/ cst01/educ71a-eng.htm.

7. Canadian Federation of Students, "Sexual Violence on Campus Fact Sheet," 2015, http://cfsontario.ca/wp-content/uploads/sites/50/2016/06/Sexual-Assault -Factsheet.pdf.

8. Daniel Schwartz, "Truth and Reconciliation Commission: By the Numbers," *CBC News*, June 23, 2015, http://www.cbc.ca/news/indigenous/truth-and -reconciliation-commission-by-the-numbers-1.3096185.

9. Parshuram Tamang, "An Overview of the Principle of Free, Prior and Informed Consent and Indigenous Peoples in International and Domestic Law and Practices," *Australian Indigenous Law Reporter* (2005).

10. Marie Battiste and James Youngblood Henderson, *Protecting Indigenous Knowledge and Heritage: A Global Challenge* (Vancouver: University of British Columbia Press, 2000), 90.

11. Donna J. Haraway, "A Cyborg Manifesto: Science, Technology, and Socialist-Feminism in the Late Twentieth Century," in *Simians, Cyborgs and Women: The Reinvention of Nature* (New York: Routledge, 1991), 150.

12. Battiste and Henderson, *Protecting Indigenous Knowledge*, 90.

13. Kim Anderson, *A Recognition of Being: Reconstructing Native Womanhood* (Toronto: Canadian Scholars' Press, 2000).

14. Stephen Joseph Harper, "Prime Minister Harper Offers Full Apology on Behalf of Canadians for the Indian Residential Schools System," Office of the Prime Minister, June 11, 2008.

15. Richard Florizone, January 9 Update to Community, Task Force on Misogyny, Sexism and Homophobia in the Faculty of Dentistry, Dalhousie University, 2015, https://www.dal.ca/cultureofrespect/background/updates.html.

16. Cindy Blackstock, "Reconciliation Means Not Saying Sorry Twice: Lessons from Child Welfare in Canada," in *From Truth to Reconciliation: Transforming the Legacy of Residential Schools* (Ottawa: Aboriginal Healing Foundation, 2008), 163.

17. Paul Tasker, "RCMP's Recent History of Harassment, Abuse, and Discrimination," *CBC News*, February 18, 2016, http://www.cbc.ca/news/politics/rcmp-sexual-harassment-history-1.3453413.

18. Voices-Voix, "Sisters in Spirit," accessed February 12, 2016, http://voices-voix.ca/en/facts/profile/sisters-spirit.

19. American Association of University Professors, *On Trigger Warnings*, 9.

20. Florizone, January 9 Update to Community.

21. *CBC News*, "Dalhousie Dentistry Complaints Date back to Summer, Student Says," last modified December 16, 2015, http://www.cbc.ca/news/canada/nova-scotia/dalhousie-dentistry-complaints-date-back-to-summer-student-says.

22. Simona Choise, "Dalhousie Dentistry Students Scrambled to Contain Damage after Comments Became Public," *The Globe and Mail*, January 6, 2015, 7, http://www.theglobeandmail.com/news/national/dalhousie-rejects-calls-to-name-students-involved-in-facebookscandal/article22317027/.

23. Constance Backhouse, Donald McRae, and Iyer Nitya, *Report of the Task Force on Misogyny, Sexism and Homophobia in Dalhousie University Faculty of Dentistry* (Halifax, NS: Dalhousie University, 2015).

24. *CBC News*, "Saint Mary's Pro-Rape Chant Sparks 20 New Recommendations," December 19, 2013, http://www.cbc.ca/news/canada/nova-scotia/saint-mary-s-pro-rape-chant-sparks-20-new-recommendations.

Bibliography

American Association of University Professors, Committee A on Academic Freedom and Tenure. *On Trigger Warnings*. August 2014. http://www.aaup.org/report/trigger-warnings.

Anderson, Kim. *A Recognition of Being: Reconstructing Native Womanhood*. Toronto: Canadian Scholars' Press, 2000.

Backhouse, Constance, Donald McRae, and Iyer Nitya. *Report of the Task Force on Misogyny, Sexism and Homophobia in Dalhousie University Faculty of Dentistry*. Halifax, NS: Dalhousie University, 2015.

Battiste, Marie, and James Youngblood Henderson. *Protecting Indigenous Knowledge and Heritage: A Global Challenge*. Vancouver: University of British Columbia Press, 2000.

Blackstock, Cindy. "Reconciliation Means Not Saying Sorry Twice: Lessons from Child Welfare in Canada." In *From Truth to Reconciliation: Transforming the Legacy of Residential Schools*. Ottawa: Aboriginal Healing Foundation, 2008, 163–78.

Canadian Federation of Students. "Sexual Violence on Campus Fact Sheet." 2015. http://cfsontario.ca/wp-content/uploads/sites/50/2016/06/Sexual-Assault-Factsheet.pdf.

CBC News. "Dalhousie Dentistry Complaints Date back to Summer, Student Says." Last modified December 16, 2015. http://www.cbc.ca/news/canada/nova-scotia/dalhousie-dentistry-complaints-date-back-to-summer-student-says.

———. "Saint Mary's Pro-Rape Chant Sparks 20 New Recommendations." December 19, 2013. http://www.cbc.ca/news/canada/nova-scotia/saint-mary-s-pro-rape-chant-sparks-20-new-recommendations.

Choise, Simona. "Dalhousie Dentistry Students Scrambled to Contain Damage after Comments Became Public." *The Globe and Mail*, January 6, 2015, 7. http://www.theglobeandmail.com/news/national/dalhousie-rejects-calls-to-name-students-involved-in-facebookscandal/article22317027/.

Darder, Antonia. *Teaching as an Act of Love: Reflections on Paulo Freire and His Contributions to Our Lives and Our Work*. Covina: California Association for Bilingual Education, 1998.

Filipovic, Jill. "We've Gone Too Far with 'Trigger Warnings.'" *The Guardian*, March 5, 2014. https://www.theguardian.com/commentisfree/2014/mar/05/trigger-warnings-can-be-counterproductive.

Florizone, Richard. January 9 Update to Community, Task Force on Misogyny, Sexism and Homophobia in the Faculty of Dentistry. Dalhousie University, 2015. https://www.dal.ca/cultureofrespect/background/updates.html.

Haraway, Donna J. "A Cyborg Manifesto: Science, Technology, and Socialist-Feminism in the Late Twentieth Century." In *Simians, Cyborgs and Women: The Reinvention of Nature*. New York: Routledge, 1991, 150.

Harper, Stephen Joseph. "Prime Minister Harper Offers Full Apology on Behalf of Canadians for the Indian Residential Schools System." Office of the Prime Minister. June 11, 2008. https://www.aadnc-aandc.gc.ca/eng/1100100015644/1100100015649.

Schwartz, Daniel. "Truth and Reconciliation Commission: By the Numbers." *CBC News*, June 2, 2015. http://www.cbc.ca/news/indigenous/truth-and-reconciliation-commission-by-the-numbers-1.3096185.

Statistics Canada. "Postsecondary Enrollments by Institution Type, Registration Status, Province and Sex." CANSIM, table 477-0019, 2016. Last modified November 23, 2016. http://www.statcan.gc.ca/tables-tableaux/sum-som/l01/cst01/educ71a-eng.htm.

Tamang, Parshuram. "An Overview of the Principle of Free, Prior and Informed Consent and Indigenous Peoples in International and Domestic Law and Practices." *Australian Indigenous Law Reporter*, 2005.

Tasker, Paul. "RCMP's Recent History of Harassment, Abuse, and Discrimination." *CBC News*, February 18, 2016. http://www.cbc.ca/news/politics/rcmp-sexual-harassment-history-1.3453413.

Voices-Voix. "Sisters in Spirit." Accessed February 12, 2016. http://voices-voix.ca/en/facts/profile/sisters-spirit.

CHAPTER SIX

AN "APP" FOR THAT
The Case against the "Equal Access"
Argument for Trigger Warnings
Bonnie Washick

The migration of trigger warnings—or notifications of content that might elicit or "trigger" an adverse psychosomatic response—from marginal social media to university classrooms has generated a broad public debate on their efficacy and effects. Those taking issue with trigger warnings argue that they have a deadening effect on discussion and cultivate demanding yet intellectually and emotionally enfeebled students and readers. Proponents have suggested that trigger warnings are centrally about equal access. In short, they argue that trigger warnings can be thought of as tools that enable individuals with posttraumatic stress disorder (PTSD) and other mental illnesses to engage a text, a topic, or course that might otherwise elicit a disabling response.

As a tool, the trigger warning (1) prevents harm that might result from an unanticipated encounter with triggering content, and (2) enables its receiver to make informed decisions regarding when and how to engage potentially triggering content. Finally (3), as a tool of equal access,[1] the trigger warning is figured as a reasonable accommodation that has little or no impact on those for whom it is not intended: a broader reading, viewing, listening public who engages the same content without being either triggered or forewarned. This does not mean this broader public is irrelevant. To the contrary, the "normal" reader (viewer, listener) of this broader public implicitly functions to establish the "equal" or peer, to whom an individual with psychosomatic triggers is enabled to realize their status (equal) with the aid of a trigger warning.

This chapter undertakes a sympathetic critique of what I have termed the "equal access" argument for trigger warnings. I argue that the strengths of the equal access framing cannot be disentangled from a central weakness: an individualizing model of harm and accommodation. While an individualizing model of harm and accommodation fits neatly with hegemonic or commonsense understandings of the same, worldly uses of trigger warnings fit poorly with such a model.[2] I argue that this ill fit reflects the ways in which worldly uses of trigger warnings *publicize* both harm attributable to structural violence and accommodation. "Publicize" here means to "make public," both in the sense of "making known," and to "make the public's responsibility."

The problem with the equal access framing is not simply conceptual. Framed as an individualizing tool of equal access, discussions of trigger warnings center on the tool itself, rather than structural violence that trigger warnings name by way of a trace: trauma and its durable effects. What's more, framing trigger warnings as an equal access tool renders them amenable to co-optation by a neoliberal rationality, potentially generating an expectation of individuals with triggers to privately "manage" their well-being or underwriting a technical fix—for example a computer application or "app"—that student-consumers might use to tailor their college experience to their taste. Drawing out the ways in which they publicize harm attributable to structural violence, I argue trigger warnings are better understood as a counter-public practice, or a means of cultivating subjects through public address that challenges normative visions of the democratic subject.

The chapter proceeds as follows: I open by delving into the history and development of trigger warnings. Section II elaborates how student advocates articulated affinities between the equal access argument for trigger warnings and the promise of accommodation, nondiscrimination, and inclusion in institutions of higher education by figuring trigger warnings as equal access tools. I argue that articulating these affinities was crucial in elevating the trigger warning to a topic of national concern even as it vastly circumscribed that discussion. In Section III, I develop the case for conceptualizing trigger warnings as a counter-public practice. I conclude by reflecting on the ways in which viewing trigger warnings as a counter-public practice raises different questions and makes possible new alliances.

Section I: Trigger Warnings in Computer-Mediated Communication

In this section I examine how and where trigger warnings have been used and discuss their movement across communicative spaces. I argue that framing trigger warnings as tools enabling access has a long history but does not capture all the ways in which trigger warnings have been advocated. Additionally, I attend to the changing nature of the interest and criticism that trigger warnings drew as they moved from private sites of communication to marginal feminist social justice media. In attending to these changes I find support for my claim that trigger warnings are better understood as a counter-public practice, a claim I return to in Section III.

Defining Trigger Warnings

Trigger warnings are a common feature of feminist blogging and other computer-mediated communication (CMC) that aspires to create "safe spaces" for feminist—and also often antiracist, anti-ableist, and queer—speech. Using a trigger warning has typically entailed typing "Trigger Warning," "Trigger," "TW," or "Warning" followed by an explanation of what content may be triggering. Many sites moved away from the language of "trigger warnings" to that of "content notes" or "content warnings"—abbreviated to "CN" or "CW," respectively—before trigger warnings became a topic of broad public debate.

For the most part, trigger warnings traffic in general categories of trauma that may be predicted based on statistics (e.g., the prevalence of sexual assault) and/or context (e.g., in a forum for those recovering from an eating disorder, one can anticipate readers who might be "triggered" by an account of purging). These warnings typically appear in the title or at the top of a post—sometimes in bold and placed in brackets, or between asterisks—or alongside linked content that contains triggering material. On many sites, comment policies detailing moderation practices include a request for commenters to consider whether the use of a trigger warning is necessary before posting. The use of trigger warnings by commentators may also be modeled or enforced by a moderator who edits a comment to add or remove a trigger warning.

Trigger Warnings in Private Computer-Mediated Communication

Before trigger warnings showed up on feminist blogs they were being used in online "self-help" communities intended to support individuals struggling with or recovering from suicidal ideation, self-harm, eating disorders, and interpersonal violence, including sexual assault. *Bodies under Siege* (*BUS*), founded in 1996, appears to have been one of the first to use trigger warnings.[3] *BUS* administrators confirmed that trigger warnings were in use on *BUSlist*, the private listserv that, in 2001, became a password-protected online forum.[4]

When sequestered in "private" CMC, or CMC that is not immediately accessible and open to all, including *BUSlist* and the password-protected *BUS* forum, trigger warnings drew little attention from a broader public. Perhaps the earliest scholarship touching on trigger warnings—produced in the early 2000s by psychologists interested in the benefits and risks of CMC for those struggling with self-harm—depicts trigger warnings in a relatively benign light.[5] While trigger warnings were not found to be perfectly effective,[6] their absence was more concerning.[7] In these specialized, private spaces of communication it was accepted—indeed it was a motivating premise of these psychological studies—that participants might have a harmful response to content encountered and that the good of both individual participants and the communities depended, to some extent, on how they responded to this possibility. In this context, trigger warnings appear as a tool "enabl[ing] group members to make a choice" about whether and how to engage potentially harmful, triggering content.[8]

Even so, trigger warnings were not depicted as easy for writers to use, as can be seen in the discussion that accompanied the move from content warnings to trigger warnings on *BUS*. *BUS* appears to have been one of the first to make this transition in the early 2000s. The change in language was motivated by the failure of some writers to indicate the nature of potentially triggering material as well as a perceived overuse of warnings tags. Both of these "failures" reflect some confusion about who the trigger warning was "for"—that is, whether it conveyed something of the author's state of mind, indicated the "importance and validity of [a] post" to the community, or was intended to let readers "know what to expect before they start[ed] reading a post."[9] In the hope of better achieving the last goal, *BUS* adopted the more ubiquitous term *content* to prompt writers to indicate what—if any—sort of content might be triggering. Paired with a new, limited list of content that moderators indicated warranted a warning, the move from the language of "trigger warning" to "content warning" on *BUS* can be seen as an effort to circumscribe the use of trigger warnings so that they remained specialized to the private community and its espoused concerns.

Trigger Warnings in Marginal Public CMC

It is unclear if feminist bloggers adopted trigger warnings in response to requests from readers or incorporated them as writers, drawing from their experience in other forums, but, by the mid-2000s, one can find trigger warnings used without explanation on popular feminist blogs like *Feministe* and *Shakesville*. What is clear is that feminist bloggers and their audiences argued for trigger warnings on grounds that they prevented harm and helped survivors engage content healthfully. However, this was not the only ground upon which their use was advocated.

A blog post authored by Melissa McEwan, founder and primary contributor to the feminist blog *Shakesville*, provides an example of the ways in which feminist bloggers' reasons for using trigger warnings included but were not fully captured by their use as tools enabling access. In a post explaining—and defending—the use of trigger warnings, McEwan initially describes trigger warnings as tools enabling access and functioning as described in my introduction. First, McEwan interprets what it means to be triggered—for example, one might experience "a full-blown panic attack"—thereby giving form to the harm that the use of trigger warnings prevents.[10] McEwan then describes how trigger warnings enable survivors to make informed decisions about when and how to engage potentially triggering content:

> We provide trigger warnings because they give survivors of various stripes the option to assess whether they're in a state of mind to deal with triggering material before they stumble across it. Just like someone who isn't easily triggered can nonetheless have, say, a shorter temper when stressed or tired or hungry, a person whose history of trauma makes some material triggering for them can often navigate triggering material without a problem, except when stressed or tired or hungry. Trigger warnings give them a moment to consider whether they want to deal with potentially triggering material *right now*.[11]

Finally, McEwan implies trigger warnings have little impact on those for whom they are not intended by characterizing their use as "polite," or a reasonable social nicety, and indicating that writers have no good reasons not to use them—only "carelessness or laziness or ignorance."[12]

However, later in the same blog post, McEwan writes: "We provide trigger warnings because we know that 1 out of every 6 women and 1 out of every 10 men is a survivor of sexual assault or attempted sexual assault, many of them having survived *multiple* sexual assaults, and just because the larger culture doesn't acknowledge the existence of this vast population of people doesn't mean we don't have to."[13] McEwan's prose now centers on writers' knowledge and actions, rather than what trigger warnings do. More precisely, the action shifts from the trigger warning that "give[s]" to a blogging "we" that "know[s]" and "acknowledge[s]" forms of harm that tend to remain private even as a "vast population" share them.

Admittedly, this acknowledgment might be helpful, even therapeutic, to individuals who have experienced sexual assault,[14] but McEwan's prose suggests that she sees the use of trigger warnings as doing something more than providing a tool for survivors of trauma. Discursively linking the lack of public acknowledgment of sexual assault and the commonness of sexual assault, McEwan's explanation for why writers use trigger warnings suggests their use constitutes a form of activism. This marks a departure from their use in private forums like *BUS*.

Another area in which we can observe a departure in feminist bloggers' use and understanding of trigger warnings from their use in private CMC like *BUS* is in the reasons given for the movement away from the language of trigger warnings to that of content warnings or content notes. As discussed above, the move to the language of content warnings on *BUS* circumscribed the tagging practice so that it remained specialized to the niche community and its espoused concerns. By contrast, on feminist and other social justice blogs framed as "safe spaces," the move to the language of content notes or warnings appears to have been motivated by an effort to flag structural inequality and symbolic violence as at least potentially traumatizing, even if not synonymous with the notion of being triggered. Rather than a limited list of content requiring warnings, the shift to content warnings or notes in feminist and social justice blogging accommodated or accompanied an expansion of tagged content. So, for example, on the feminist blog, *Shakesville*, one can find content notes for "heterosexism," "fat hatred," and "racism," in addition to more conventional warnings for sexual assault or graphic depictions of violence.[15]

In Section III, I expand on an alternative approach to conceptualizing trigger warnings that attends to the ways in which trigger warnings might both facilitate access and constitute a form of activism. For now, it suffices to say that the equal access argument for trigger warnings does not fully explain how and why feminist and other social justice bloggers took up trigger warnings.

And taken up they were: They became immensely popular on Tumblr's micro-blogging platform, founded in 2007, owing to an interface that "offers no warning—not even a headline" for material that might be triggering.[16] At the same time that trigger warnings spread through a growing feminist and, more broadly, social justice–oriented blogosphere, they became common on *LiveJournal* for both fanfiction and personal journaling.[17]

By 2010, feminists' use of trigger warnings in online contexts was common enough to draw critical attention from Susannah Breslin, writing for the now defunct, online-only news site *True/Slant*.[18] Breslin's post addresses a broader public and satirizes "a ponderously feminist blog," *Feministe*, and its unusual "bloggy style"; that is, the use of trigger warnings.[19] Breslin depicts trigger warnings as absurd, the badge of a "dead" political movement that, having already won the day, now tilted at windmills ("an enemy that I never seem quite able to locate"[20]).

Breslin received substantial pushback for dismissing trauma survivors and a tool intended for them. In reply, Breslin moved away from figuring trigger warnings as absurd and contemptible to confused or wrong-minded: a counterproductive tool that perversely compelled trauma survivors to read on, rather than turn away.[21] While Breslin remained critical of trigger warnings, the equal access framing compelled her to take them seriously, a point I return to in Section II.

Even so, as trigger warnings migrated from "private"—members-only listservs and password-protected CMC—to "public"—formally open-access CMC like blogs—they prompted little concern for the well-being of those who read for them and even less for a broader public. This does not mean that all members of these marginal, public CMC platforms wholeheartedly embraced the use of trigger warnings. There were internal discussions about problematic *usages*, including overuse,[22] and there were those who personally found trigger warnings off-putting and opted not to use them, including those who had triggers.[23] Breslin's posts thus present an exception to CMC, that addressed a broad public, most of which remained uninterested or unconcerned by the use of trigger warnings in marginal feminist and social justice CMC, and to *LiveJournal*, a platform associated with young women and girls and trivial discourse.[24] In the following section I discuss the migration of trigger warnings to college classrooms and the means by which they became a topic of broad, sustained debate.

Section II: Trigger Warnings on Campus

It was not simply the change of medium—from social media to college classrooms—that made trigger warnings a topic of broad, sustained deliberation. Earlier instances of individual students requesting trigger warnings and of college instructors discussing how to productively use trigger warnings in the classroom did not prompt a national debate.[25] This remained true even after the use of trigger warnings in the classroom was noted in a December 2013 *Slate* article in which Amanda Marcotte identified a growing "mainstream" awareness of the concept of a trigger warning.[26]

Writing just before trigger warnings became a problem warranting national discussion, Marcotte at once named trigger warnings a "mainstream concept" and concluded that if they became "ubiquitous . . . odds are that most people will end up tuning them out like we do similarly intended parental warnings slapped on movie posters and TV shows."[27] As further evidence against the notion that it was the change of venue that prompted the debate, one can observe that it remains common for critics—sympathetic and otherwise—to indicate it is "perfectly reasonable" for individual "survivors of violence" to request warnings for specific triggers.[28]

I argue that it was students' advocacy of trigger warnings as a systemic solution that elevated trigger warnings to a topic of national debate. More precisely, it was the articulation of affinities between trigger warnings as a tool of equal access and the institutionalization of the American Disabilities Act (ADA); Title IX, which bars discrimination on the basis of sex; and diversity[29] on college campuses that made it possible to imagine that the use of trigger warnings could come to be required, expected, or simply normal.[30]

Indeed, the threat of a new normal looms large in Jenny Jarvie's March 2014 *New Republic* article, "Trigger Happy," which can be credited with prompting the debate over trigger warnings. Jarvie writes:

> Now that they've entered university classrooms, it's only a matter of time before warnings are demanded for other grade levels. As students introduce them in college newspapers, promotional material for plays, even poetry slams, it's not inconceivable that they'll appear at the beginning of film screenings and at the entrance to art exhibits. Will newspapers start applying warnings to articles about rape, murder, and war? Could they even become a regular feature of speech? "I was walking down Main Street last night when—trigger warning—I saw an elderly woman get mugged."[31]

Whereas Marcotte could imagine trigger warnings as both "ubiquitous" and irrelevant to "most people" who would simply "tun[e] [them] out" (possibly reflecting her own experience as a feminist blogger-cum-mainstream journalist who "do[es] not" use trigger warnings), Jarvie paints a future wherein "most people" are using trigger warnings and "public life [is structured] around the most fragile personal sensitivities."[32] Two early instances of advocacy for trigger warnings in the classroom that were cited in Jarvie's account clarify how this dramatic change occurred: the publication of a guide for Oberlin College's faculty encouraging the use of trigger warnings[33] and a University of California, Santa Barbara (UCSB) student government resolution "mandat[ing]" the use of trigger warnings.[34] I discuss these briefly below.

Oberlin's short-lived "Support Resources for Faculty" was produced by a task force comprised of students, faculty, and administrators from the Office of Equity Concerns, one site of the institutionalization of Title IX at Oberlin.[35] The Oberlin guide lists "[u]nderstand[ing] triggers, avoid[ing] unnecessary triggers, and provid[ing] trigger warnings" as a means of "mak[ing] . . . classroom[s] more inclusive for survivors of sexualized violence."[36] Triggers were then described as harmful, "disrupt[ive] [to] a student's learning."[37] Faculty were encouraged to exclude content that contained triggering material but that "d[id] not contribute directly to the course learning goals" and to otherwise utilize a trigger warning "so that [students] can prepare for or choose to avoid the trigger."[38] Potential triggers were not limited to content related to sexual assault but extended to "racism, classism, sexism, heterosexism, cissexism, ableism, and other issues of privilege and oppression."[39]

The UCSB student resolution similarly opens by defining triggers, in this case as "a symptom of PTSD." The resolution notes that "UCSB Disabled Students Program recognizes PTSD as a disability" and frames trigger warnings as an appropriate accommodation.[40] Trigger warnings are introduced as tools preventing harm—including "severe emotional, mental, and even physical distress"—and enabling "informed" choices.[41]

In both cases, institutional affiliation, language used, and examples selected suggest that trigger warnings are tools preventing harm and enabling access of student survivors of trauma and that their adoption in classrooms would constitute an appropriate expression of colleges' commitments regarding reasonable accommodations, nondiscrimination, and inclusion. With that said, these commitments are reflected in somewhat ambivalent ways. On the one hand, both the Oberlin faculty guide and the UCSB student resolution discount the "use" of trigger warnings by anyone other than those for whom they might facilitate access and any effect they might have on writers and other readers. Indeed, the UCSB resolution asserts that "[i]ncluding trigger warnings is not a form of criticism or censorship of content" and "does not restrict academic freedom," thereby anticipating and disavowing what will become familiar charges relating to the impact trigger warnings have on a broader public.[42]

On the other hand, both documents more or less implicitly articulate a relationship between structural violence, for which a broader public bears responsibility, and individual experiences of trauma, harm, and disability. For example, the Oberlin guide notes that classrooms may include survivors of sexual assault as well as those "who have committed some form of sexual misconduct, or who hold views that may contribute to a culture and climate where sexualized violence is more likely to occur."[43] This observation is followed by the assertion that "Oberlin's community cannot afford to ignore sexualized violence."[44] In this context, I suggest that trigger warnings function not only as a tool for individuals with triggers, but also as a means of challenging "a culture and climate" that normalizes certain forms of violence and thereby participates in the making of trauma survivors. In the following section I elaborate why this other argument "for" trigger warnings fails to gain significant traction.

Effects of the Equal Access Framing: Traction and Intractable Debate

Articulating trigger warnings as tools fulfilling college mandates regarding accommodation, nondiscrimination, and inclusion made it possible for proponents to suggest trigger warnings were tools whose appropriateness had already been debated, determined, and institutionalized and for critics like Jenny Jarvie to imagine a world "structur[ed] around the most fragile personal sensitivities."[45] But while the articulation of these affinities was effective, it would at the same time dramatically circumscribe the debate that unfolded. Hegemonic conceptions of harm and accommodation as individualized, or detached from a broader public, made it both difficult and necessary for proponents to explain how a tool that required others' (e.g., writer and instructors) participation, was non-exclusive (i.e., one would encounter the tool whether or not one had triggers) and was fiercely resisted could nonetheless be characterized as causing no undue hardship to those for whom it was not intended.

Concretely, this manifested as a narrow public discussion centered on the question of what sort of tool trigger warnings constituted. Many introduced trigger warnings as tools for *avoiding* content rather than tools *enabling* engagement with content in different, more healthful ways. Some further indicated that trigger warnings were used to avoid content that was merely discomforting.[46]

Critics who granted that students used trigger warnings for valid reasons nonetheless asserted that they were *ineffective* tools. Increasingly, this claim is supported by reference to scientific literature suggesting "exposure therapy" has been most effective in helping those with triggers, which relies upon a misleading contrast between the terms "avoidance" and "exposure."[47] Others suggested that the fact that triggers are varied and often deeply personal meant that using a trigger warning amounts to a false, even harmful, promise of safety.[48]

Opponents likewise depicted trigger warnings as an *unreasonable accommodation* that tasked instructors with the impossible and could have a significant adverse effect on a broader public. The fact that triggers can be diverse and deeply personal was presented as proof of the impossibility of implementing trigger warnings.[49] The negative impact that trigger warnings constituted for a broader public has been variously depicted as producing a "chilling effect,"[50] creating a "repressive, 'chilly' climate,"[51] and "censorship,"[52] but shares in suggesting that freedom of speech and expression are threatened by the use of trigger warnings.

Others suggest it is freedom of interpretation[53] or even experience that is threatened.[54] The implication of this line of criticism is not only that one might read and experience content that is forewarned as traumatic or traumatizing, but that this interpretation or experience would be artificial or insincere, an effect of social priming and not one's own thoughts and feelings. Finally, some have argued that trigger warnings disproportionately affect and so also stigmatize already marginal disciplines and course content, such as gender studies and women's studies and books authored by people of color, respectively.[55]

Arguments "for" trigger warnings following their elevation to a topic of public consideration have spent a great deal of time refuting the charges above. Proponents discuss what it means to be triggered, focusing on persuading the reader that trigger warnings are intended to prevent or mitigate harm and not mere discomfort.[56] Related, they illustrate the ableist notions of trauma, and those with trauma triggers, that underwrite many criticisms of the trigger warning.[57] They explain how trigger warnings enable student engagement with content, often focusing on persuading the reader that trigger warnings are not centrally about avoidance.[58] They liken trigger warnings to other accommodations for disabilities.[59]

Challenging the varied claims that trigger warnings would have a significant, adverse effect on others, proponents describe using trigger warnings as "easy."[60] They discount the possibility of a "chilling" effect on speech or expression, often suggesting that discussion might be improved by their use.[61] And finally, they challenge the notion that trigger warnings might (further) stigmatize marginal literatures and fields of study.[62]

Proponents typically shy away from asserting that trigger warnings might work on and also be "for" a broader public. To do so would be to destabilize commonsense conceptions of harm and accommodation as individualized and so also to "politicize" a tool that only became imaginable as common outside private or marginal communications spaces on grounds that it reflected a prior political consensus. Proponents thus find themselves in the challenging position of arguing that a tool that requires others, is non-exclusive, and is opposed by many should nonetheless be seen as having little impact on those for whom it is not intended. In the following section I discuss risks of this position.

Risks of the Equal Access Framing: "Better" Tools and Neoliberal Co-optation

Aside from leading to a rather intractable debate, the awkwardness of figuring trigger warnings as an equal access tool causing no undue hardship presents opportunities for "better" tools that accomplish the functions of preventing harm and enabling healthful engagement with minimal or no involvement from a broader public of writers and readers. It is not difficult to imagine individually tailored, technical fixes enabling students with triggers to identify and prepare for potentially triggering content. For example, a user-installed plug-in, or "app," could scan assigned texts for keywords or categories input by the user.[63] Alternatively, individuals could privately check required readings against a database of trigger warned texts.

A trigger warning app would likely be a more effective tool for mitigating harm and enabling access of those with triggers for the same reason that such fixes would circumvent one of the central criticisms of trigger warnings: that individual triggers are often deeply personal and thus evade the generalized categories in which trigger warnings traffic. However, such an app would fit poorly with proponents' inadequately articulated concern with a "culture and climate"[64] that participates in making "survivors."

My hypothetical trigger warning app also appears at odds with the form that requests for trigger warnings in the classroom may take: Students often request or suggest the addition of a trigger warning on content that they did not personally experience as triggering, but rather imagined as triggering to others. Queer theorist Jack Halberstam reads this practice as evidence that "trigger warning[s] conform to a normative structure of surveillance," presented as "a structure of paternalistic normativity within which some people make assumptions about harm, and about right and wrong, on behalf of others who supposedly cannot make such decisions for themselves."[65]

Halberstam's interpretation may reflect the common—and, I would argue, overly simplistic—likening of trigger warnings to movie and TV ratings.[66] As Halberstam notes, movie and TV ratings were intended to facilitate parents' control over content viewed by children who were understood to be unfit if not unable to make decisions for themselves. By contrast, trigger warnings are addressed to a general audience, imagined as including those who have experienced trauma; those with triggers are not imagined to require a third party to assess their fitness for engaging potentially triggering content. However, a third party's (writerly) use of a trigger warning could make it possible for those with triggers to make decisions for themselves, and, in that sense, the request by a fourth or fifth party on behalf of an imagined other may likewise participate in the access of an individual with triggers who looks for trigger warnings. This collective practice is difficult to square with the hypothetical app in which one would individually and privately manage triggering content.

Finally, the equal access argument for trigger warnings is particularly vulnerable to neoliberal co-optation. Neoliberalism, understood as a distinct "political rationality," elevates the market to an organizing logic, *"extending and disseminating market values to all institutions and social action."*[67] Neoliberal political rationality "constructs and interpellates individuals as entrepreneurial actors . . . [and] in so doing . . . carries responsibility for the self to new heights."[68] At the same time, neoliberalism can support vast bureaucratic apparatuses aimed at "maximizing" individual performance and thus also cultivating and normalizing neoliberal subjects. The threat of neoliberalism "permeat[ing]" college campuses seems particularly acute as students (or their parents) are increasingly treated as customers purchasing, at once, an experience and set of skills that will ensure their future gainful employment.[69]

Framed as equal access tools, trigger warnings lend themselves to an individualized model of harm and accommodation. As suggested above, proponents' advocacy of trigger warnings seems often to undermine this individualizing tendency and thus also renders the equal access argument less coherent. The same could not be said for the hypothetical app. One can imagine the provision of such an app used to market accommodation and inclusion that impinges least on others. Or, the availability of the app creating an expectation for students to privately manage their well-being. Or, students using such an app to avoid content they found uncomfortable, including challenging discussions of privilege. In the following section I explore an alternative approach to thinking about trigger warnings that might avoid some of these pitfalls.

Section III: Counter-Public Theory

Rather than conceptualizing trigger warnings as equal access tools exclusively for individuals with PTSD and other mental illnesses, we might consider trigger warnings as a counter-public practice, a term informed by the work of Michael Warner's *Publics and Counterpublics*. Warner defines "publics" as the modern phenomena by which strangers are constituted as particular sorts of subjects—e.g., Americans,[70] men of reason,[71] queers[72]— by means of generic form, style, mode of delivery, protocols, and the content of discursive claims. In this sense, Warner argues that public address is always a form of "poetic world making" or party to materializing the world and the subjects it presumes already exist.[73]

Publics undergird and are productive of relations of power, organizing the world and subjects such that some individuals, topics, modes of speech, and so on seem appropriate for "the public,"[74] while others seem out of place. Typically, Warner explains, the poetic function of public speech is obscured by the constitutive presumption of a public's existence—that is, that public address presumes the audience it creates—and by "the dominant tradition of the public sphere."[75]

In the dominant tradition, it is reason—and not force or power—that determines the outcome of public debate over common concerns.[76] One's words are imagined as *freest* and, related, as *expressive* of an ideal democratic subject—discrete, independent, sovereign—to the extent that they participate in a reason imagined as universal. Inequalities between speakers are imagined as bracketable and bracketed. Concretely, speakers perform this bracketing through speech that abstracts from their embodied particularity and anticipates (and so also, cultivates) an audience that does the same, affecting a meeting of minds or of Mind. Finally, one's obligation to strangers addressed is limited to sincere intentions to communicate and to listen to reason.

To understand this mode of address as dominant, one need look no further than the debate around trigger warnings themselves. In their effort to avoid "politicizing" the use of trigger warnings by articulating them as also "for" a broader public, proponents buy into, or work within a paradigm wherein reason is opposed to (and undone) by power. Meanwhile, critics routinely avow a relationship between speakers and speech that conforms to the dominant tradition in imagining writers' and readers' thoughts and experiences as wholly their own unless and until incited or impinged upon by trigger warnings.

A *counter*-public challenges dominant expectations of writers and readers and thereby the subjects and world that is brought into being through address. Because of this, Warner argues that counter-public speech "will circulate up to a point," but will eventually "meet intense resistance," especially beyond "special, protected venues."[77] The changing nature of interest and criticism that trigger warnings drew as they moved from *private* sites of communication to the *marginal publics* of feminist and social justice blogging, and then to a *broader public* via discussion of their (mostly imagined) normalization in college classrooms, supports my framing of trigger warnings as a counter-public practice. In the section that follows I elaborate how I understand trigger warnings to challenge a dominant public's cultivation of writers and readers.

Cultivating Embodied, Interdependent, Non-Sovereign Democratic Subjects

Considering trigger warnings as a counter-public practice requires that one examine the ways in which they cultivate writers' orientations to strangers and anticipate—and so also cultivate—readers. I argue that the use of trigger warnings can function to "publicize" structural violence; that is, to make it both known and to make it a broader public's responsibility. In this sense trigger warnings cultivate a writer and her audience that avows what Judith Butler has termed the "social ontology" of the body. Butler states: "To be a body is to be exposed to social crafting and form. . . . In other words, the body is exposed to socially and politically articulated forces as well as to claims of sociality—including language, work, and desire—that make possible the body's persisting and flourishing."[78] Trigger warnings can be understood as a practice of public speech that models and cultivates ways of moving in the world premised on the precariousness of the self and its ineluctable dependence on others that dominant modes of public speech disavow.

Trigger warnings cultivate writers whose obligations to strangers extend beyond good intentions to encompass an awareness of structural violence and its local manifestations. Using a trigger warning requires writers to pause and reflect on the possible effects of their words given the persistence of inequality of differentially situated and embodied readers. Indeed, the fact that one can anticipate certain things as potentially triggering—such as a graphic account of sexual assault—*turns on* an understanding of the connection between the content depicted or discussed and structural violence and inequality that manifests as individualized harm and trauma. As a writerly practice, trigger warnings could be thought of as enacting some small portion of responsibility and inviting—or compelling—readers to do the same.

Trigger warnings anticipate an audience inclusive of individuals with triggers. Rhetoric and disability studies scholar Melanie Yergeau argues that trigger warnings "anticipate a *disabled* response, at a guttural and embodied/enminded level" and, in doing so, "actively *decenter* normative audience expectations."[79] Observing the same, Halberstam suggests that trigger warnings "project[t] . . . the student as a fragile organism with no intellectual immune system" and "giv[e] rise to an understanding of self . . . vulnerable to paternalistic modes of protection."[80] I think Halberstam is correct to suggest that trigger warnings anticipate and so also cultivate readers who are vulnerable, but it does not follow that the trigger warning's audience lacks the means of coping with any challenging content or is ripe for paternalism.

As noted earlier, Halberstam describes what trigger warnings do by reference to TV and movie ratings, leading him to conclude that trigger warnings presume readers who are unable to make their own decisions. Pressing on distinctions between parental guidelines and trigger warnings presents an alternative interpretation: In anticipating a disabled response from a "general" audience, trigger warnings trouble a vision of "normal" democratic subjects as the developmental outcome of protective parents empowered by the state and entertainment industries. In so doing, they might illuminate the all-too-normal reality of systemic inequality, much of which manifests in individuated instances of sexual assault, racialized violence, ableist exclusion, and so on.

Halberstam also discounts the productive possibility of readers imagining other readers as vulnerable. Students requesting the use of a trigger warning for someone other than themselves thus becomes a practice of surveillance and paternalism even as the means by which this request co-opts the decision making of the imagined reader is neither obvious nor specified. There is an alternative: The student's request could be understood as "publicizing" structural violence and taking some small portion of responsibility for changing the ways in which such violence is perpetuated through silence and the disarticulation of harm it causes from power and privilege. Indeed, this is how "Jules," commenting in response to a blog post on the topic of trigger warnings, describes his or her own relationship to trigger warnings as a reader who does not have triggers:

> Seeing the trigger warning often reminds me that the freedom I have to not be triggered by graphic material is a privilege. It reinforces the pervasive nature of trauma and raises my level of empathy/consideration for those who have survived sexual assaults/domestic violence, etc. It takes me only a second to read the words "trigger warning" but the lessons about the nature of PTSD are more lasting, and it reminds me that there are people out there reading the same thing I am reading for whom THIS IS PERSONAL.[81]

As with Melissa McEwan's earlier account, Jules's comment suggests that the work that trigger warnings do includes publicizing harm that reflects structural violence and inequality. Through the act of reading, "Jules" is drawn into alliance with those "who have survived sexual assaults/domestic violence" and other forms of violence.

To be blunt, I experience Jules's prose—framing "not be[ing] triggered" as a "privilege" and trauma as "pervasive," as well as the use of all capital letters to assert that something they have not experienced "IS PERSONAL"—as rather irksome. Critical responses to trigger warnings suggest many share this response. Mainstream feminist blogger, Jill Filipovic, might characterize Jules's comment as "performative feminism," or a "low-stakes way to use the right language to identify yourself as conscious of social justice issues."[82] Others might characterize it as approval-seeking behavior or "cookie-seeking."

The more interesting question for me is this: (How) do such comments structure relationships between strangers and what role does affect play in drawing us toward, or repelling us from Jules? It seems that part of what makes the comment grating is precisely Jules's taking some small portion of ownership of harm of which he or she has no personal experience. This does not mean that status acquired through use of "the right language" is irrelevant, but it does invite some reflection on when we raise such questions. Put otherwise: We might wonder why Filipovic's feminist criticism is not also "performative feminism" or evaluate what relationship between strangers Filipovic's speech presumes and enacts. In the following section I reflect on the feelings of discomfort that frequently accompany encounters with trigger warnings and what they might tell us about the efficacy and effects of counter-public speech.

Public Feelings and Vulnerable Address

Halberstam posits vulnerability as an undesirable or dangerous understanding of the self and a "resilient" self as a desirable alternative.[83] He is hardly alone in doing so. However, I want to suggest that the appeal of resilience—of aspiring to invulnerability—may reflect a desire to be or be seen as a normative democratic subject; that is, discrete, independent, sovereign. Roxane Gay's thoughtful discussion of trigger warnings allows me to elaborate. Gay writes:

> I used to think I didn't have triggers because I told myself I was tough. I was steel. I was broken beneath the surface, but my skin was forged, impenetrable. Then I realized I had all kinds of triggers. . . . There are things that rip my skin open and reveal what lies beneath, but I don't believe in trigger warnings.[84]

More precisely, Gay does not believe in the reality of safety that she takes trigger warnings to promise. As a survivor of sexual assault with her own deeply personal triggers, Gay knows any such promise cannot be perfectly realized. Gay concludes by meditating on the connection between her not "feel[ing] safe" or "believing in safety" and her "fascinat[ion]" with "enduring": "Human endurance fascinates me, probably too much because more often than not, I think of life in terms of enduring instead of living."[85]

This complex compulsion to "endure" rather than "live," to be "impenetrable," functions defensively. But while aspiring to invulnerability facilitates Gay's ability to "endur[e]," it simultaneously circumscribes that existence, narrowing its frame, and precludes "liv[ing]." My point in noting this is not to criticize Gay for not "believ[ing] in safety or trigger warnings," but to show how her aversion is attached to a desire to be unaffected by the violence that had been enacted upon her, at least in the eyes of others ("the surface").

I want to suggest that Gay's desire is normal, both in the sense of being understandable and in the sense that it functions normatively to shape appropriate ways of being and speaking in public. Gay's aspiring to a "normal" relationship to harm, trauma, and the body may well come with the benefit of inclusion.[86] And one can imagine that it might also prevent a painful dismissal of one's pain as an overreaction or, in Gay's case as evidence "typifying" black women.[87]

However, recent work on affect suggests that we ought to examine the broader effects of these "normal" desires. Sara Ahmed's *The Promise of Happiness* directs us to consider the value and function of Gay's "endurance" not only at the individual level, but at the societal level, where it may participate in the delineation of "happy" survivors and political subjects from those whose "unhappiness" might offer a more thoroughgoing challenge to the status quo.[88] In *Cruel Optimism*, Lauren Berlant argues that when "survival" supplants visions of living well, it often affords some minimal, individualized protection even as it perpetuates structural inequality.[89] Attachment to survival can be "cruel" precisely because, as an ideal, "survival" participates in producing conditions that assure there will always be more to survive, more survivors. Black, queer, feminist blogger Robin Boylorn makes a similar point, suggesting that to value and admire "withstand[ing] . . . suffering" not only fails to challenge the structural conditions that multiply opportunities to "withstand suffering" but also reflects a broader societal resistance to, in particular, black Americans "feeling pain and expressing it" that ought to be interrogated.[90]

Vulnerability is both a human inevitability and something that is disproportionately born by marginal populations.[91] Trigger warnings constitute one practice of public speech that acknowledges both these things. In so doing they posit non-, or rather counter-, normative responses to vulnerability and avow a social ontology of the body.

Conclusion

Conceptualizing trigger warnings as a counter-public practice clarifies when and why trigger warnings became a matter for broad public discussion: At the moment, trigger warnings could be imagined as an expected, normal practice of speech. It also illuminates characteristics of that debate, notably, a generalized disparity in institutional rank and publication prestige between critics and advocates, with critics writing from positions of (more) authority and published on the front page of national newspapers and magazines.

But considering trigger warnings as a counter-public practice does more than set the record straight; it might also change the conversation by clarifying goals and illuminating possible alliances. Viewed as a counter-public practice, trigger warnings challenge the discrete, sovereign, independent subject of modern democratic thought. In its place, feminist bloggers' and others' use of trigger warnings cultivates a non-sovereign, interdependent democratic subject. This does not mean that "access" of those with triggers is irrelevant, but it does suggest the need to reframe this goal. Concretely, one might say that access is an *effect* of the collaboration of writers and readers, mediated by particular platforms and their affordances, rather than an outcome achieved by an individual armed with a tool.

One might nonetheless ask: Do we want trigger warnings in the classroom? The answer, I think, depends upon the means by which trigger warnings might appear in the classroom, as well as who the "we" addressed in the question includes. A counter-public practice presents a norm that challenges dominant ways of understanding ourselves in relation to strangers. I do not think that such a practice could meaningfully survive the transformation into a form of bureaucratic box ticking.[92]

Those drawn to a vision and practice of the speaking subject as a discrete, independent, sovereign being whose words and thoughts are freest when (imagined as) unhindered by embodied, vulnerable addressees' will surely continue to bristle at trigger warnings. Those—feminists, queers, new materialists, post-humanists—who are interested in imagining the subject as constitutively outside itself might find in trigger warnings a resource for the cultivation of subjects who act as if this were the case. At the very least, studying responses to trigger warnings may clarify the ways in which viscerally felt attachments to "normal" ways of seeing and moving in the world might challenge or even undercut our principled, perhaps richly theoretical, commitment to liberatory politics.

Notes

1. It is important to note a distinction between "equal access" and "universal design," which aspires to universal access. This third function of the trigger warning tool places it in the former camp as it marks those for whom it is intended as abnormal, requiring accommodations that an imagined "most people" do not

require. However, from another perspective, the access and comfort of "most people" are accommodated routinely. For example, ambulatory people typically expect chairs as a form of accommodation accompanying a lecture, whereas an individual in a wheelchair would require no such accommodation. Promulgating the perspective that accommodation is normal, universal design aims to make "all products, buildings and exterior spaces . . . usable by all people to the greatest extent possible." See: Ronald L. Mace, Graeme J. Hardie, and Jaine P. Place, "Accessible Environments: Toward Universal Design," in *Design Intervention: Toward a More Humane Architecture*, edited by W. E. Preiser, J. C. Vischer, and E. T. White, 2 (New York: Van Nostrand Reinhold, 1991).

2. My understanding of hegemony is drawn from Ernesto Laclau and Chantal Mouffe's germinal work, *Hegemony and Socialist Strategy: Towards a Radical Democratic Politics*. Laclau and Mouffe argue that there is no uncontestable, foundational, or "given" content to social-political identities, movements, and claims. The content and justification for social-political categories are contingent, acquiring meaning through their articulation in relation to other categories and from within a discursive structure. A particular articulation is hegemonic to the extent it "dominate[s] the field of discursivity" and "arrest[s] the flow of differences," so that it functions like common sense and precludes alternatives. In this case, worldly uses of trigger warnings function as "disruptive" elements that cannot be fully—or at least easily—incorporated into liberalism's concept and commitment to individualism or to neoliberalism's hyper-individualism. See: Ernesto Laclau and Chantal Mouffe, *Hegemony and Socialist Strategy: Towards a Radical Democratic Politics* (New York: Verso, 2001), 112.

3. "Skada" commenting on Amanda Hess, "Trigger Warnings and Being an Asshole," *The Sexist: A Washington City Paper Blog*, April 16, 2010, accessed September 17, 2016, http://www.washingtoncitypaper.com/blogs/sexist/2010/04/16/trigger-warnings-and-being-an-asshole/. Communications and women's studies scholar Raechel Tiffe has indicated that trigger warnings were simultaneously being used in feminist zines. In the 2000s one can find trigger warnings used on feminist zines with a digital presence like *Hoax* (see: http://hoaxzine.tumblr.com/).

4. E-mail correspondence, 2016.

5. Janis L. Whitlock, Jane L. Powers, and John Eckenrode, "The Virtual Cutting Edge: The Internet and Adolescent Self-Injury," *Developmental Psychology* 42, no. 3 (2006): 1–11; Craig D. Murray and Jezz Fox, "Do Internet Self-Harm Discussion Groups Alleviate or Exacerbate Self-Harming Behaviour?" *Australian e-Journal for the Advancement of Mental Health* 5, no. 3 (2006): 1–9; Janis Whitlock, Wendy Lader, and Karen Conterio, "The Internet and Self-Injury: What Psychotherapists Should Know," *Journal of Clinical Psychology: In Session* 63, no. 11 (2007): 1135–43.

6. Murray and Fox, "Do Internet Self-Harm Discussion Groups," 6.

7. Whitlock et al., "The Virtual Cutting Edge," 9–10; Murray and Fox, "Do Internet Self-Harm Discussion Groups," 8.

8. Murray and Fox, "Do Internet Self-Harm Discussion Groups, 6.

9. Proximity, "Putting Warnings on Your Posts," *Bodies under Siege*, April 30, 2006 (edited May 2, 2006), accessed September 13, 2016, http://buslist.org/phpBB/viewtopic.php?p=2047540#p2047540. As a private forum, the overwhelming majority of *BUS*'s posts are not appropriate for publication. The cited post is one of few public *BUS* posts that do not require a password to view and represents an update to *BUS*'s posting guidelines published in 2002.

10. Melissa McEwan, "I Write Letters," *Shakesville*, April 13, 2010, accessed September 17, 2016, http://www.shakesville.com/2010/04/i-write-letters_13.html. See also: Jill Filipovic, "You Know You're Kind of a Jerk When You Write a Blog Post Basically Mocking Rape Survivors," *Feministe*, April 13, 2010, accessed September 12, 2016, http://www.feministe.us/blog/archives/2010/04/13/you-know-youre-kind-of-a-jerk-when-you-write-a-blog-post-basically-mocking-rape-survivors/; Jill Filipovic, "Trigger Warning: Insufferable Dingbat Ahoy," *Feministe*, April 14, 2010, accessed September 12, 2016, http://www.feministe.us/blog/archives/2010/04/14/trigger-warning-insufferable-dingbat-ahoy/.

11. McEwan, "I Write Letters." See also: "abby" commenting on Hess, "Trigger Warnings and Being an Asshole"; Filipovic, "You Know You're Kind of a Jerk"; Filipovic, "Trigger Warning: Insufferable Dingbat Ahoy."

12. McEwan, "I Write Letters." Others were even more direct in asserting the ease of using a trigger warning. See: Filipovic, "You Know You're Kind of a Jerk."

13. McEwan, "I Write Letters."

14. The reader posting as "abby," who acknowledges having "severe PTSD," writes that "blogs that put trigger warnings on certain posts tend to be ones that expect and welcome readers with histories of trauma, and that think of them as people who matter, not just points to be made in arguments." See: "abby" commenting on Hess, "Trigger Warnings and Being an Asshole."

15. Many sites continued to use the language of trigger warnings even while tagging a broader range of content.

16. Ali Vingiano, "How the 'Trigger Warning' Took over the Internet," *BuzzFeedNews*, May 5, 2014, accessed September 30, 2016, https://www.buzzfeed.com/alisonvingiano/how-the-trigger-warning-took-over-the-internet?utm_term=.ph5AGvMEW#.pn0ZJbnLX.

17. Ibid. It is worth noting that *LiveJournal* was and remains a venue for social justice discussion and work. Thanks to Sarah Gram for her insights on this point.

18. Susannah Breslin, "Trigger Warning: This Blog Post May Freak You the F*** Out," *True/Slant*, April 13, 2010, accessed October 1, 2016, http://trueslant

.com/susannahbreslin/2010/04/13/trigger-warning-this-blog-post-may-freak-you-the-f-out/.

19. Ibid.

20. Ibid.

21. Susannah Breslin, "Trigger Warnings Don't Work. Here's Why," *True/Slant*, April 14, 2010, accessed October 1, 2016, http://trueslant.com/susannah-breslin/2010/04/14/trigger-warnings-dont-work-heres-why/. Interestingly, this concern was shared—and, to a very limited extent, observed—by psychologists studying online communities for those struggling with the desire to engage in self-harm. See: Murray and Fox, "Do Internet Self-Harm Discussion Groups."

22. Choire Sicha, "When 'Trigger Warning' Lost All Its Meaning," *The Awl*, May 30, 2012, accessed October 3, 2016, https://theawl.com/when-trigger-warning-lost-all-its-meaning-31acf9a2012d#.e4fobl6er.

23. Roxane Gay, "The Illusion of Safety/The Safety of Illusion," *The Rumpus*, August 28, 2012, accessed October 3, 2016, http://therumpus.net/2012/08/the-illusion-of-safetythe-safety-of-illusion/.

24. Melissa C. Gregg, "Posting with Passion: Blogs and the Politics of Gender," in *Uses of Blogs*, edited by Axel Bruns and Joanne Jacobs, 151–60 (New York: Peter Lang, 2006).

25. Ruxandra Looft, "How Do Trigger Warnings Fit into the Classroom Lesson Plan?" *Shakesville*, February 12, 2013, accessed October 1, 2016, http://www.shakesville.com/2013/02/how-do-trigger-warnings-fit-into.html; Raechel Tiffe, "Pedagogy of a Trigger," *Rebel Grrrl Academy*, September 4, 2012, accessed October 1, 2016, https://rebelgrrlacademy.wordpress.com/2012/09/04/pedagogy-of-a-trigger/.

26. Amanda Marcotte, "The Year of the Trigger Warning," *Slate*, December 30, 2013, accessed September 27, 2016, http://www.slate.com/blogs/xx_factor/2013/12/30/trigger_warnings_from_the_feminist_blogosphere_to_shonda_rhimes_in_2013.html.

27. Ibid.

28. Jill Filipovic, "We've Gone Too Far with 'Trigger Warnings,'" *The Guardian*, March 5, 2014, accessed September 26, 2016, https://www.theguardian.com/commentisfree/2014/mar/05/trigger-warnings-can-be-counterproductive/.

29. Sara Ahmed, *On Being Included: Racism and Diversity in Institutional Life* (Durham, NC: Duke University Press, 2012), 57–60.

30. Queer theorist Jack Halberstam notes the coincidence of "the call for trigger warnings on college campuses . . . with new sets of regulations around sexual interactions, sexual assault, and teacher-student relationships," but does not discuss the relevance of ADA or diversity. See: Jack Halberstam, "Trigger Happy: From Content Warning to Censorship," *Signs* 42, no. 2 (Winter 2017):

advanced online publication, accessed October 1, 2016, http://signsjournal.org/currents-trigger-warnings/halberstam/.

31. Jenny Jarvie, "Trigger Happy," *New Republic*, March 2, 2014, accessed October 1, 2016, https://newrepublic.com/article/116842/trigger-warnings-have-spread-blogs-college-classes-thats-bad.

32. Ibid.

33. Office of Equity Concerns, "Sexual Offense Resource Guide: Support Resources for Faculty," Oberlin College, 2013, accessed October 2, 2016, http://web.archive.org/web/20131122144749/http://new.oberlin.edu/office/equity-concerns/sexual-offense-resource-guide/prevention-support-education/support-resources-for-faculty.dot.

34. Nikki Calderon and Derek Wakefield, Student Sponsor: Bailey Loverin, "A Resolution to Mandate Warnings for Triggering Content in Academic Settings (02262014:61)," Associated Student Senate, University of California, Santa Barbara, 2014, https://www.as.ucsb.edu/senate/resolutions/a-resolution-to-mandate-warnings-for-triggering-content-in-academic-settings/. The language of "mandate" is quite misleading as the approved resolution would require faculty approval.

35. Office of Equity Concerns, "Sexual Offense Resource Guide: Support Resources for Faculty." It has been mistakenly suggested that the task force did not include or solicit faculty input (see: Jennifer Medina, "Warning: The Literary Canon Could Make Students Squirm," *New York Times*, May 17, 2014, accessed September 26, 2016, http://www.nytimes.com/2014/05/18/us/warning-the-literary-canon-could-make-students-squirm.html). In addition to faculty members on the task force, the authors solicited feedback at two public forums. Nonetheless, many Oberlin faculty learned of the guide only after it had become a topic of national discussion. See: Madeline Peltz, "College's Trigger Warning Proposal Incites Media Backlash," *Oberlin Review*, April 13, 2014, accessed November 17, 2016, http://oberlinreview.org/5485/news/colleges-trigger-warning-proposal-incites-media-backlash/; Adiel Kaplan, "Sexual Offense Policy Task Force Report Due by End of Semester," *Oberlin Review*, March 1, 2013, accessed November 17, 2016, http://oberlinreview.org/2036/news/sexual-offense-policy-task-force-report-due-by-end-of-semester/.

36. Office of Equity Concerns, "Sexual Offense Resource Guide: Support Resources for Faculty."

37. Ibid.

38. Ibid.

39. Ibid.

40. Calderon and Wakefield, "A Resolution to Mandate Warnings for Triggering Content in Academic Settings (02262014:61)."

41. Ibid. See also: Bailey Loverin, "Trigger Warnings Avert Trauma: Opposing View," *USA Today*, April 21, 2014, accessed September 26, 2016, http://www.usatoday.com/story/opinion/2014/04/21/trigger-warnings-ptsd-bailey-loverin-editorials-debates/7985479/; Bailey Loverin, "Trigger Warnings Encourage Free Thought and Debate," *New York Times*, May 19, 2014, accessed September 26, 2016, http://www.nytimes.com/roomfordebate/2014/05/19/restraint-of-expression-on-college-campuses/trigger-warnings-encourage-free-thought-and-debate.

42. Calderon and Wakefield, "A Resolution to Mandate Warnings for Triggering Content in Academic Settings (02262014:61)."

43. Office of Equity Concerns, "Sexual Offense Resource Guide: Support Resources for Faculty."

44. Ibid.

45. Jarvie, "Trigger Happy."

46. Committee on Academic Freedom and Tenure, "On Trigger Warnings," American Association of University Professors, August 2014, accessed October 3, 2016, http://www.aaup.org/report/trigger-warnings; Laurie Essig, "Trigger Warnings Trigger Me," *Chronicle of Higher Education*, March 10, 2014, accessed October 2, 2016, http://www.chronicle.com/blogs/conversation/2014/03/10/trigger-warnings-trigger-me/.

47. Jonathan Chait, "Not a Very P.C. Thing to Say," *New York*, January 27, 2015, accessed October 3, 2016, http://nymag.com/daily/intelligencer/2015/01/not-a-very-pc-thing-to-say.html; Greg Lukianoff and Jonathan Haidt, "The Coddling of the American Mind," *The Atlantic*, September 2015, accessed September 26, 2016, http://www.theatlantic.com/magazine/archive/2015/09/the-coddling-of-the-american-mind/399356/; Richard J. McNally, "Hazards Ahead: The Problem with Trigger Warnings, according to the Research," *Pacific Standard*, May 20, 2014, accessed September 26, 2016, http://www.psmag.com/health-and-behavior/hazards-ahead-problem-trigger-warnings-according-research-81946; Susan P. Robbins, "From the Editor—Sticks and Stones: Trigger Warnings, Microaggressions, and Political Correctness," *Journal of Social Work Education* 52, no. 1 (2016): 1–5.

48. 7 Humanities Professors, "Trigger Warnings Are Flawed," *Inside Higher Ed*, May 29, 2014, accessed October 1, 2016, https://www.insidehighered.com/views/2014/05/29/essay-faculty-members-about-why-they-will-not-use-trigger-warnings; Filipovic, "We've Gone Too Far with 'Trigger Warnings'"; Jessica Valenti, "Feminists Talk Trigger Warnings: A Round-Up," *Nation*, March 6, 2014, accessed October 3, 2016, https://www.thenation.com/article/feminists-talk-trigger-warnings-round/.

49. Jarvie, "Trigger Happy."

50. 7 Humanities Professors, "Trigger Warnings Are Flawed"; Jay Caspian Kang, "Trigger Warnings and the Novelist's Mind," *The New Yorker*, May 21, 2014, accessed September 17, 2016, http://www.newyorker.com/books/page-turner/trigger-warnings-and-the-novelists-mind; Medina, "Warning: The Literary Canon Could Make Students Squirm."

51. Committee on Academic Freedom and Tenure, "On Trigger Warnings."

52. Essig, "Trigger Warnings Trigger Me."

53. Kang, "Trigger Warnings and the Novelist's Mind."

54. Filipovic, "We've Gone Too Far with 'Trigger Warnings.'"

55. 7 Humanities Professors, "Trigger Warnings Are Flawed;" Lisa Duggan, "On Trauma and Trigger Warnings, in Three Parts," *Bully Bloggers*, November 23, 2014, accessed September 18, 2016, https://bullybloggers.wordpress.com/2014/11/23/on-trauma-and-trigger-warnings-in-three-parts/; Filipovic, "We've Gone Too Far with 'Trigger Warnings'"; Tressie McMillan Cottom, "The Trigger Warned Syllabus," *TressieMC*, March 5, 2014, accessed October 3, 2016, https://tressiemc.com/2014/03/05/the-trigger-warned-syllabus/.

56. Angela Carter, "Teaching with Trauma: Trigger Warnings, Feminism, and Disability Pedagogy," *Disability Studies Quarterly* 35, no. 2 (2015), http://dsq-sds.org/article/view/4652/3935; Bailey Loverin, Interview with Patt Morrison, "UC Students Vote to Mandate Warnings for 'Triggering' Content in Classrooms," AirTalk (KPCC), March 12, 2014, accessed September 26, 2016, http://www.scpr.org/programs/airtalk/2014/03/12/36431/uc-students-vote-to-mandate-warnings-for-triggerin/; Loverin, "Trigger Warnings Avert Trauma: Opposing View"; Loverin, "Trigger Warnings Encourage Free Thought and Debate"; Kate Manne, "Why I Use Trigger Warnings," *New York Times*, September 19, 2015, accessed October 2, 2016, http://www.nytimes.com/2015/09/20/opinion/sunday/why-i-use-trigger-warnings.html?_r=0/; Melissa McEwan, "Triggered," *Shakesville*, March 4, 2014, accessed September 11, 2016, http://www.shakesville.com/2014/03/triggered.html.

57. Carter, "Teaching with Trauma"; Melanie Yergeau, "Disable All the Things: On Affect, Metadata, and Audience," Keynote Address, Computers and Writing Conference, Washington State University, Pullman, WA, June 6, 2014.

58. Carter, "Teaching with Trauma"; Manne, "Why I Use Trigger Warnings"; Sarah Orem and Neil Simpkins, "Weepy Rhetoric, Trigger Warnings, and the Work of Making Mental Illness Visible in the Writing Classroom," *Enculturation: A Journal of Rhetoric, Writing and Culture* (December 16, 2015), accessed September 21, 2016, http://enculturation.net/weepy-rhetoric; Yergeau, "Disable All the Things."

59. Carter, "Teaching with Trauma"; Manne, "Why I Use Trigger Warnings"; Loverin, "Trigger Warnings Avert Trauma: Opposing View"; Yergeau, "Disable All the Things."

60. McEwan, "Triggered." See also: Manne, "Why I Use Trigger Warnings."

61. McEwan, "Triggered"; Loverin, "Trigger Warnings Encourage Free Thought and Debate"; Kai Johnson, Tanika Lynch, Elizabeth Monroe, and Tracey Wang, "Our Identities Matter in Core Classrooms," *Columbia Spectator*, April 30, 2015, accessed September 26, 2016, http://columbiaspectator.com/opinion/2015/04/30/our-identities-matter-core-classrooms.

62. Orem and Simpkins, "Weepy Rhetoric."

63. A tool not unlike this was created for Tumblr and advocated in place of trigger warnings. It does not appear to have stemmed the use of trigger warnings on Tumblr, which suggests that such a tool might well miss a great deal of the work trigger warnings do. See: Choire Sicha, "When 'Trigger Warning' Lost All Its Meaning."

64. Office of Equity Concerns, "Sexual Offense Resource Guide: Support Resources for Faculty."

65. Halberstam, "Trigger Happy."

66. See, for example: McEwan, "Triggered," and Loverin, "Trigger Warnings Avert Trauma." Some of the confusion here likely reflects a change in the way audiences think about and use movie and TV ratings. For example, in 2013, Shonda Rhimes tweeted agreement with fans indicating a trigger warning would have been appropriate before an episode of *Scandal* including a rape scene. In point of fact, Rhimes and her fans were speaking of the use (or creative misuse) of the TV Parental Guidelines advising "viewer discretion." See: Marcotte, "The Year of the Trigger Warning."

67. Wendy Brown, *Edgework: Critical Essays on Knowledge and Power* (Princeton, NJ: Princeton University Press, 2005), 40. Author's emphasis.

68. Ibid., 42.

69. Ibid., 43.

70. Benedict Anderson, *Imagined Communities: Reflections on the Origin and Spread of Nationalism* (New York: Verso, 1991). In this classic, Anderson argues that print publication and the development of national vernacular was essential to constructing the sense that one belonged to a nation.

71. Michael Warner, *Publics and Counterpublics* (New York: Zone Books, 2002), 107–16; Iris Marion Young, *Justice and the Politics of Difference* (Princeton, NJ: Princeton University Press, 2011), 109.

72. Warner, *Publics and Counterpublics*, 120.

73. Ibid., 114.

74. Warner writes that a public that stands in as "the public" is a dominant public. Ibid., 107.

75. Ibid., 114–15.

76. Ibid., 47–51, 115.

77. Ibid., 120.

78. Judith Butler, *Frames of War: When Is Life Grievable?* (New York: Verso, 2010), 3.

79. Yergeau, "Disable All the Things." Author's emphasis.

80. Halberstam, "Trigger Happy."

81. "Jules" commenting on Hess, "Trigger Warnings and Being an Asshole."

82. Filipovic, "We've Gone Too Far with 'Trigger Warnings.'"

83. Jack Halberstam, "You Are Triggering Me! The Neo-Liberal Rhetoric of Harm, Danger and Trauma," *Bully Bloggers*, July 5, 2014, accessed September 26, 2016, https://bullybloggers.wordpress.com/2014/07/05/you-are-triggering-me -the-neo-liberal-rhetoric-of-harm-danger-and-trauma/.

84. Gay, "The Illusion of Safety/The Safety of Illusion."

85. Ibid.

86. Young, *Justice and the Politics of Difference*, 134.

87. Ibid.

88. Sara Ahmed, *The Promise of Happiness* (Durham, NC: Duke University Press, 2010), 195–98.

89. Lauren Berlant, *Cruel Optimism* (Durham, NC: Duke University Press, 2011).

90. Robin Boylorn, "Unbreakable or the Problem with Praising Blackgirl Strength," *The Crunk Feminist Collective*, July 22, 2014, accessed September 27, 2016, http://www.crunkfeministcollective.com/2014/07/22/unbreakable-or-the -problem-with-praising-blackgirl-strength/.

91. Butler, *Frames of War*.

92. My response is informed by Ahmed's *On Being Included*.

Bibliography

Ahmed, Sara. "Against Students." *The New Inquiry*, June 29, 2015. Accessed October 2, 2016. http://thenewinquiry.com/essays/against-students/.

———. *On Being Included: Racism and Diversity in Institutional Life*. Durham, NC: Duke University Press, 2012.

———. *The Promise of Happiness*. Durham, NC: Duke University Press, 2010.

Anderson, Benedict. *Imagined Communities: Reflections on the Origin and Spread of Nationalism*. Revised Edition. New York: Verso, 1991 [1983].

Berlant, Lauren. *Cruel Optimism*. Durham, NC: Duke University Press, 2011.

Boylorn, Robin. "Unbreakable or the Problem with Praising Blackgirl Strength." *The Crunk Feminist Collective*, July 22, 2014. Accessed September 27, 2016. http://www.crunkfeministcollective.com/2014/07/22/unbreakable-or-the-problem-with-praising-blackgirl-strength/.

Breslin, Susannah. "Trigger Warning: This Blog Post May Freak You the F*** Out." *True/Slant*, April 13, 2010. Accessed October 1, 2016. http://trueslant.com/susannahbreslin/2010/04/13/trigger-warning-this-blog-post-may-freak-you-the-f-out/.

———. "Trigger Warnings Don't Work. Here's Why." *True/Slant*, April 14, 2010. Accessed October 1, 2016. http://trueslant.com/susannahbreslin/2010/04/14/trigger-warnings-dont-work-heres-why/.

Brodsky, Alexandra. "Pathological, Noticeable: Another Note on Trigger Warnings." *Feministing*, May 22, 2015. Accessed September 9, 2016. http://feministing.com/2015/05/22/pathological-noticeable-another-note-on-trigger-warnings/.

Brown, Wendy. *Edgework: Critical Essays on Knowledge and Power*. Princeton, NJ: Princeton University Press, 2005.

Butler, Judith. *Frames of War: When Is Life Grievable?* New York: Verso, 2010.

Calderon, Nikki, Derek Wakefield, and Bailey Loverin (Student Sponsor). "A Resolution to Mandate Warnings for Triggering Content in Academic Settings (02262014:61)." Associated Student Senate, University of California, Santa Barbara. 2014. Accessed October 1, 2016. https://www.as.ucsb.edu/senate/resolutions/a-resolution-to-mandate-warnings-for-triggering-content-in-academic-settings/.

Carter, Angela. "Teaching with Trauma: Trigger Warnings, Feminism, and Disability Pedagogy." *Disability Studies Quarterly* 35, no. 2 (2015). http://dsq-sds.org/article/view/4652/3935.

Chait, Jonathan. "Not a Very P.C. Thing to Say." *New York*, January 27, 2015. Accessed October 3, 2016. http://nymag.com/daily/intelligencer/2015/01/not-a-very-pc-thing-to-say.html.

Committee on Academic Freedom and Tenure. "On Trigger Warnings." American Association of University Professors, August 2014. Accessed October 3, 2016. http://www.aaup.org/report/trigger-warnings.

Cottom, Tressie McMillan. "The Trigger Warned Syllabus." *TressieMC*, March 5, 2014. Accessed October 3, 2016. https://tressiemc.com/2014/03/05/the-trigger-warned-syllabus/.

DiAngelo, Robin. "White Fragility." *International Journal of Critical Pedagogy* 3, no. 3 (2011): 54–70.

Duggan, Lisa. "On Trauma and Trigger Warnings, in Three Parts." *Bully Bloggers*, November 23, 2014. Accessed September 18, 2016. https://bully

bloggers.wordpress.com/2014/11/23/on-trauma-and-trigger-warnings-in
-three-parts/.

Eosphoros, Cyrus. "Content Warnings Needed as Accommodations." *Oberlin
Review*, February 27, 2015. Accessed November 22, 2016. http://oberlin
review.org/7562/opinions/content-warnings-needed-as-accommodations/.

Essig, Laurie. "Trigger Warnings Trigger Me." *Chronicle of Higher Education*,
March 10, 2014. Accessed October 2, 2016. http://www.chronicle.com/
blogs/conversation/2014/03/10/trigger-warnings-trigger-me/.

Filipovic, Jill. "Trigger Warning: Insufferable Dingbat Ahoy." *Feministe*, April
14, 2010. Accessed September 12, 2016. http://www.feministe.us/blog/
archives/2010/04/14/trigger-warning-insufferable-dingbat-ahoy/.

———. "We've Gone Too Far with 'Trigger Warnings.'" *The Guardian*, March
5, 2014. Accessed September 26, 2016. https://www.theguardian.com/com
mentisfree/2014/mar/05/trigger-warnings-can-be-counterproductive/.

———. "You Know You're Kind of a Jerk When You Write a Blog Post Basically Mocking Rape Survivors." *Feministe*, April 13, 2010. Accessed
September 12, 2016. http://www.feministe.us/blog/archives/2010/04/13/
you-know-youre-kind-of-a-jerk-when-you-write-a-blog-post-basically
-mocking-rape-survivors/.

Gay, Roxane. "The Illusion of Safety/The Safety of Illusion." *The Rumpus*, August 28, 2012. Accessed October 3, 2016. http://therumpus.net/2012/08/
the-illusion-of-safetythe-safety-of-illusion/.

Gregg, Melissa C. "Posting with Passion: Blogs and the Politics of Gender." In
Uses of Blogs, edited by Axel Bruns and Joanne Jacobs, 151–60. New York:
Peter Lang, 2006.

Halberstam, Jack. "Trigger Happy: From Content Warning to Censorship."
Signs 42, no. 2 (Winter 2017). Advanced online publication. Accessed
October 1, 2016. http://signsjournal.org/currents-trigger-warnings/halber
stam/.

———. "You Are Triggering Me! The Neo-Liberal Rhetoric of Harm, Danger and Trauma." *Bully Bloggers*, July 5, 2014. Accessed September 26,
2016. https://bullybloggers.wordpress.com/2014/07/05/you-are-triggering
-me-the-neo-liberal-rhetoric-of-harm-danger-and-trauma/.

Herzog, Don. *Poisoning the Minds of the Lower Orders*. Princeton, NJ: Princeton
University Press, 1998.

Hess, Amanda. "Trigger Warnings and Being an Asshole." *The Sexist: A Washington City Paper Blog*, April 16, 2010. Accessed September 17, 2016. http://
www.washingtoncitypaper.com/blogs/sexist/2010/04/16/trigger-warnings-
and-being-an-asshole/.

Jarvie, Jenny. "Trigger Happy." *New Republic*, March 2, 2014. Accessed October 1, 2016. https://newrepublic.com/article/116842/trigger-warnings-have-spread-blogs-college-classes-thats-bad.

Johnson, Kai, Tanika Lynch, Elizabeth Monroe, and Tracey Wang. "Our Identities Matter in Core Classrooms." *Columbia Spectator*, April 30, 2015. Accessed September 26, 2016. http://columbiaspectator.com/opinion/2015/04/30/our-identities-matter-core-classrooms.

Kang, Jay Caspian. "Trigger Warnings and the Novelist's Mind." *The New Yorker*, May 21, 2014. Accessed September 17, 2016. http://www.newyorker.com/books/page-turner/trigger-warnings-and-the-novelists-mind.

Kaplan, Adiel. "Sexual Offense Policy Task Force Report Due by End of Semester." *Oberlin Review*, March 1, 2013. Accessed November 17, 2016. http://oberlinreview.org/2036/news/sexual-offense-policy-task-force-report-due-by-end-of-semester/.

Laclau, Ernesto, and Chantal Mouffe. *Hegemony and Socialist Strategy: Towards a Radical Democratic Politics*. New York: Verso, 2001.

Looft, Ruxandra. "How Do Trigger Warnings Fit into the Classroom Lesson Plan?" *Shakesville*, February 12, 2013. Accessed October 1, 2016. http://www.shakesville.com/2013/02/how-do-trigger-warnings-fit-into.html.

Loverin, Bailey. Interview with Patt Morrison. "UC Students Vote to Mandate Warnings for 'Triggering' Content in Classrooms." AirTalk (KPCC), March 12, 2014. Accessed September 26, 2016. http://www.scpr.org/programs/airtalk/2014/03/12/36431/uc-students-vote-to-mandate-warnings-for-trig gerin/.

———. "Trigger Warnings at UCSB." *Daily Nexus*, March 11, 2014. Accessed September 26, 2016. http://dailynexus.com/2014-03-11/trigger-warnings-at-ucsb/.

———. "Trigger Warnings Avert Trauma: Opposing View." *USA Today*, April 21, 2014. Accessed September 26, 2016. http://www.usatoday.com/story/opinion/2014/04/21/trigger-warnings-ptsd-bailey-loverin-editorials-debates/7985479/.

———. "Trigger Warnings Encourage Free Thought and Debate." *New York Times*, May 19, 2014. Accessed September 26, 2016. http://www.nytimes.com/roomfordebate/2014/05/19/restraint-of-expression-on-college-cam puses/trigger-warnings-encourage-free-thought-and-debate.

Lukianoff, Greg, and Jonathan Haidt. "The Coddling of the American Mind." *The Atlantic*, September 2015. Accessed September 26, 2016. http://www.theatlantic.com/magazine/archive/2015/09/the-coddling-of-the-american-mind/399356/.

Mace, Ronald L., Graeme J. Hardie, and Jaine P. Place. "Accessible Environments: Toward Universal Design." In *Design Intervention: Toward a More Humane Architecture*, edited by W. E. Preiser, J. C. Vischer, and E. T. White, 1–44. New York: Van Nostrand Reinhold, 1991.

Manne, Kate. "Why I Use Trigger Warnings." *New York Times*, September 19, 2015. Accessed October 2, 2016. http://www.nytimes.com/2015/09/20/opinion/sunday/why-i-use-trigger-warnings.html?_r=0/.

Marcotte, Amanda. "The Year of the Trigger Warning." *Slate*, December 30, 2013. Accessed September 27, 2016. http://www.slate.com/blogs/xx_factor/2013/12/30/trigger_warnings_from_the_feminist_blogosphere_to_shonda_rhimes_in_2013.html.

McEwan, Melissa. "I Write Letters." *Shakesville*, April 13, 2010. Accessed September 17, 2016. http://www.shakesville.com/2010/04/i-write-letters_13.html.

———. "Triggered." *Shakesville*, March 4, 2014. Accessed September 11, 2016. http://www.shakesville.com/2014/03/triggered.html.

McNally, Richard J. "Hazards Ahead: The Problem with Trigger Warnings, according to the Research." *Pacific Standard*, May 20, 2014. Accessed September 26, 2016. http://www.psmag.com/health-and-behavior/hazards-ahead-problem-trigger-warnings-according-research-81946.

Medina, Jennifer. "Warning: The Literary Canon Could Make Students Squirm." *New York Times*, May 17, 2014. Accessed September 26, 2016. http://www.nytimes.com/2014/05/18/us/warning-the-literary-canon-could-make-students-squirm.html.

Murray, Craig D., and Jezz Fox. "Do Internet Self-Harm Discussion Groups Alleviate or Exacerbate Self-Harming Behaviour?" *Australian e-Journal for the Advancement of Mental Health* 5, no. 3 (2006): 1–9. http://www.auseinet.com/journal/vol5iss3/murray.pdf.

Office of Equity Concerns. "Sexual Offense Resource Guide: Support Resources for Faculty." Oberlin College, 2013. Accessed October 2, 2016. http://web.archive.org/web/20131122144749/http://new.oberlin.edu/office/equity-concerns/sexual-offense-resource-guide/prevention-support-education/support-resources-for-faculty.dot.

Orem, Sarah, and Neil Simpkins. "Weepy Rhetoric, Trigger Warnings, and the Work of Making Mental Illness Visible in the Writing Classroom." *Enculturation: A Journal of Rhetoric, Writing and Culture* (December 16, 2015). Accessed September 21, 2016. http://enculturation.net/weepy-rhetoric.

Peltz, Madeline. "College's Trigger Warning Proposal Incites Media Backlash." *Oberlin Review*, April 13, 2014. Accessed November 17, 2016. http://ober

linreview.org/5485/news/colleges-trigger-warning-proposal-incites-media
-backlash/.

Proximity. "Putting Warnings on Your Posts." *Bodies under Siege*, April 30, 2006, edited May 2, 2006. Accessed September 13, 2016. http://buslist.org/ phpBB/viewtopic.php?p=2047540#p2047540.

Robbins, Susan P. "From the Editor—Sticks and Stones: Trigger Warnings, Microaggressions, and Political Correctness." *Journal of Social Work Education* 52, no. 1 (2016): 1–5.

Schmidt, Peter. "Many Instructors Embrace Trigger Warnings, Despite Their Peers' Misgivings." *Chronicle of Higher Education*, June 16, 2015. Accessed November 7, 2016. http://www.chronicle.com/article/Many-Instructors -Embrace/230915.

7 Humanities Professors. "Trigger Warnings Are Flawed." *Inside Higher Ed*, May 29, 2014. Accessed October 1, 2016. https://www.insidehighered .com/views/2014/05/29/essay-faculty-members-about-why-they-will-not -use-trigger-warnings.

Sicha, Choire. "When "Trigger Warning" Lost All Its Meaning." *The Awl*, May 30, 2012. Accessed October 3, 2016. https://theawl.com/when-trigger -warning-lost-all-its-meaning-31acf9a2012d#.e4fobl6er.

Stengel, Barbara S. "The Complex Case of Fear and Safe Space." *Studies in Philosophy and Education* 29, no. 6 (November 2010): 523–40.

Tiffe, Raechel. "Pedagogy of a Trigger." *Rebel Grrrl Academy*, September 4, 2012. Accessed October 1, 2016. https://rebelgrrlacademy.wordpress .com/2012/09/04/pedagogy-of-a-trigger/.

Valenti, Jessica. "Feminists Talk Trigger Warnings: A Round-Up." *Nation*, March 6, 2014. Accessed October 3, 2016. https://www.thenation.com/ article/feminists-talk-trigger-warnings-round/.

Vingiano, Ali. "How the 'Trigger Warning' Took over the Internet." *BuzzFeed-News*, May 5, 2014. Accessed September 30, 2016. https://www.buzzfeed.com/ alisonvingiano/how-the-trigger-warning-took-over-the-internet?utm_ term=.ph5AGvMEW#.pn0ZJbnLX.

Warner, Michael. *Publics and Counterpublics*. New York: Zone Books, 2002.

White, Gary. "Message from the Director." University of California, Santa Barbara Disabled Students Program. Accessed October 1, 2016. http:// dsp.sa.ucsb.edu/home/directors-message.

Whitlock, Janis, Wendy Lader, and Karen Conterio. "The Internet and Self-Injury: What Psychotherapists Should Know." *Journal of Clinical Psychology: In Session* 63, no. 11 (2007): 1135–43.

Whitlock, Janis L., Jane L. Powers, and John Eckenrode. "The Virtual Cutting Edge: The Internet and Adolescent Self-Injury." *Developmental Psychology* 42, no. 3 (2006): 1–11.

Wythe, Philip. "Trigger Warnings Needed in Classroom." *Daily Targum*, February 18, 2014. Accessed September 23, 2016. http://www.dailytargum.com/article/2014/02/trigger-warnings-needed-in-classroom.

Yergeau, Melanie. "Disable All the Things: On Affect, Metadata, and Audience." Keynote Address. Computers and Writing Conference, Washington State University, Pullman, WA. June 6, 2014.

Young, Iris Marion. *Justice and the Politics of Difference*. Princeton, NJ: Princeton University Press, 2011 [1990].

CHAPTER SEVEN

WRITING POLICY ABOUT TRIGGER WARNINGS

The Experience of the American Association of University Professors and the American Library Association

Barbara M. Jones

In late summer 2016, the University of Chicago's Dean of Students John "Jay" Ellison issued a letter to incoming students about an issue brewing for years in academe. Ellison attempted to clarify the University of Chicago's position on freedom of expression on campus:

> Once here you will discover that one of the University of Chicago's defining characteristics is our commitment to freedom of inquiry and expression. This is captured in the University's faculty report on freedom of expression. Members of our community are encouraged to speak, write, listen, challenge and learn, without fear of censorship. Civility and mutual respect are vital to all of us, and freedom of expression does not mean the freedom to harass or threaten others. You will find that we expect members of our community to be engaged in rigorous debate, discussion, and even disagreement. At times this may challenge you and cause discomfort.
>
> Our commitment to academic freedom means that we do not support "trigger warnings," we do not cancel invited speakers because their topics might prove controversial, and we do not condone the creation of intellectual "safe spaces" where individuals can retreat from ideas and perspectives at odds with their own.[1]

"The Chicago Letter" became an overnight national sensation and was heavily covered by social and traditional media. The American Association of University Professors (AAUP) had begun work on a report about trigger warnings and academic freedom by early 2014. In so many ways, trigger warnings were not new to groups like the AAUP, but simply an example of another strategy to grapple with the growing attempts to balance free speech with the needs of historically marginalized student groups to feel safe—and heard—on campus.

This chapter is devoted to the response of two professional associations to the issue of trigger warnings—The American Association of University Professors and the Association of College and Research Libraries (ACRL), a division of the American Library Association (ALA). The response includes the AAUP Statement on Trigger Warnings and ACRL's endorsement of this statement. Both organizations write policies that focus on faculty and librarians working in higher education. This author helped write the AAUP Committee A statement and then worked with ALA's governance process to advocate for its endorsement.

This chapter is centered on answering the question "Do trigger warnings provide a balance between what Judge Avern Cohn, in *Doe v. University of Michigan* (1989), called "'two competing values—freedom and equality'?" First, the chapter discusses the backstory to trigger warnings—the terminology in the Ellison letter is well known to those working with campus academic freedom and diversity issues. This backstory includes brief references to the major strategies, policies, and regulations as applied to the balance of academic freedom with respect for diversity—with varying degrees of success. Issues include hate speech codes, civility programs, "safe spaces," the Americans with Disabilities Act (ADA), and Title IX. These are all well-meaning attempts to improve what should be viewed as the very exciting multicultural dimension to higher education today—the growth of access to college for diverse racial and religious groups, disabled students, LGBTQ students, women, and others. Next, the chapter gives an account of how two professional associations, the AAUP and the ACRL, researched and wrote policy on trigger warnings. What is the role of professional associations? What does the policy look like? Given the associations' mission and priorities, what issues can it legitimately cover? In the concluding section, I share some thoughts about trigger warnings within the larger context of academic freedom. These thoughts are based on personal, sometimes anecdotal, experience with this issue as a librarian who made intellectual freedom her professional focus for forty years and who eventually directed the Office for Intellectual Freedom and the Freedom to Read Foundation.

Strategic Responses to Increasingly Diverse College Campuses

Today's college campuses are increasingly likely to include LGBTQ students proud to declare themselves, as well as students who are international, nontraditional, of color, "disabled" in some way, and/or economically challenged. All, including women, continue to enter fields once mostly open to white males and continue to meet a host of obstacles. As students, staff, administrators, and faculty increasingly identified with and celebrated their diversity, campuses tried to acknowledge the changes and ensure a more inclusive environment.

While studies show that diversity provides students an ideal environment for learning life lessons and for enjoying a myriad of campus cultural programs, the reality is far more complex. For example, this author has previously worked with college students of color who were consistently singled out in class to represent the point of view for their entire culture. Some women in engineering or physics, as another example, are still unable to get their advisors to take their career placement seriously. One tragic example happened in 2010 when an eighteen-year-old gay Rutgers student, Tyler Clementi, jumped to his death on the George Washington Bridge. His roommate caught him on a hidden webcam kissing another man and posted the video on social media. This incident ripped open wounds of other students who felt marginalized and threatened. Across the country, students and faculty alike are now naming many of their grievances—macroaggressions and white privilege are but two of them—and working for structural changes in higher education.

Over recent decades, administration, faculty, and students tried a number of strategies to address the inequality of student experiences on campuses. For example, many students of color complained early on that they did not have a voice in the classroom and were terrorized and bullied verbally on campus. And so, starting in the mid-1980s, hate speech codes were an early attempt to modulate campus discourse through regulating speech.

Hate Speech Codes

It is an unfortunate fact of our constitutional system that the ideals of freedom and equality are often in conflict. The difficult and sometimes painful task of our political and legal institutions is to mediate the appropriate balance between these two competing values.

—Judge Avern Cohn, in *Doe v.*
University of Michigan (721 F.Supp.852) 1989)

In the 1980s and 1990s, campuses implemented hate speech codes as a way to promote civility on campus and to prevent cruel verbal attacks on students of color. These codes did not fare well in the courts because of the First Amendment and other legal precedents to protect free speech and because they were overly broad and thus chilled potential speech.[2] During this period, I also noted that many of the hate speech codes were merely threats that chilled speech but gave no recourse; that is, the codes did not always provide due process for students or faculty accused of hate speech.

Civility Policies and Programs

As hate speech codes were being regularly struck down in the courts, higher education looked for other solutions that would not restrict protected speech but, rather, encourage dialogue. Could a culture of civility be fostered? Many campuses, including this author's, hired not-for-profit organizations to work with faculty, students, and administrators on diversity issues. Workshops included students who challenged participants to consider the pain of African American students who studied in the library under portraits of the founders—some of whom were slave owners. Another discussion centered on the trauma of women victimized by the "rape culture" of some campus fraternities. While many participants found these discussions to be helpful, the problems began when campuses tried to formally codify or mandate civility.

In 2014, the University of California at Berkeley's Chancellor Nicholas Dirks e-mailed the campus community about the fiftieth anniversary of the free speech movement:

To honor this turning point in our history, it is important that we recognize the broader social context required in order for free speech to thrive. . . .

Specifically, we can only exercise our right to free speech insofar as we feel safe and respected in doing do, and this in turn requires that people treat each other with civility. Simply put, courteousness and respect in words and deeds are basic preconditions to any meaningful exchange of ideas. . . . In this sense, free speech and civility are two sides of a single coin.[3]

Faculty around the United States were incensed that their academic freedom was being violated. *Popehat*, a legal blog, posted a line-by-line critique, trashing the coin metaphor: "Civility is not a prerequisite for free speech."[4] Joan Scott, professor emerita of Princeton's Institute for Advanced Study's School of Social Science, delivered a powerful speech that was later transformed into an article in *The Nation*.[5] Scott makes the provocative argument that if "civility" is the norm for campus discourse, the privileged will define what is "civil" and leave out marginalized voices or speech considered too raucous or outside the norm.

As the social theorist Nancy Fraser has argued, the dissident claims of minority groups go unheard in the public sphere when they are tagged as departures from the protocols of style and decorum—dismissed as evidence of irrationality and so placed outside the realm of what is taken to be reasoned deliberation. They are, by definition, uncivil, and thus beneath contempt. Once a certain space or style of argument is identified as civil, the implication is that dissenters from it are uncivilized. "Civility" becomes a synonym for orthodoxy; "incivility" designates unorthodox ideas or behavior.[6]

This argument is rarely made and needs to be made more often—that marginalized students may fare far worse in a public sphere restricted by the arbitrary rules of "civility."

Safe Spaces

The term *safe space* is difficult to pin down. When used in conjunction with *trigger warning* it defines a space cleansed of potentially trauma-inducing speech. Therefore, students in frequently intimidated groups may feel safer there. It becomes a space to speak freely or not speak at all. Some have suggested that marginalized groups sometimes like to socialize together without feeling pressured to interact with other groups on political issues. Northwestern University's president recounts an incident when white students wanted to sit with black students in a cafeteria and the black students asked to be left alone. This, the president states, is okay with him.[7]

More difficult situations arise when on public university campuses conferences or workshops are held for one race only—for example, a conference for whites—or blacks—on "white privilege." When such spaces and group segregations are formalized, problems begin. Regarding public housing accommodations, for example, a Malcolm X Dorm for one race only is likely to violate the provisions of the Civil Rights Act of 1964. Finally, students who want to discuss a topic in a "safe space" are sometimes reportedly left out. For example, recently a Jewish student was refused entry into an on-campus discussion of the Israeli-Palestinian conflict.[8] "Safe spaces" are philosophically related to "free speech zones" established on some campuses that disallow unrestricted speech to certain areas of campus. Critics of such spaces sometimes wonder why these spaces are needed and argue that free expression should exist on the entire campus.

Americans with Disabilities Act

Other attempts to create an environment of inclusion for a diverse student community come from federal law and regulation. While it has proven to be an excellent catalyst for providing equity of access for the entire campus community, the ADA is, in many respects, responsible for medicalizing disability issues. This fact is important for understanding why, as shown below, the AAUP's trigger warnings policy places the burden not on faculty, but on the student health service, for addressing students suffering from posttraumatic stress disorder (PTSD).

The ADA prohibits discrimination based on disability. In some regards, it is an extension of Title VII of the Civil Rights Act of 1964; however, it goes beyond the Civil Rights Act by requiring organizations to provide "reasonable accommodations." In other words, if a student in a wheelchair is accepted at the university, that institution must provide an accessible dormitory, access to classrooms, and library study tools or technology for reading assignments. Posttraumatic stress disorder is specifically mentioned in many of the ADA regulations. Since it was originally designed to address the needs of returning students who are veterans, in order to comply with the ADA, the campus health center or other designated offices must provide appropriate treatment options or referrals.

Title IX

Title IX "prohibits discrimination on the basis of sex in any federally funded education program or activity." It was originally designed to combat campus sexual assault and harassment. To this end, Title IX understandably calls for ridding campuses of any "hostile environment." The AAUP issued a report on the issue, *The History, Uses, and Abuses of Title IX*, which was adopted by the AAUP Council in June 2016.[9]

The AAUP believes that, in the effort to eliminate campus violence to women in particular, the law is overly broad and "compromises the meaningful educational goals that lead to sexually safe campuses." Specifically, the overly broad definitions of "hostile environment" have punished faculty exercising their protected speech rights. Title IX, they contend, has left an unclear distinction between "conduct" and "speech." The AAUP's approach to this topic will be evident in its report on trigger warnings discussed below.

Trigger Warnings

The latest policy strategy for creating a safe, inclusive campus environment has been trigger warnings. What began as a PTSD diagnosis for returning veterans and victims of violent assault has been extended (though not in the official *DSM* diagnosis) to any number of traumatic events that are very real but arguably different (for example, an undercurrent of racial bias on campus) and require different treatment. The AAUP consulted research and psychological professionals while drafting the statement on trigger warnings. As part of the three-member team drafting this document, I present below some of the research and background leading to the final report.

Posttraumatic Stress Disorder (PTSD) as a Psychological/Psychiatric Diagnosis

This chapter will not detail the evolution of the PTSD diagnosis. However, the impact of medicalizing the diagnosis in 1980 has dramatically influenced campus policies regarding posttraumatic stress and trigger warnings. PTSD first appeared in the American Psychiatric Association's third edition of the *Diagnostic and Statistical Manual of Mental Disorders*

(*DSM*) published in 1980.[10] It was the first time that trauma stressors were viewed by the medical profession—and to some extent by society at large—as external stressors and not as weakness in character. The 1980 *DSM-III* therefore defined "traumatic stressors" and "stress response." The PTSD diagnosis provided war veterans great relief when the psychiatric profession affirmed that any person could be subject to PTSD, that it was not a result of a "character deficiency" like "cowardice," and that it could be treated. This led to extension of disability benefits and treatment programs at Veterans Administration hospitals and community health centers. It is important to understand that the *DSM* is a tool for diagnosis, not treatment, and the diagnoses are numbered and tied to insurance billing.

The term, "triggering event" in *DSM* is used to describe stimuli that remind the victim of the trauma and cause replication of that trauma. However, it is not always possible to know what will trigger the trauma. For example, for an individual who experienced a deadly hurricane, a windy day might trigger the hurricane memory and cause great discomfort. When doing research for the AAUP report, psychology professionals confirmed that one would almost need to be a hermit in order to avoid what might trigger the original trauma. Further, the examples given in *DSM* as trauma include "first responders collecting human remains,"— such as the trauma of those who went into the Sandy Hook Elementary School after the massacre of school children. While racism and misogyny can certainly be disabling, they do not fit into the *DSM* framework.

The *DSM-5* continues to describe PTSD as a severe disorder. It now lives in a section called "Trauma and Stressor-Related Disorders," separate from "anxiety disorders" and "depression." For better or worse, the *DSM* does not include racism, for example, as a stressor. If a racist person violently attacks another person out of racial hatred, then the PTSD diagnosis applies to any flashbacks that victim might experience. The *DSM* does acknowledge that there are higher rates of PTSD among U.S. Latinos, African Americans, and American Indians. It might well be that these groups experience more violence and are unable to get treatment, but the *DSM* does not diagnose a deep social problem. Over the years, the *DSM* has evolved to include not only the stressors and trauma of war violence, but also rape and witnessing or even hearing about violence toward acquaintances. Another telling statistic is that the *DSM* projection for lifetime risk for PTSD in the U.S. general population up to seventy-five years is 8.7 percent. This clearly means that it does not consider the trauma of racism and other social ills in its definitions.

Trigger Warnings Go to College: The Oberlin Case

While researching to draft the AAUP statement, one of the first non-anecdotal examples of constructing "trigger warning" language was the Oberlin College case. In 2012, based on the worrisome rise in the rate of sexual assault on its campus, the Oberlin College Sexual Offense Policy Task Force (made up of students and administrators only, with no faculty) reviewed the current policy and reported back to the faculty. The report contained language and ideas that concerned the faculty deeply. At the time, the Oberlin faculty apparently had not understood the implications of the trigger warning part of the policy. (As a former faculty member at the college, I guess the faculty did not have time to fully digest the document before the faculty meeting.) The faculty now understood that if a student claimed that classroom content triggered a traumatic response, the faculty offender could be disciplined. At that point, meetings took place, faculty were included, and eventually the policy was revised. As one faculty member said: "We need to challenge students, to conduct open inquiry in classrooms, to *make* students feel uncomfortable" [emphasis mine].[11]

The National Coalition against Censorship (NCAC) Survey on Trigger Warnings[12]

It must be noted that to this day there are military leaders who reject the concept of PTSD as a result of war trauma. Little wonder that many reject it when applied to victims of the trauma of hurtful communication in academe. And how many real incidents of trauma in the classroom could be found? Was AAUP creating a problem that does not exist? Were we relying on anecdotes alone? In order to answer these questions and others, the National Coalition against Censorship teamed up with the College Art Association (CAA) and the Modern Language Association (MLA) to survey faculty members about this topic. The object was to clarify the meaning so that it could be used in chapters such as this one. The report's findings are detailed below.

First, most institutions do not have trigger warnings policies. However, 15 percent of the recipients reported the use of trigger warnings as a student-driven request. Trigger warnings are usually not faculty driven; they may be administration responding to students—not only to ensure student well-being but also to avoid the legal risk of volatile classroom situations. Another significant factor in this era is parental monitoring of their children far longer than in the past. They are placing a higher pressure on administrators for making sure their children are intellectually safe. Additionally, 62 percent of instructors surveyed think trigger warnings have a negative effect. Seventeen percent believe they can be used positively. For example, one respondent said that a trigger warning about a particularly explosive upcoming assignment prepared students for a difficult conversation.

Finally, there was widespread agreement that instructors, not administrators, should decide whether or not to use trigger warnings. Many said that it should be left informal and not enshrined in policy. This author can say anecdotally, and in interviewing faculty for this report, that no faculty member said that he or she would force students to attend a particular class or engage with course content that was traumatic for them.[13]

The AAUP Policy Response to Trigger Warnings

The AAUP decided to develop policy around the trigger warning issue, as described above, at a tipping point. Members had shared numerous anecdotal stories of their own experiences, and the academic and general press were naming and covering the phenomenon and not always clearly. And so, in 2014, Committee A on Academic Freedom began the exploration and policy formulation around the issue of trigger warnings at their regular meetings in Washington, D.C. Later on, in early 2015, the board of directors of the Association of College and Research Libraries (ACRL), a division of the American Library Association, endorsed the document. At that time, I was a consulting member of the AAUP Committee A and also a staff member at the American Library Association and therefore played a role in bringing the AAUP work to the ACRL for consideration and subsequent endorsement.

History and Mission of AAUP

The American Association of University Professors was founded in 1915 and is a product of the Progressive Era. Its aim was to enhance the status of the professoriate. The AAUP, as Hans-Joerg Tiede documents in his history of the organization,[14] was also formed to ensure that faculty had a say in the running of higher education. Academic freedom and shared governance have always been key principles; these ideals can be viewed in the trigger warnings report. The founding document (1915) on Academic Freedom and Tenure is crucial. Many U.S. associations were founded during this Progressive Era. Due to its focus on academic freedom, Committee A was the premier committee from the beginning. In 1940, an abridged statement of academic freedom and tenure was adopted and endorsed by more than one hundred groups, including the American Library Association. Subsequent policies and reports are collected in AAUP's *Redbook*, now in its eleventh edition (2015).

The 1940 Statement of Principles on Academic Freedom and Tenure is a restatement of the 1915 principles and remains a guiding document for such issues as trigger warnings' impact on the professoriate. It was adopted by dozens of associations, including the American Library Association, as adapted for librarians, in 1946:

> Freedom in research is fundamental to the advancement of truth. Academic freedom in its teaching aspect is fundamental for the protection of the rights of the teacher in teaching and of the student to freedom in learning. It carries with it duties correlative with rights.
>
> Teachers are entitled to freedom in the classroom in discussing their subject, but they should be careful not to introduce into their teaching controversial matter which has no relation to their subject. Limitations of academic freedom because of religious or other aims of the institution should be clearly stated in writing at the time of the appointment.

In 1970, a clarification was added: "The intent of this statement is not to discourage what is 'controversial.' Controversy is at the heart of the free academic inquiry which the entire statement is designed to foster." It must be noted that good policy is based on past principles and the above principles and policies are relevant to understanding the development of the trigger warnings report.

BARBARA M. JONES

Campus Sexual Assault: AAUP Suggested Policies and Procedures

The AAUP policy on campus sexual assault was written in the aftermath of the sexual assaults at Penn State University in 2011. It reflects AAUP's approach regarding the faculty role in the growing problem of campus violence. The following excerpts from this policy are crucial for understanding the AAUP approach to trigger warnings:

> The American Association of University Professors has long recognized that the freedom to teach and to learn is inseparable from the maintenance of a safe and hospitable learning environment. Several Association documents identify important elements of such an environment. The Joint Statement on Rights and Freedoms of Students, formulated in 1967 (revised 1990–92), states that the "freedom to learn depends upon appropriate opportunities and conditions in the classroom, on the campus, and in the larger community." The 1966 Statement on Professional Ethics (revised in 1987 and 2009) emphasizes the responsibility of faculty members to "avoid any exploitation . . . of students." "Sexual Harassment: Suggested Policy and Procedures for Handling Complaints" (1995) reiterates this ethical responsibility, asserting that acts of harassment clearly violate expected standards of campus conduct. The same statement emphasizes that the success of any policy requires campus leadership to "provide appropriate ethical standards and to provide suitable internal procedures to secure their observance."

II. Consequences of Sexual Assault (excerpts)

The consequences of sexual assault are potentially very serious. An immediate concern is physical injury, which may be extensive enough to require medical treatment or hospitalization.

Pregnancy and sexually transmitted diseases (STDs), including HIV, are additional concerns. Emotional damage may be serious and equally requiring of treatment. Sexual assault may affect students' academic achievement as well as their capacity to contribute to the campus community. College students who have survived sexual assault rarely perform at their prior academic levels, are sometimes unable to carry a normal course load, and frequently miss classes. These changes stem sometimes from social withdrawal, sometimes from a desire to avoid the perpetrator. Assaulted students regularly drop courses altogether, leave school, or transfer. Along with decline in academic performance and social withdrawal, long-term outcomes may include increased risk of depression, substance abuse, self-harm, eating disorders, post-traumatic stress, personality disorders, and suicide. . . .

VI. Faculty Responsibilities

While the foregoing suggestions are generally applicable to campus-wide strategies for managing sexual assault, the role of faculty members in protecting student rights and freedoms is distinctive and merits further discussion. As advisers, teachers, and mentors, faculty members may be among the most trusted adults in a student's life and often are the persons in whom students will confide after an assault. A faculty member may also be the first adult who detects changes in a student's behavior that stem from a sexual assault and can encourage the student to talk about it. Faculty members may thus find themselves in the role of "first responders" to reports of sexual assault, yet few consider themselves adequately equipped for the role—in part because they are the least likely campus constituency to receive information about sexual assault and guidance about reporting and responding to it.

The reporting question is important. The Clery Act mandates that campus crime statistics be gathered from "campus police or security, local law enforcement, and other school officials who have 'significant respon-sibility for student and campus activities' such as judicial affairs directors." It is the view of this committee that faculty members, as a general rule, do not fall into this category and are therefore not mandated Clery reporters. As a consequence, faculty members are thus usually not expected to be trained investigators, nor, except in specific circumstances as defined by individual institutions, are they normally expected to be mandated report-ers of incidents about which they are told or happen to learn. But they can provide other important forms of support and assistance.

This policy is heavily quoted here, and included in the main text, because it shows clearly the focus of AAUP policy on issues that relate to trigger warnings. First, it clearly limits faculty involvement to those areas in which faculty are experts. Second, it assigns roles to other campus organizations, such as the police and the health service, for issues outside faculty purview—or issues that because of law and regulation are handled by other departments on campus. Third, this policy protects faculty from liability in doing the wrong thing in a well-meaning attempt to help the student. Finally, the policy assigns responsibility and gives faculty an im-portant but not exclusive role. It also clearly delineates that sexual violence means the act itself—not its depiction in classroom discussions, paintings, or readings. This is important for understanding both the AAUP and ACRL policy approaches to trigger warnings.

With clear and consistent references to their mission and other policy statements, the *AAUP Report on Trigger Warnings* was finalized and is included in the appendix to this chapter. As a participant in the discussions and crafting of the document, this author was impressed that the AAUP focused on its mission as an association. While certainly the Title IX policy emphasizes the impact of sexual assault on individual students, the AAUP must be sure that the policy protects faculty academic freedom and their role on campus. This includes direction to faculty on what they should and should not do in regard to student health issues. With the trigger warnings policy, the drafting group researched information from medical professionals who understood PTSD and from those who understood how the ADA should be applied on campus. Faculty should not diagnose or treat medical conditions. There are also privacy issues to consider. This policy is one indication that there may be some problems on campus that are unquestionably severe and need to be addressed, but that legal remedies might not work in all cases. Campuses need to consider whether protecting one student is preventing the rest of the class from learning, and dealing emotionally with, essential but sometimes disturbing information.

The AAUP statement distinguishes between speech and action. While the Title IX statement clearly deals with what to do if someone is sexually assaulted, the trigger warnings statement does not treat hurtful speech in the same way. This is because of how the U.S. Supreme Court has interpreted what speeches and actions the First Amendment does and does not protect. Given the current rise in authoritarian governments in the United States and elsewhere, do we as a society want to dispose of speech protection? Does the chilling of speech uncomfortable to some remedy the challenges of campus diversity and inclusion on campus?

The American Library Association and Association of College and Research Libraries Policy Response to Trigger Warnings

The American Library Association was founded in 1876 and today is the oldest and largest library membership organization in the world. ALA includes such divisions as ACRL, which will be explained below as the home of academic and research librarians. Within the general

ALA structure (not a division) is the Office for Intellectual Freedom (OIF), which celebrates its fiftieth birthday in 2017. Together the two sections have the portfolio for intellectual freedom, privacy, academic freedom, ethics, and tenure issues for librarians. As noted, during the trigger warnings debate, I served on the AAUP Committee A. It is not a space necessarily reserved for librarians, but a happy confluence for this important shared problem.

The Association of College and Research Libraries: A Division of ALA

ACRL became an official division of ALA in 1938, after there were enough academic librarians to form a critical mass to branch off from ALA. Their purpose is "to lead academic and research librarians and libraries in advancing learning and scholarship."[15] ACRL has long advocated that academic freedom must apply to academic library content and services. In addition, academic librarians want to be recognized as professionals along with faculty, and in many academic libraries, librarians do, indeed, have faculty status or the equivalent. Therefore, ACRL and AAUP have two joint statements about faculty status that show that librarians with or without faculty status must be afforded the same rights of academic freedom as faculty in order to do their job according to the ALA's ethical principles and practices regarding intellectual freedom.[16]

ALA's Office for Intellectual Freedom—Another AAUP Policy Partner

The ACRL's work with the AAUP is coordinated with and through the ALA Office for Intellectual Freedom. OIF supports ALA member policy making on such committees as the Intellectual Freedom Committee ([IFC]; much the same as AAUP's Committee A). IFC develops policies for approval by the ALA Governing Board and Council.

The Office for Intellectual Freedom was founded in 1967 to deal with the ever-growing number of censorship incidents in libraries, or the chilling effect brought on in the McCarthy era that caused many librarians to lose their jobs. It has a long tradition of working with academic librarians. In fact, many of the most profoundly complex intellectual freedom issues today come from the academic library world. While in the past library censorship was often a public library removing a book from the collection, in today's academic library it can be a campus-wide Internet filtering policy affecting the entire campus. The culture wars are sometimes fought at the university library too, as some have been threatened with losing state funding if they purchase LGBTQ information.

OIF's *Intellectual Freedom Manual*, now in its ninth edition, is similar to AAUP's *Redbook*. Policies are crafted by members and committees and approved by ALA Council in a process very similar to that of AAUP. Like AAUP, the Office for Intellectual Freedom and its Intellectual Freedom Committee were professionally experiencing, or receiving anecdotal evidence about, trigger warnings. These reports confirmed the experiences of OIF staff on the road on such campuses as Iowa State University, where a young female student asked the OIF speaker what to do about her parents' monitoring her syllabus and reading list. This confirmed the office's anecdotal evidence about parents increasingly extending the period of parenting to monitoring their children's reading habits in college. However, it must be said that while the OIF received no evidence of book labeling on the academic level, we saw the potential connection immediately. What if a campus administrator, faculty member, or student asked that trigger warnings be applied to certain books? In fact, the American Library Association had for decades proscribed such practices in its interpretation on labeling and ratings systems (see the introduction to this volume).

It is clear from reading the AAUP and ALA policies that several foundational principles are shared:

- Protecting the freedom of librarians and teachers to express their opinions and provide content that is controversial, because that is how students learn to think critically.

- Refusing to filter content reflects that librarians do not want to impose someone else's framework of appropriateness onto students.

- Avoiding labeling of content because it predisposes students to think a particular way about content.

- In the case of AAUP, giving practical guidance on what faculty can and cannot do in a difficult situation—giving them latitude to assist a student in particular ways, and to make a referral. My experience is that libraries do the very same thing. If a student would approach the reference desk and ask for help with stress, the librarian would refer that student (if the student agreed) to the campus health facility. Similarly, a teacher asked by a student to be excused from a particular session because of potentially traumatic content often makes individual arrangements with a student but does not prevent the other students from engaging with that material in the syllabus.

Conclusion

Based on my academic library practice, along with a research agenda on intellectual freedom in academic libraries for forty years, here are some thoughts on policy making for trigger warnings. You will note in this conclusion that trigger warnings are barely mentioned, as I believe they are a symptom of a much larger systemic problem with racism and other discriminatory behavior in U.S. society, which is then reflected in the structure and practice of higher education.

- *Without academic freedom, college and university campuses will lose their potential and meaning for students and society at large. In the United States, academic freedom is a strong tradition and its loss would be a tragedy for the entire world.*

As stated many times in this chapter, college is the time for students to engage, hopefully in a supportive community. They can test out their ideas, join clubs and movements, and find people to spar with intellectually. It may be harder for some students than others, and that inequity (often of temperament) can be addressed without trigger warnings. As with libraries, some classroom content *should* make students uncomfortable. The difference is that in college, one is surrounded by at least some like-minded students and organizations. At college, a student can test ideas without getting fired. Students can learn to live with diverse people and ideas and cultural difference. To avoid such opportunities out of fear of discomfort is a missed opportunity.

This does not mean that controversial content need be taught or made available with no context. Teachers and librarians are professionals, bound by their own ethical standards and experience and expertise. They will undoubtedly give the controversial material a context by providing references and other readings and might even point out that the book was banned at one time, for example, or that it caused great unrest. The library can provide this content. The classroom is an opportunity for engaging with others, compared to reading alone. It is up to the instructor to make sure that one voice doesn't dominate—including that of the instructor. In an ideal discussion, the instructor makes sure that those who are silent are asked if they wish to contribute, to make sure that if they want to speak, they have that opportunity as part of the group. Creating an alternative space robs the class of an important perspective.

Librarians, too, provide context for the classroom by conducting information literacy sessions in the classroom. They can point out content from a variety of perspectives. They can recommend historical materials to provide background to the controversial material. Rather than labeling or "warning" someone about a particular painting or reading, the librarian can surround it—or not—with other perspectives. Placing controversial ideas into a context creates a comfort zone.

- *Every student comes to college with a unique and important background and potential contribution to the development of knowledge and ideas.*

In some cases, this background can make a profound contribution. One student might be an Iraq war veteran with PTSD, among predominantly antiwar classmates. This author recalls a conversation in a library lunch room among student workers who were the first in their families to attend college. Thanksgiving at home was not fun for them. They were often attacked for thinking they were smarter than the rest of the family. They did not get nurturing support from their parents. I recall in horror another incident in which an African graduate student approached me and said, "I have never used a library like this one. Where do I start?" My response to a colleague was, "If he didn't know what to do, he has no right to be here." More students come to college ill-prepared. Many, like Tyler Clementi, come to college and encounter other students who are cruel and bullying regarding LGBTQ issues. It is the first time that many students encounter a very diverse group of classmates. Campuses must continue to try strategies to make sure that students can get whatever assistance or safety net they need. It might be tutoring. It might be counseling at the health service. As a friend said recently, "I didn't know what I needed as a student, I was trying to come out but didn't know that, so I treated a lot of people badly." Trigger warnings will not help in these cases. Rather, an inclusive group of people willing to listen empathetically will help. Not to mention a course with challenging texts about LGBTQ issues.

- *Students calling for trigger warnings might have deeper concerns.*

I am reminded of an incident in October 2016 of a student leaving for class and looking back to see her door painted with "nigger." Yes, a hate speech conduct code might prohibit this, but it doesn't solve the larger systemic racism of students on that campus.

The responses from Columbia University students demanding trigger warnings is revealing. When interviewed by the *Washington Post* about the call for trigger warnings on such classics as Ovid's *Metamorphoses*, it was revealed that one of the students had been sexually assaulted. She was disturbed by the *Metamorphoses* but remained for the entire class. But when she approached her instructor to share her thoughts, she felt "essentially dismissed." Remember that in their call for trigger warnings at Columbia, the students asked for teachers to be more aware of their backgrounds and emotional status: "Given these tools, professors will be able to add in the inclusion of student voices which presently feel silenced." Talk about a missed opportunity and botched up communication! What if the student had been recognized by the teacher in the first place? What if at the next class session the teacher had encouraged discussion of not only the beauty, but also the brutality, of the text? It sounded as if the students were asking for trigger warnings because they didn't know what else to do to have their concerns recognized.

And what about the Chicago letter? What if Jay Ellison had included in that letter an enthusiastic report of University of Chicago's diverse campus as an opportunity to learn? Didn't the letter's tone have something to do with the outrage? Recently Robert Jones, the new chancellor at the University of Illinois at Urbana-Champaign, told a group that he was very proud that one out of seven of new freshmen at UIUC was the first in his or her family to attend college. He stated that in a celebratory manner—as an opportunity. It might also mean that faculty and librarians need to be aware that some students do not come to college with the same background. This is sometimes a change and a challenge, but this is what college is for, in my view.

This author came to college during the time of the Vietnam War protests and the U.S. civil rights movement. She met students who could barely speak English. She had her beliefs shaken up. One of her dorm mates had never been told at home about sexual intercourse. She engaged in long discussions with people with dramatically different backgrounds and economic status. Those conversations and lessons on the lawn were part and parcel of learning. A shelter was not what she wanted. And she was told by a professor that women would be discriminated against in PhD programs. He told her about a woman whose husband was a machinist and just didn't fit in. There were programs discouraged. There were assumptions about careers for women. Thinking through these challenges is the only way to face the world of work and family and lifelong engagement with the world.

- *Policies are one strategy among many to create an inclusive campus.*

Just as the *Diagnostic and Statistical Manual for Mental Disorders* is not a good fit for addressing course content, policies also do not address or solve the entire problem of campus inclusion. They are not meant to! The AAUP policy, as endorsed by ACRL, focuses on those issues important to their members when it comes to the topic of trigger warnings. Their members are faculty and librarians who have a specific role to play in promoting campus safety and diversity and academic freedom. I am reminded of my last academic library job, when students would study in the library and often approach the librarian on duty to talk about having problems of stress. The librarian knew, from campus sessions, to refer that student immediately to the campus health service, well equipped to handle the stress of final exams. And the ADA mandates that campuses be able to support students under stress. While, as seen in AAUP statements, teachers do have a role, it is limited and could have legal repercussions if they overstep or try to offer expertise they do not have and are not expected to have.

The Freeh Report at Penn State clearly stated that written policy about sexual harassment could have prevented some of the abuse. In the case of no written policy, nobody felt responsible. By the same token, not all campus interactions can be solved by a law, regulation, or policy. One of my fondest stories is about a colleague as school librarian in a religiously and politically conservative school district. When she added controversial books to the collection, she invited parents to a brown bag lunch (scheduled at various times to meet the shift needs of the parents). They discussed the books, and this librarian never experienced a challenge to her collection. All the parents wanted was a voice. How about students? Communications skills, along with good policy, accountability to such laws as the ADA, and a caring environment together make trigger warnings unnecessary.

- *Trigger warnings are a quick fix for a systemic problem.*

Trigger warnings are so much like book banning. Many well-meaning people challenge books because they want to help in one small way with a contemporary problem. It might be teen suicide. It might be racism. It is their way of expressing their concern in making the world a better place. On the other hand, they must be shown that censorship creates barriers for others. And to remove themselves to a safe space is a real loss to dialogue. Avoiding a topic does not make it go away. In fact, engaging in uncomfortable content, at college, where one is surrounded by peers and support groups, is the best way. College trains students for a workplace far colder than the classroom. The best way to alleviate trauma is to work through them. I am reminded of the "fishbowl" discussion sessions that are held at Holy Cross University to address controversial topics with a process that gives everyone an opportunity to speak. They even had a fishbowl on trigger warnings![17] We need engagement, not retreat.

Appendix: *AAUP Report on Trigger Warnings*

This report was drafted by a subcommittee of Committee A on Academic Freedom and Tenure in August 2014 and has been approved by Committee A.

A current threat to academic freedom in the classroom comes from a demand that teachers provide warnings in advance if assigned material contains anything that might trigger difficult emotional responses for students. This follows from earlier calls not to offend students' sensibilities by introducing material that challenges their values and beliefs. The specific call for "trigger warnings" began in the blogosphere as a caution about graphic descriptions of rape on feminist sites, and has now migrated to university campuses in the form of requirements or proposals that students be alerted to all manner of topics that some believe may deeply offend and even set off a post-traumatic stress disorder (PTSD) response in some individuals. Oberlin College's original policy (since tabled to allow for further debate in the face of faculty opposition) is an example of the range of possible trigger topics: "racism, classism, sexism, heterosexism, cissexism, ableism, and other issues of privilege and oppression." It went on to say that a novel like Chinua Achebe's *Things Fall Apart* might "trigger readers who have experienced racism, colonialism, religious persecution, violence, suicide and more." It further cautioned faculty to "[r]emove triggering material when it does not contribute directly to the course learning goals."

As one report noted, at Wellesley College students objected to "a sculpture of a man in his underwear because it might be a source of 'triggering thoughts regarding sexual assault.' While the [students'] petition acknowledged that the sculpture might not disturb everyone on campus, it insisted that we share a 'responsibility to pay attention to and attempt to answer the needs of all of our community members.' Even after the artist explained that the figure was supposed to be sleepwalking, students continued to insist it be moved indoors." [Useful resource: Jenny Jarvie, "Trigger Happy" at http://www.newrepublic.com/article/116842/trigger-warnings-have-spread-blogs-college-classes-thats-bad.]

The presumption that students need to be protected rather than challenged in a classroom is at once infantilizing and anti-intellectual. It makes comfort a higher priority than intellectual engagement and—as the Oberlin list demonstrates—it singles out politically controversial topics like sex, race, class, capitalism, and colonialism for attention. Indeed, if such topics are associated with triggers, correctly or not, they are likely to be marginalized if not avoided altogether by faculty who fear complaints for offending or discomforting some of their students. Although all faculty are affected by potential charges of this kind, non-tenured and contingent faculty are particularly at risk. In this way the demand for trigger warnings creates a repressive, "chilly climate" for critical thinking in the classroom.

Our concern extends to academic libraries, the repositories of content spanning all cultures and types of expression. We think the statement of the American Library Association regarding "labeling and rating systems" applies to trigger warnings. "Prejudicial labels are designed to restrict access, based on a value judgment that the content, language, or theme of the material, or the background or views of the creator(s) of the material, render it inappropriate or offensive for all or certain groups of users. . . . When labeling is an attempt to prejudice attitudes, it is a censor's tool."

Institutional requirements or even suggestions that faculty use trigger warnings interfere with faculty academic freedom in the choice of course materials and teaching methods. Faculty might feel pressured into notifying students about course content for fear that some students might find it disturbing. Of course there may be instances in which a teacher judges it necessary to alert students to potentially difficult material and that is his or her right. Administrative requirements are different from individual faculty decisions. Administration regulation constitutes interference with academic freedom; faculty judgment is a legitimate exercise of autonomy.

There are reasons, however, for concern that even voluntary use of trigger warnings included on syllabi may be counterproductive to the educational experience. Such trigger warnings conflate exceptional individual experience of trauma with the anticipation of trauma for an entire group, and assume that individuals will respond negatively to certain content. A trigger warning might lead a student to simply not read an assignment or it might elicit a response from students they otherwise would not have had, focusing them on one aspect of a text and thus precluding other reactions. If, for example, *The House of Mirth* or *Anna Karenina* carried a warning about suicide, students might overlook the other questions about wealth, love, deception, and existential anxiety that are what those books are actually about. Trigger warnings thus run the risk of reducing complex literary, historical, sociological and political insights to a few negative characterizations. By calling attention to certain content in a given work, trigger warnings also signal an expected response to the content (e.g., dismay, distress, disapproval), and eliminate the element of surprise and spontaneity that can enrich the reading experience and provide critical insight.

Some discomfort is inevitable in classrooms if the goal is to expose students to new ideas, have them question beliefs they have taken for granted, grapple with ethical problems they have never considered, and, more generally, expand their horizons so as to become informed and responsible democratic citizens. Trigger warnings suggest that classrooms should offer protection and comfort rather than an intellectually challenging education. They reduce students to vulnerable victims rather than full participants in the intellectual process of education. The effect is to stifle thought on the part of both teachers and students who fear to raise questions that might make others "uncomfortable."

The classroom is not the appropriate venue to treat PTSD, which is a medical condition that requires serious medical treatment. Trigger warnings are an inadequate and diversionary response. Medical research suggests that triggers for individuals can be unpredictable, dependent on networks of association. So color, taste, smell, and sound may lead to flashbacks and panic attacks as often as the mention of actual forms of violence such as rape and war. The range of any student's sensitivity is thus impossible to anticipate. But if trigger warnings are required or expected, anything in a classroom that elicits a traumatic response could potentially expose teachers to all manner of discipline and punishment.

It is probably not coincidental that the call for trigger warnings comes at a time of increased attention to campus violence, especially to sexual assault that is often associated with the widespread abuse of alcohol. Trigger warnings are a way of displacing the problem, however, locating its solution in the classroom rather than in administrative attention to social behaviors that permit sexual violence to take place. Trigger warnings will not solve this problem, but only misdirect attention from it and, in the process, threaten the academic freedom of teachers and students whose classrooms should be open to difficult discussions, whatever form they take.

Notes

1. Quoted in Pete Grieve, "University to Freshmen: Don't Expect Safe Spaces or Trigger Warnings," *Chicago Maroon*, August 24, 2016, https://www.chicago

maroon.com/2016/08/24/university-to-freshmen-dont-expect-safe-spaces-or
-trigger-warnings/.

2. David L. Hudson Jr., "Hate Speech and Campus Speech Codes," First Amendment Center, September 13, 2002, http://www.firstamendmentcenter .org/hate-speech-campus-speech-codes.

3. Ken White, "How the University of Chicago Could Have Done a Better Job Defending Free Speech," *Popehat*, August 24, 2016, https://popehat .com/2016/08/29/how-the-university-of-chicago-could-have-done-a-better-job -defending-free-speech/.

4. Ibid.

5. Joan W. Scott, "The New Thought Police: Why Are Campus Administrators Invoking Civility to Silence Critical Speech?" *The Nation*, April 15, 2015.

6. Ibid.

7. Morton Schapiro, "I'm Northwestern's President. Here's Why Safe Spaces for Students Are Important," *Washington Post*, January 15, 2016, https://www.wash ingtonpost.com/opinions/how-to-create-inclusive-campus-communities-first- create-safe-places/2016/01/15/069f3a66-bb94-11e5-829c-26ffb874a18d_story .html?utm_term=.8bc8004f3ebf.

8. Anthony Berteaux, "In the Safe Spaces on Campus, No Jews Allowed," *Washington Post*, September 15, 2016, https://www.washingtonpost .com/news/acts-of-faith/wp/2016/09/15/in-the-safe-spaces-on-campus-no-jews -allowed/?utm_term=.35b3560efb56.

9. See *The History, Uses, and Abuses of Title IX*, https://www.aaup.org/report/ history-uses-and-abuses-title-ix.

10. American Psychiatric Association, *Diagnostic and Statistical Manual of Mental Disorders*, 3rd ed. (Washington, DC: American Psychiatric Association, 1980), #309.89.

11. Oberlin Office of Equity Concerns, *Sexual Offense Resource Book* (2013 draft), http://web.archive.org/web/20131222174936/http:/new.oberlin.edu/ office/equity-concerns/sexual-offense-resource-guide/prevention-support-edu cation/support-resources-for-faculty.dot.

12. National Coalition against Censorships, *What's All This about Trigger Warnings?* December 2015, http://ncac.org/wp-content/uploads/2015/11/ NCAC-TriggerWarningReport.pdf.

13. Carlo Davis, "Oberlin Amends Its Trigger-Warning Policy," *New Republic*, April 9, 2014, https://newrepublic.com/article/117320/oberlin-amends-its -trigger-warning-policy.

14. Hans-Joerg Tiede, *University Reform: The Founding of the AAUP* (Baltimore, MD: Johns Hopkins University Press, 2015). Tiede also served on Committee A when the trigger warnings policy was written.

15. Association of College and Research Libraries, Plan for Excellence, 2011, http://www.ala.org/acrl/aboutacrl/strategicplan/stratplan.

16. Association of College and Research Libraries, Joint Statement on Faculty Status of College and University Librarians, 2012, http://www.ala.org/acrl/standards/jointstatementfaculty.

17. See: McFarland Center for Religion, Ethics and Culture, College of the Holy Cross, "Fishbowl Discussions: Trigger Warnings in the Classroom," https://www.holycross.edu/mcfarland-center-religion-ethics-and-culture/fishbowl-discussions.

Bibliography

American Psychiatric Association. *Diagnostic and Statistical Manual of Mental Disorders*, 3rd ed. Washington, DC: American Psychiatric Association, 1980.

Association of College and Research Libraries. Joint Statement on Faculty Status of College and University Librarians, 2012. http://www.ala.org/acrl/standards/jointstatementfaculty.

———. Plan for Excellence, 2011. http://www.ala.org/acrl/aboutacrl/strategicplan/stratplan.

Berteaux, Anthony. "In the Safe Spaces on Campus, No Jews Allowed." *Washington Post*, September 15, 2016. https://www.washingtonpost.com/news/acts-of-faith/wp/2016/09/15/in-the-safe-spaces-on-campus-no-jews-allowed/?utm_term=.35b3560efb56.

Davis, Carlo. "Oberlin Amends Its Trigger-Warning Policy." *New Republic*, April 9, 2014. https://newrepublic.com/article/117320/oberlin-amends-its-trigger-warning-policy.

Grieve, Pete. "University to Freshmen: Don't Expect Safe Spaces or Trigger Warnings." *Chicago Maroon*, August 24, 2016. https://www.chicagomaroon.com/2016/08/24/university-to-freshmen-dont-expect-safe-spaces-or-trigger-warnings/.

Hudson, David L., Jr. "Hate Speech and Campus Speech Codes." First Amendment Center, September 13, 2002. http://www.firstamendmentcenter.org/hate-speech-campus-speech-codes.

National Coalition against Censorship. *What's All This about Trigger Warnings?* December 2015. http://ncac.org/wp-content/uploads/2015/11/NCAC-TriggerWarningReport.pdf.

Oberlin Office of Equity Concerns. *Sexual Offense Resource Book* (2013 draft). http://web.archive.org/web/20131222174936/http:/new.oberlin.edu/office/

equity-concerns/sexual-offense-resource-guide/prevention-support-educa
tion/support-resources-for-faculty.dot.

Schapiro, Morton. "I'm Northwestern's President. Here's Why Safe Spaces for
Students Are Important." *Washington Post*, January 15, 2016. https://www
.washingtonpost.com/opinions/how-to-create-inclusive-campus-commu-
nities-first-create-safe-places/2016/01/15/069f3a66-bb94-11e5-829c-26ff
b874a18d_story.html?utm_term=.8bc8004f3ebf.

Scott, Joan W. "The New Thought Police: Why Are Campus Administrators
Invoking Civility to Silence Critical Speech?" *The Nation*, April 15, 2015.

Tiede, Hans-Joerg. *University Reform: The Founding of the AAUP*. Baltimore,
MD: Johns Hopkins University Press, 2015.

White, Ken. "How the University of Chicago Could Have Done a Better
Job Defending Free Speech." *Popehat*, August 24, 2016. https://popehat
.com/2016/08/29/how-the-university-of-chicago-could-have-done-a-bet
ter-job-defending-free-speech/.

Part II
CASE STUDIES

CHAPTER EIGHT

INSTITUTION-WIDE TRIGGER WARNINGS
A Case Study of a University's "Common Reading"
Joe C. Martin and Brandi N. Frisby

From the advent of their usage, "trigger warnings" have been a point of controversy in education. Designed to protect individuals from potentially distressing content, trigger warnings are currently being utilized and debated in academia.[1] Some argue that trigger warnings are both a courtesy and a necessity, empowering those who have experienced traumatic events such as rape or warfare to make informed decisions about whether to expose themselves to content that could be triggering.[2] Others view trigger warnings as a potential encroachment upon academic freedom, an impediment to the personal and intellectual growth of students, and even a threat to their mental health.[3] Though there are sharp distinctions in their views, those on both sides of this issue would agree that trigger warnings are an immensely important point of discussion.

This case study explores existing and newly collected data associated with a common reading selection and the trigger warning rhetoric associated with the selection of *Picking Cotton*, using triangulated data and the theory of cognitive dissonance. Specifically, this event will be examined at an institutional level (i.e., university messages, president's message, responses to surveys created for this study by administrators who selected the book) and classroom level (e.g., responses to surveys created for this study by faculty who utilized the book), using relevant existing assessment data from the program responsible for the selection and implementation of the book: the University of Kentucky's Common Reading Experience office.

Perspectives on Trigger Warnings

The existing scholarly literature on the subject of trigger warnings in higher education is best described as "scant." Though trigger warnings have received notable attention in popular outlets, a similar level of consideration is yet to develop in academic publications. That is not to say that trigger warnings have not been both employed or rejected in academe. In fact, the academic interest in trigger warnings reached a climax in the late summer of 2016 when University of Chicago Dean of Students John "Jay" Ellison sent a letter to incoming first-year students warning them that trigger warnings are not a supported practice at the institution, nor is facilitating students' ability to "retreat from ideas and perspectives at odds with their own."[4] Others in academic circles have advanced criticisms of trigger warnings for similar reasons. For example, in a report "On Trigger Warnings," the American Association of University Professors posits that "the presumption that students need to be protected rather than challenged in a classroom is at once infantilizing and anti-intellectual."[5]

While much of the criticism of trigger warnings centers on their alleged ability to inhibit students' personal and intellectual development, another set of concerns involves asserted incompatibilities between trigger warnings and free speech. Recently, the National Coalition against Censorship (NCAC) published results from a survey of more than seven hundred educators, reporting that 62 percent of respondents believed trigger warnings will "have a negative effect on academic freedom."[6] Some have argued that while trigger warnings may not directly violate free speech rights, they may still have a "chilling effect on classroom discussions," especially for students who hold opinions unpopular in the broader culture.[7]

Although there is certainly no shortage of criticism for trigger warnings among academics, the practice of issuing trigger warnings also enjoys considerable support. In fact, some instructors are repulsed by the opposition to trigger warnings, perceiving that any outrage concerning them is feigned and in service to "a desire to have the gatekeepers remain in place."[8] Northwestern University president Morton Schapiro used terms like "idiots" and "lunatics" to describe opponents of trigger warnings and "safe spaces" as well as those who reject ideas like "microaggressions."[9] Though there is undoubtedly impassioned activism in favor of trigger warnings, some proponents consider them simply to be matters of "sound pedagogy."[10] Clearly, there is often a deep ideological and intellectual gulf between advocates and opponents of trigger warnings. In order to better understand trigger warnings and the competing viewpoints they inspire in students, faculty, and administrators, an exploration of the phenomenon through the lens of cognitive dissonance is warranted.

A Theoretical Understanding

Trigger warnings, as well as the situations that bring about their usage, are situated within communication contexts. Potentially triggering information must be communicated in order to trigger others, to issue a trigger warning is to communicate, and even the response of the triggered individual sends messages (either intentionally or unintentionally). Despite the fact that trigger warnings are clearly communicative phenomena, they do not fit neatly into any existing communication theories. One potential theoretical framework for trigger warnings is the theory of cognitive dissonance. Originally proposed by Leon Festinger, cognitive dissonance is "the existence of nonfitting relations among cognitions" in an individual's mind.[11] After asserting that dissonance is an uncomfortable state, Festinger argues that, in addition to trying to reduce experiences of dissonance, an individual will "actively avoid situations and information which would likely increase the dissonance."[12]

The experience of cognitive dissonance is similar to that of being triggered in at least two ways. First, both experiences involve "nonfitting relations among cognitions." While the exact nature of dissonance varies from episode to episode, all triggering events incite competing simultaneous notions such as: "I am well/I am unwell." While much of cognitive dissonance theory describes the way in which individuals cope with or seek to alleviate the experience of cognitive dissonance, Festinger notes that in "certain circumstances there are also strong and important tendencies to avoid increases of dissonance or to avoid the occurrence of dissonance."[13] Thus, trigger warnings can be viewed as a formal mechanism, or avoidance behavior, designed to reduce the experience of cognitive dissonance among students.

Context: The University of Kentucky's Common Reading Trigger Warning

Many individuals and institutions have found themselves in situations where they must make a practical decision about whether to use trigger warnings. One such instance took place at the University of Kentucky. Each year, the University of Kentucky's Common Reader Selection Committee adopts one book that all incoming freshmen must read before beginning their first semester; in 2015, that book was *Picking Cotton*, by Jennifer Thompson-Cannino, Ronald Cotton, and Erin Torneo.[14] Centering on the true story of a wrongful conviction, *Picking Cotton* addresses subjects ranging from systematic racial discrimination to sexual assault. In the book's opening chapters, a graphic firsthand account of a rape at knifepoint is described in detail by the victim herself. Not only are the specifics and consequences of this rape revisited throughout the book, other rapes are described and the wrongfully convicted male protagonist is threatened with rape while in prison. Furthermore, accounts and descriptions of systemic racial prejudice were a prominent theme in the book. In light of the above, administrators at the University of Kentucky issued a trigger warning at the institutional level for *Picking Cotton*.

After *Picking Cotton* was chosen, the Common Reader Selection Committee distributed a "Note" to the campus community that began with the following words:

> The University of Kentucky and the Common Reading Experience program recognize *Picking Cotton* needs to be read and utilized on campus with great sensitivity due to the issues it raises, such as sexual assault and racial dynamics. The book carries a trigger warning.[15]

The "carrying" of a trigger warning turned out to be true in a literal sense, as each copy of the book distributed on campus included a blue card imprinted with a content warning to readers (including the above quotation). As a further measure, the university's president, Eli Capilouto, recorded a video message for students and faculty that warned readers about the contents of the book:

> The process of reading it, I believe, will elicit sometimes searing responses or memories, and call us to question subtle perspectives and our

many differences. As we process their stories, we need to be conscious of all the dynamics the story involves. We want this to be a safe and shared experience, and the challenge and opportunity of a campus like ours is that this experience will take place among a diverse collection of backgrounds, viewpoints, and characteristics.[16]

Other institutional messaging surrounded the distribution of *Picking Cotton*. Specifically, students were informed of Title IX regulations regarding sexual assault and confidentiality when communicating details regarding an assault to UK faculty, staff, and student workers. Information was also provided to students on appropriate steps to take if they were the victim of sexual assault or racial discrimination on campus. Students were offered alternative readings and assignments if they deemed the book to be potentially triggering. For instance, students were offered an exception to the Common Reader Experience requirement that allowed them to opt not to read any of the book's chapters written by the rape victim (approximately half of the book) and potentially triggering sections of the wrongfully accused's chapters. Students were also instructed to contact administrative staff if they wished to discuss "other alternatives." Messages like those above served as the impetus for this case study and were examined using triangulated methodology.

Method

To examine the form, function, and implementation of trigger warnings related to the 2015–2016 University of Kentucky Common Reading, *Picking Cotton*, we collected data from a variety of sources. We utilized publicly available information (e.g., President Capilouto's announcement) as well as previously gathered assessment data from the 2015–2016 first-year class at the University of Kentucky. Additionally, after receiving approval from our Institutional Review Board, we provided open-ended surveys to Common Reading Experience (CRE) committee members, CRE administrators, and instructors who implemented the CRE book in their classes. Snowball sampling was used to aid in the distribution of both surveys.

The research question that guided our inquiry was: What are student, faculty, and administrator perceptions of institution-wide trigger warnings?

Results

The data gathered for this case study represent insights from students, faculty, and administration. First, we examined a survey sent to all first-year students that evaluated the CRE. We found their perspectives on potentially triggering content fell into two basic categories: *Concerned* and *Praiseful*. It should also be noted that none of the student respondents indicated being triggered by the material, but this reality is less surprising in light of the extensive "warning" messaging surrounding the book's distribution.

The first category, *Concerned*, contained students who expressed concerns that the book could be potentially "triggering" to others. One such student wrote, "The book was a good read overall. The only problem I would say is if past rape victims have to read the book, it may be hard for them relating to their past." Another indicated:

> I also think that the school should be choosing books that everyone can read (i.e., without triggering content). I understand that it is on a topic that people should be aware of and educated on and that's fine but I think if you are going to pick a book for everyone to read, it should be a book that everyone can read free from content that could bring up bad memories/feelings and even possibly cause panic or anxiety attacks.

In addition to showing concern for others, these responses further illustrate the avoidance behaviors that are often associated with cognitive dissonance. These students expressed a belief that others should be free to avoid the dissonant experience of being triggered.

The second type of response, *Praiseful*, consisted of students who praised the selection of the book, specifically in light of its potentially triggering content:

> *Picking Cotton* really surprised me. I thought UK wouldn't pick a book like that, maybe something boring or something that would effect [*sic*] us or teach us an actual lesson. *Picking Cotton* was the exact opposite and I'm glad it was the CRE book.

Another student appreciated the way the book connected to campus resources for victims of sexual assault: "I thought it was a very well chosen book, especially to show us a real life example of everything we learned in the VIP centers program, Haven." One respondent indicated initially being sensitive to the book's potentially triggering qualities, but after reading it, appreciated the book for the same reasons:

> At first when I read the discription [sic] of the book I was a bit confused on why we would real [sic] a book about rape, considering it is a common problem with students our age, and would make someone very uncomfortable when they read it. But as I read the book I was hooked and was thought this was such a good common reading experience book. I think everyone needs to read this book, to understand and realize that rape is a serious matter.

The response of the student above highlights the belief that if the reading made a student "uncomfortable," it would be deemed a poor choice. Additionally, the fact that this particular student overcame an initial cognitive dissonance while reading the book was a key component of the student's reasoning for evaluating it positively (i.e., the initial reason for perception of the selection as a negative choice led to the student being able to justify the selection).

In addition to the administrative messaging and student perspectives examined above, members of the Common Reading Committee shared their views regarding trigger warnings via our open-ended survey. One respondent shared the experience with the construction of the institutional messaging, noting that an attempt to use "fairly standard language" was made in the generation of the trigger warning. Additionally, the same respondent indicated that the university's counseling center was consulted in the message creation process.

Committee members expressed widely differing experiences and attitudes toward trigger warnings. One point of difference was in their understanding of how the trigger warnings affected the university as a whole. While one member noted that the warning (as well as the book) had a "positive" impact, another stated that "it generated broader discussion about college students and the 'need' for trigger warnings in the first place."

Committee member attitudes differed widely in regard to their "opinion" of trigger warnings. One member expressed a pragmatic perspective by indicating, "If it helps even a few students, I think it's worth it." Another committee member was less positive and expressed a view critical of the idea of trigger warnings:

> I'm not knowledgeable enough about victims/survivors of assault to know if trigger warnings have proven useful or not. It does seem a slippery slope in the context of college-level texts in the sense that most literature/art struggles with challenging issues, so at what point are trigger warnings unnecessary or in and of themselves potentially triggering?

Survey responses from faculty members who incorporated the book into their curriculum also provided insight into their students' reactions to the trigger warnings. Although several faculty members reported that the trigger warning appeared to have no effect on the class, with no students disclosing information about past assaults/injustices or asking to complete an alternative assignment, others were able to identify tangible differences compared to other CRE and teaching experiences. One faculty member reported a student who "took [the trigger warning] to heart in light of her past very negative experience." Another faculty member commented on how the trigger warning changed classroom dynamics: "It was the first encounter for most on actual trigger warnings on assignments that they were getting. Everyone was uncomfortable." The same faculty member noted that faculty status as a compulsory Title IX reporter would mean that asking for an alternative assignment would necessitate administrative intervention, a fact that resulted in cognitive dissonance between competing notions of accommodation and legal responsibility: "It became more uncomfortable when I revealed that to ask for the alt assignment was to say that you had been sexually assaulted and I would have to report it." Another instructor remarked on the perception of the book's content on students: "All of the female students were terrified of getting raped, and all of the males were scared of being accused of rape." Clearly, this instructor perceived that the content of the book negatively impacted the classroom environment, despite the administrative efforts to alleviate such outcomes.

In addition to university-supplied trigger warnings, many faculty instructors reported supplying their students with additional warnings, "I think I made sure to warn the students (verbal reminders) prior to the class sessions where we'd be discussing the book." Another echoed, "They were in the syllabus when we reviewed that at the first class session plus we reviewed them again immediately preceding discussion of the book." Yet another faculty member reiterated that alternative readings were available: "I told them . . . if they didn't want to, for any reason, read the book, they didn't have to."

Finally, instructor responses also revealed that they held varying views regarding trigger warnings. One instructor seemed almost to be "triggered" by the expression itself adding: "I really hate the expression trigger warning. The word trigger just makes me think of gun violence." Some respondents held a generally favorable view of trigger warnings: "I think they are good to include because it lets people know what to expect, so they aren't shocked when reading or viewing material." Some attempted to navigate dissonance regarding their support of trigger warnings: "I find trigger warnings to be a good courtesy for people who may suffer from combat, sexual abuse or wartime PTSD. That said, I am a strong supporter of academic freedom and the First Amendment." One respondent, effectively illustrating the range of opinions on this subject, dismissed trigger warnings as "loads of bollocks."

Implications

This case study helps to illuminate the continued importance of discussing trigger warnings in higher education, their distinctly communicative nature, and the ways in which trigger warnings may be explained by the theory of cognitive dissonance. While questions remain as to the validity of such warnings, as well as what effect they may have on free speech and intellectual and personal development, our results reinforce the notion that trigger warnings remain an issue worthy of scholarly attention. With this continued discussion comes increasing awareness, and with awareness comes the continuing disappearance of neutral ground regarding trigger warnings. As seen among the respondents in our sample, even some students are now demonstrating an understanding of potentially "triggering" phenomena and come to college with opinions and expectations regarding the use of warnings by instructors and administrators. Additionally, as seen in the above case study, some administrations have implemented trigger warnings at the institutional level. If this trend continues, instructors may increasingly be required to shift their focus from whether or not they should utilize trigger warnings to how they should deal with trigger warnings already implemented. Thus, those who work in academic contexts, regardless of their opinion on such warnings (or even their willingness to use them at all), cannot avoid the reality of trigger warnings. Though it is not known what role trigger warnings may have in the future of higher education, their influence in this present moment is clearly apparent.

The authors express their thanks to Kasey Borchardt, assistant director of the University of Kentucky's New Student and Family Programs, for her significant assistance in this project.

Notes

1. Jordan Doll, "Trauma and Free Speech in Higher Education: Do Trigger Warnings Threaten First Amendment Rights?" (Electronic Thesis, Oberlin College, 2016), https://etd.ohiolink.edu/pg_10?0::NO:10:P10_ACCESSION _NUM:oberlin1463557689.

2. Kate Manne, "Why I Use Trigger Warnings," *New York Times*, September 19, 2015, http://www.nytimes.com/2015/09/20/opinion/sunday/why-i-use -trigger-warnings.html?_r=0.

3. Greg Lukianoff and Jonathan Haidt, "The Coddling of the American Mind," *The Atlantic*, September 2015, http://www.theatlantic.com/magazine/archive/ 2015/09/the-coddling-of-the-american-mind/399356/.

4. Richard Pérez-Peña, Mitch Smith, and Stephanie Saul, "University of Chicago Strikes Back against Campus Political Correctness," *New York Times*, August 26, 2016, http://www.nytimes.com/2016/08/27/us/university-of-chi -cago-strikes-back-against-campus-political-correctness.html.

5. American Association of University Professors, "On Trigger Warnings," 2014, https://www.aaup.org/report/trigger-warnings.

6. National Coalition against Censorship, *What's All This about Trigger Warnings?* December 2015, http://ncac.org/wp-content/uploads/2015/11/NCAC- TriggerWarningReport.pdf.

7. A. Levinovitz, "Trigger Warnings and Safe Spaces on College Campuses Can Silence Religious Students," *The Atlantic*, August 30, 2016, http://www.theatlantic. com/politics/archive/2016/08/silencing-religious-students-on-campus/497951/.

8. Kevin Gannon, "UChicago's Anti-Safe Spaces Letter Isn't about Academic Freedom. It's about Power," *Vox*, August 26, 2016, http://www.vox .com/2016/8/26/12657684/chicago-safe-spaces-trigger-warnings-letter.

9. Peter Kotecki, "Schapiro to Freshmen: People Criticizing Safe Spaces 'Drives Me Nuts,'" *The Daily Northwestern*, September 20, 2016, accessed December 16, 2016, https://dailynorthwestern.com/2016/09/21/campus/schapiro -to-freshmen-people-criticizing-safe-spaces-drives-me-nuts/.

10. Angus Johnston, "Why I'll Add a Trigger Warning," *Inside Higher Ed*, May 29, 2014, https://www.insidehighered.com/views/2014/05/29/essay-why-profes sor-adding-trigger-warning-his-syllabus.

11. Leon Festinger, *A Theory of Cognitive Dissonance* (Stanford, CA: Stanford University Press, 1957), 3.

12. Ibid.

13. Ibid., 29–30.

14. Jennifer Thompson-Cannino, Ronald Cotton, and Erin Torneo, *Picking Cotton: Our Memoir of Injustice and Redemption* (New York: St. Martin's Press, 2009).

15. University of Kentucky, "Important Notice for Readers of *Picking Cotton*," April 30, 2016, https://bluegrassblade.files.wordpress.com/2015/03/cre -insert2015.pdf.

16. University of Kentucky, "Pres. Capilouto Talks about UK's 2015 Common Reading Experience," uploaded March 11, 2015, https://www.youtube.com/ watch?v=Vr4nHzh5V_A&feature=youtu.be.

Bibliography

American Association of University Professors. "On Trigger Warnings." 2014. https://www.aaup.org/report/trigger-warnings.

Doll, Jordan. "Trauma and Free Speech in Higher Education: Do Trigger Warnings Threaten First Amendment Rights?" Electronic Thesis, Oberlin College, 2016. https://etd.ohiolink.edu/pg_10?0::NO:10:P10_ACCES SION_NUM:oberlin1463557689.

Festinger, Leon. *A Theory of Cognitive Dissonance*. Stanford, CA: Stanford University Press, 1957.

Gannon, Kevin. "UChicago's Anti-Safe Spaces Letter Isn't about Academic Freedom. It's about Power." *Vox*, August 26, 2016. http://www.vox.com/2016/8/ 26/12657684/chicago-safe-spaces-trigger-warnings-letter.

Johnston, Angus "Why I'll Add a Trigger Warning." *Inside Higher Ed*, May 29, 2014. https://www.insidehighered.com/views/2014/05/29/essay-why -professor-adding-trigger-warning-his-syllabus.

Kotecki, Peter. "Schapiro to Freshmen: People Criticizing Safe Spaces 'Drives Me Nuts.'" *The Daily Northwestern*, September 20, 2016. Accessed December 16,

2016. https://dailynorthwestern.com/2016/09/21/campus/schapiro-to-fresh
men-people-criticizing-safe-spaces-drives-me-nuts/.

Levinovitz, A. "Trigger Warnings and Safe Spaces on College Campuses Can
Silence Religious Students." *The Atlantic*, August 30, 2016. http://www
.theatlantic.com/politics/archive/2016/08/silencing-religious-students-on
-campus/497951/.

Lukianoff, Greg, and Jonathan Haidt. "The Coddling of the American Mind."
The Atlantic, September 2015. http://www.theatlantic.com/magazine/
archive/2015/09/the-coddling-of-the-american-mind/399356/.

Manne, Kate. "Why I Use Trigger Warnings." *New York Times*, September
19, 2015. http://www.nytimes.com/2015/09/20/opinion/sunday/why-i-use
-trigger-warnings.html?_r=0.

National Coalition against Censorship. *What's All This about Trigger Warnings?* December 2015. http://ncac.org/wp-content/uploads/2015/11/NCAC
-TriggerWarningReport.pdf.

Pérez-Peña, Richard, Mitch Smith, and Stephanie Saul. "University of Chicago
Strikes Back against Campus Political Correctness." *New York Times*, August 26,
2016. http://www.nytimes.com/2016/08/27/us/university-of-chicago-strikes
-back-against-campus-political-correctness.html.

Thompson-Cannino, Jennifer, Ronald Cotton, and Erin Torneo. *Picking Cotton:
Our Memoir of Injustice and Redemption*. New York: St. Martin's Press, 2009.

University of Kentucky. "Important Notice for Readers of *Picking Cotton*." April
30, 2016. https://bluegrassblade.files.wordpress.com/2015/03-insert2015.
pdf.

———. "Pres. Capilouto Talks about UK's 2015 Common Reading Experience."
Uploaded March 11, 2015. https://www.youtube.com/watch?v=Vr4nHzh5V_
A&feature=youtu.be.

CHAPTER NINE

ON PRIVILEGE, AUTHORITY, AND ABUSES OF PROFESSORIAL POWER

Jami McFarland

Our feminist political hopes rest with over-sensitive students. Over-sensitive can be translated as: Sensitive to that which is not over.

—Sara Ahmed, "Against Students"[1]

Content warning: cissexism, transphobic violence, colonial violence, child abuse (sexual and physical), ableism, and molestation.

I am both an eager student and an aspiring educator. As an undergraduate student, I never had strong opinions about the use of trigger warnings—visual and/or verbal indicators that both describe content and notify audiences of forthcoming violence—in the university classroom. As a young student, trigger warnings—sometimes referred to as content warnings—were just extra text on a syllabus. I understood that if they were not for me, they were likely present for the benefit of someone else. Perhaps unsurprisingly, I was introduced to trigger warnings in women's studies courses, where subjective knowledge is valued and validated, and power, in all its various manifestations, is named and challenged. As a graduate student and an emerging educator, I have had to reconsider the pedagogical use of trigger warnings in the classroom. Pedagogically, it is my business as an educator, to care about trigger warnings. Regardless of my own politics on the subject, making the classroom accessible to all of my students is simply a component of the job, a part of responsible and attentive teaching. Not all educators, however, share a teaching philosophy that recognizes accessibility concerns.

In this case study, I offer my experience of asking a professor to consider the use of trigger warnings on the syllabus, reactions to the request, and the ensuing consequences of this request. The importance of this case study lies in the volatile interaction that transpired between student and educator and—perhaps most significantly—the disproportionate ramifications I, as the student in this particular interaction, experienced. Focusing on some of the most recent academic scholarship on trigger warnings, namely Wendy Wyatt's article "The Ethics of Trigger Warnings,"[2] while also exploring the consequences of my experience, I challenge the notion that students should be burdened with the responsibility of approaching professors with sensitive and personal information for the purpose of authenticating a request for trigger warnings to alert them to violent and/or distressing content in the course. Instead, I argue that institutions, including universities, should be held responsible for proactively endeavoring to protect the well-being of their members, including students and educators.

Literature on the topic of the use of trigger warnings in university classrooms is largely polarized. On one side, opponents of the use of trigger warnings are quick to construct the application of trigger warnings as a matter of "censorship."[3] For instance, in a 2016 letter addressed to the incoming Class of 2020,[4] John "Jay" Ellison, Dean of Students in the College at the University of Chicago, disparaged and prohibited the use of trigger warnings in the classroom and safe spaces on campus. In the letter, Dr. Ellison suggested that trigger warnings and safe spaces are antithetical to "freedom of expression," "academic freedom," and "the free exchange of ideas."[5] However, as Kevin Gannon[6] and Aaron Hanlon[7] have argued, prohibiting the use of trigger warnings in the university setting ironically censors the diversity of opinion and preserves a superficial and limited intellectual climate. On the other side of the trigger warning debate, supporters of this practice insist that the use of trigger warnings in classrooms, and on course syllabi specifically, presents factual information about content[8] at worst while at best it reduces the potential for harm to victims of systemic violence.[9]

In her article, "The Ethics of Trigger Warnings," Wyatt argues that trigger warnings are neither necessary nor unreasonable.[10] In response to such polarized discourses, emerging literature like that of Wyatt has endeavored to offer a more nuanced approach to the ethical application of trigger warnings. Wyatt proposes a "pluralistic"[11] approach that centers on "considerations of content, of context and the mutual obligations that arise from professor-students relationships."[12] Refusing to settle "on one extreme"[13] pole of the trigger warning debate, Wyatt's analysis "results in an approach that rejects trigger warnings as policy but recognizes that they may, at times, be ethically required."[14] While I appreciate Wyatt's desire for a more nuanced conversation about the application of trigger warnings, I am skeptical of a resolution that places a neoliberal onus on the individual rather than the institution. For the purpose of this case study, I would like to focus specifically on the implications and limitations of Wyatt's third category of consideration, "the mutual obligations that arise from professor-students relationships,"[15] to make a case for the institutionalization of trigger warnings in universities. For Wyatt, "ethical decision-making around the use of trigger warnings"[16] *must* be informed by a mutually shared responsibility, between professor and student, to learning. Students, Wyatt aptly notes, are agentic beings who are "capable of advocating on their own behalf" and, therefore, "should take responsibility early in each semester to connect with their professors and share their concerns."[17] What, however, are the consequences of asking students to divulge *their concerns*? Moreover, if the student does take up this responsibility, are Wyatt's expectations realistic, or even just, given the inherent power dynamic of the student-professor relationship as well as the current fraught nature of accessing disability accommodations? In what follows, I proffer my experience of asking for trigger warnings as a cautionary tale to demonstrate the limitations of Wyatt's approach, which burdens the individual and overwhelmingly places the student at risk, and to envision and agitate for the institutionalization of trigger warnings in the university classroom. Provision of trigger warnings, I argue, must be the obligation of the institution, not a mere allowance of the professor, or request by the student.

My own request for trigger warnings happened in a cross-listed women's studies graduate course. The course readings addressed many institutionally sanctioned systemic violences, including, but not limited to, colonialism, racism, misogyny, genocide, sexual assault, child abuse, and homophobia. For any student of women's studies, this is familiar thematic territory. Largely, students know that we will be addressing graphic descriptions of violence in our courses. By enrolling in courses that give critical and thoughtful space to these issues, students willingly attend to the compositions and contours of those violences to make power visible and work toward social justice. Students are, however, also often victims of the violences we study. When students ask for trigger warnings, they are asking for people and institutions to recognize that their embodied experiences are not simply thought experiments, but lived realities that have left both visible and invisible damage. When professors mistakenly interpret requests for trigger warnings as a sign of discomfort rather than as a form of accommodation, the trigger warning debate, as Angela M. Carter argues, continues to be focused on the "able-bodyminded among us."[18] Trigger warnings, thus, make visible "bodily symptoms that are characteristically invisible."[19] Although this is fairly established practice and knowledge in women's studies courses, it is neither mandated nor evenly agreed upon.

Several weeks into the course and after more than a few contentious, yet unaddressed, student disruptions within the class, I, along with my fellow classmates, began to read the assigned text for the upcoming class on the legacies of residential schools in Canada. Fittingly, the text assigned was Tomson Highway's semiautobiographical novel, *Kiss of the Fur Queen*,[20] which recounts the colonial terrors experienced by two Cree brothers who are forced into residential schools in Manitoba. Among other graphic violences, the novel, in artful prose, describes the physical and sexual abuse experienced by the semifictional Indigenous child brothers. As I read the novel, I was surprised by the violence described in the text. As a witness to too many testimonies of this particular violence, I imagined the triggered reactions of friends and colleagues, mostly women and people of color, to texts such as this one. I reread the syllabus to see if any overlooked indicators had been provided and became increasingly concerned that the professor had not provided a brief warning—either verbally in class or visually on the syllabus—that the book would explore such content. Already irritated by the professor's general lack of sensitivity to the topics we discussed, I decided to ask if the professor would consider, especially if she were to teach in women's studies again, using trigger warnings in the future.

In my initial e-mail to the professor of the course, I did the following: I asked of the professor if she would consider using trigger warnings in the future, stated briefly the purpose and importance of trigger warnings to students who suffer from systemic forms of violence, implied that I was aware that many professors avoided the use of trigger warnings in spite of substantial accessibility concerns, and finally, requested that she refrain from initiating a discussion about trigger warnings with me in person due to my own personal abilities and limitations. The professor swiftly responded; thanked me for my e-mail; and, in spite of my request to avoid a discussion in person, dismissively asked if I would consider meeting with her to have a discussion in person. In the same e-mail, she implied that I had drawn unnecessary conclusions about her and indirectly suggested that she, the professor, may also personally relate to the topics taught in class.

There must be no doubt or confusion here. I was certainly not, as many opponents of trigger warnings will inevitably argue, suggesting that *Kiss of the Fur Queen* be removed from the course. This speaks to what Sarah Orem and Neil Simpkins call the "additive" rather than "subtractive" nature of trigger warnings.[21] I did not demand that a text be *removed*; rather, I asked if trigger warnings, additional text, could be *added*. Highway's piece is invaluable literature for learning about Canada's colonial violences. It is necessarily an uncomfortable read. What I was instead suggesting was that the inclusion of trigger/content warnings on the syllabus may aid survivors of child abuse and/or colonial violence (or both) in navigating the emotional, psychosomatic terrain that is uniquely unlike the discomfort felt by the majority of the class.

To be clear, I do not want to police or delineate the contours of the experience of being triggered. Nor am I invested in policing the line between triggered feelings and feelings of discomfort, because traditionally these conversations often seek to validate narrow rather than expansive conceptualizations of trauma. However, as Carter argues, a substantial amount of literature in opposition to trigger warnings misleadingly conflates triggered feelings with any feelings of discomfort and thus this dissociation must be made when we discuss how and for whose benefit trigger warnings are being utilized within the classroom.[22] As several critical disability scholars and academics living with disabilities have already thoughtfully argued,[23] such conflations that misconstrue trauma and mental health illness "as simple discomfort instead of a true disability"[24] work to silence and invalidate legitimate accessibility and accommodation concerns. If trigger warnings were institutionalized like other accessibility needs—ramps, for instance—students would not have to substantiate their request for trigger warnings. Without an institutional trigger warning policy, students with invisible disabilities, such as post-traumatic stress disorder and/or generalized anxiety disorder, are required to press institutions for their inclusion. As Orem and Simpkins have demonstrated,[25] this overwhelmingly places students living with mental health conditions at risk for greater harm because requests for disability accommodations are often met with attitudes of condescension and dis-belief from professors, but, more importantly, from society at large.

For Wyatt, offering trigger warnings is "ethically straightforward."[26] Employing examples of her own discretion regarding trigger warnings, Wyatt suggests that there is certain content that *obviously* warrants cau-tion. Unfortunately, this has not been the case for many professors, some of whom cannot and should not be trusted with the decision of how and when to appropriately apply trigger warnings to course readings. Con-sider, for example, the psychology professor Jordan Peterson, from the University of Toronto, who most recently garnered attention for his com-ments that denounced the use of the plural pronoun "they" as singular for gender nonbinary identities in his YouTube "lecture," "Professor against Political Correctness."[27] Professors like Peterson—who make bigoted ar-guments and refuse to acknowledge the humanity or even the existence of gender nonconforming and trans folks—cannot be trusted with deciding which violences matter and which do not. In this particular case, it is clear that if a trans and/or a gender-nonconforming student were to approach Peterson with a request for alerts for transphobic content in course read-ings, Peterson would not comply.[28] Wyatt suggests that professors witness the concerns of students with respect; however, the "difficult truth," as Kimberly Dark so nicely puts it, "is that not all professors are setting up a culture of respect and environments of study that are conducive to deep and respectful learning."[29] In effect, some instances of violence are vali-dated while others are repudiated and subsequently perpetuated.

Barring overtly prejudiced professors, deciding on what material warrants such warnings may be fraught with uncertainty for even those educators who may be well intentioned. Many professors[30] argue that the question of *when* to use trigger warnings and for *what* material is confus-ing, situational, and potentially risky for educators. Thus, what is ethically straightforward for one educator, like Wyatt, may not be so for another.

Professors suggest as much when they make frank, yet simplistic arguments such as, "Faculty cannot predict in advance what will be triggering for students."[31] An argument like this diverts focus from the societal to the personal and treats violences directed at particular bodies as individual rather than systemic. Educators *can* name systemic violences like racism or homophobia even if they cannot know how those violences will affect and/or manifest in students individually. If scholars concerned with the ethics and implications of trigger warnings are to take arguments like the one presented above seriously, we must find solutions for *both* educator and student. However, if educators cannot truly discern which forms of oppression and systemic violences warrant a warning, then institutionalizing a collectively agreed-upon list of systemic violences may actually be the most beneficial solution for uncertain educators and vulnerable identities and/or bodies.

As an emerging queer educator who lives with an anxiety disorder, I am well aware of how close we are to the topics we teach and the largely inaccessible classrooms we teach them in. My intention was never to exclude educators from the discussion about individual and collective trauma but to signal toward a very immediate demand from students for trigger warnings in the classroom. My fear was that if I did indeed meet with this professor for the purpose of a seemingly inessential and ill-defined discussion, I would find myself in the complicated, power-laden position of either disclosing sensitive and personal information or being witness to her own. Prior to my request for trigger warnings, my professor had never previously indicated that she had wanted to meet with me. Aware of the power differential between educator and student, I did not want to have to substantiate or authenticate my request for trigger warnings, nor did I want to explore in private her suggestion that teachers may also be affected by the material they teach. Ultimately, given the invasive and mentally taxing nature of authenticating disabilities, especially 'invisible' disabilities,[32] I wanted to avoid an intimate and potentially harmful discussion with the professor. After seeking advice from other educators and direction from the university's disability services, I sent a response to the professor, repeating that an in-person discussion would not be best because of my own limitations. In addition to this, I suggested that if she thought that the conversation was absolutely necessary that we then might have it via e-mail so I could be cooperative while working within my abilities.

Moreover, prior to sending my response, I electronically submitted an assignment to the professor in an entirely different e-mail thread. In both e-mail threads, one conversational and one professional, the professor pressed me, yet again, for an in-person meeting. If I had not felt pressure to satiate professorial authority before, I certainly did when the professor's groundless requests began to permeate my academic work. Whether consciously or unconsciously executed, the message was clear: This conversation was happening in a power dynamic in which I was the evaluated and she was the evaluator. At this point, I had no idea how much this power dynamic would be exercised to her benefit.

Although this was not my objective, I knew that when I asked the professor to consider the use of trigger warnings that I was implicitly challenging her pedagogy and consequently her authority. Trigger warnings, Orem and Simpkins suggest, "*do* allow students to challenge professors' traditional authority" because "[t]hey represent a site where students are rejecting a passive role in the classroom."[33] Perhaps, my request for trigger warnings became a site of conflict precisely because "[t]rigger warnings work to equalize the traditionally hierarchal relationship between professors and students in the classroom."[34] However, if met with condescending or doubtful attitudes, requests for trigger warnings within the existing student-professor power dynamic have the potential to be harmful. Although Wyatt makes clear that professors "must be cognizant"[35] of the power dynamic present between student and professor, many professors may be unaware of how the power differential is felt and embodied by their students.

What was once uncomfortable yet manageable had become overwhelmingly threatening. Put simply, I felt I was being aggressively hailed to explain my request and my inability to discuss this request in person. To avoid the seemingly unavoidable conversation with the professor, I made the decision to skip the next class with the hope that the conversation would be abandoned. This resulted in yet another, albeit (likely) well-intentioned, e-mail from the professor. She explained, in her e-mail, that she noticed that I was absent from class and cared about my academic success and well-being. The professor might have demonstrated that she "cared" by respecting my set limitations as a student with an anxiety disorder. Moreover, she might have interpreted my request for trigger warnings as an expression of me proactively maintaining my "well-being." Instead, she habitually referred me to mental health resources on campus.

The content of her e-mail was indicative of the advice listed in the op-ed, "Trigger Warnings Are Flawed," in which seven humanities professors suggest that educators should refer students to "counseling resources, support groups, advising, [and] relevant student organizations."[36] The dangerous and misinformed assumption being drawn in their instruction is that students are not taking care of their mental health, and if they are, they are doing it incorrectly because it shows in their actions. Correspondingly, trigger warnings, by their conceptualization, are constructed as simple fixes to trauma and mental illness rather than one of many tools available to students who are living with trauma and/or disability. Her response was mechanical, yet it mirrored the dominant academic response typical of "concerned" professors. In the future, established responses, like that of my professor, will require further critical and reflective intervention from educators and scholars who theorize trigger warnings and their use.

I decided that perhaps it was best to reassert my boundaries and limitations in person while thanking her for the work I could see her doing—even if that work was more taxing than helpful for me. To be cooperative, within my abilities, I approached her the following week in class, during our short break. I thanked her for her e-mails, assured her that I was taking care of my mental health as I saw fit, and reiterated that a meeting was unnecessary. At first, she conceded that an in-person meeting probably was not best because she could see that the suggestion had caused me distress. I felt relieved. I started to envision a return to an inadequate, yet manageable, classroom. It appeared at first that she was going to respect my limitations, even if she did not understand them. Finally, my simple request for her to *consider* the use of trigger warnings, which had spiraled into an invasive probing for answers, meaning, and intelligibility, was coming to a close. "But why?" she wanted to know, would I not meet with her? She continued to ask questions and insinuated that if I was able-minded enough to attend class, then I was able to have a "professional" meeting with her. I was dumbfounded by her conclusions. I reiterated that my anxiety disorder would not allow for a meeting and that I would consider an in-person meeting once outside of the student-professor power dynamic. This disclosure greatly affected the professor. She became visibly upset and the conversation moved from invasive and suspicious to hostile and accusatory. I apologized for upsetting her and returned to class where I started to experience discernable panic attacks. I removed myself before the class resumed to ensure that I was not a distraction to the professor and/or my peers.

The actions taken following this conversation can only be described as an abuse of professorial power. Immediately after class, the professor notified me via e-mail that my behavior was inappropriate and warranted my removal from her class. In addition to this, she asserted that I would not be allowed back into the classroom unless I met with her in private so she could outline what was expected of me in her classroom. Panicked and frightened, I sent all of her e-mails—there were several—to both my department and a third party official to, first, confirm if she could exercise her power to ban me from class and, second, make a complaint about her behavior. The professor's behavior and classroom were deemed inappropriate and hostile by outside officials. Consequently, I was removed from the physical space of her classroom and fulfilled the remainder of the course requirements from home. My assignments, some of which had already been completed or started, were altered and re-weighted to match the new arrangement. The opportunity to learn alongside my peers was seized. I avoided parts of campus that she frequented in fear of confrontation. These are just a few of the consequences I have faced after approaching a professor with my concerns. I imagine that this conflict had repercussions for my professor as well. I can, of course, only speculate that this conflict would not have taken place had trigger warnings been mandated by my university.

If, as Wendy Wyatt suggests, the decision of when to use trigger warnings and for what content is "ethically straightforward" and even "ethically obligatory," [37] why are specific trigger warnings not already institutionalized? If trigger warnings were uniformly obvious to professors, why was a trigger warning missing for content that described the sexual molestation of a child in my course? Moreover, why should students be burdened with explaining to professors why this might be disabling to some students? In this paper, I have argued that the well-intentioned albeit imprudent approach of Wyatt, which requires students to divulge personal and potentially re-traumatizing material to a professor, has the capacity to be dangerous for both student and professor. As argued throughout, it is overwhelmingly the student who is placed at risk in the power-laden student-professor relationship. I have offered my experience to suggest that the use of trigger warnings should be informed by university policy, as acknowledged by a collectively agreed upon, preestablished list of systemic violences, rather than simply left to the discretion of the individual professor who may carry conscious or unconscious prejudices. Such an approach to the application of trigger warnings, I suggest, minimizes the likelihood of inflicting further harm to victims of systemic violence, while simultaneously protecting both student and educator.

Notes

1. Sara Ahmed, "Against Students," *New Inquiry*, June 29, 2015.
2. Wendy Wyatt, "The Ethics of Trigger Warnings," *Teaching Ethics* 16, no. 1 (2016): 17–35.
3. *The Berkshire Eagle*, "Our Opinion: 'Trigger Warnings' ahead," June 3, 2014, accessed September 12, 2016, http://www.berkshireeagle.com/stories/our-opinion-trigger-warnings-ahead, 371759.
4. Leonor Vivanco and Dawn Rhodes, "U. of C. Tells Incoming Freshmen It Does Not Support 'Trigger Warnings' or 'Safe Spaces,'" *Chicago Tribune*, August 25, 2016, accessed October 3, 2016. http://www.chicagotribune.com/news/local/breaking/ct-university-of-chicago-safe-spaces-letter-met-20160825-story.html.
5. Ibid.
6. Kevin Gannon, "UChicago's Anti-Safe Space Letter Isn't about Academic Freedom. It's about Power," *Vox*, August 26, 2016, accessed September 15, 2016, http://www.vox.com/2016/8/26/12657684/chicago-safe-spaces-trigger-warnings-letter. html.
7. Aaron R. Hanlon, "How to Fix Our Toxic Debate about Political Correctness on Campus," *New Republic*, September 7, 2016, accessed September 15, 2016, https://newrepublic.com/article/136600/fix-toxic-debate-political-correctness-campus.html.
8. Lindy West, "Trigger Warnings Don't Hinder Freedom of Expression; They Expand It," *The Guardian*, August 18, 2016, accessed September 14, 2016. https://www.theguardian.com/education/commentisfree/2015/aug/18/trigger-warnings-dont-hinder-freedom-expression.html.
9. Bailey Loverin, "Trigger Warnings Avert Trauma: Opposing View," *USA Today*, April 21, 2014, accessed September 14, 2016, http://www.usatoday.com/story/opinion/2014/21/trigger-warnings-ptsd-bailey-loverin-editorials-debates/7985479/.
10. Wyatt, "The Ethics of Trigger Warnings."
11. Ibid., 19.

12. Ibid., 31.

13. Ibid., 32.

14. Ibid., 31.

15. Ibid.

16. Ibid., 25.

17. Ibid., 29.

18. Angela M. Carter, "Teaching with Trauma: Trigger Warnings, Feminism, and Disability Pedagogy," *Disability Studies Quarterly* 36, no. 4 (2016).

19. Sarah Orem and Neil Simpkins, "Weepy Rhetoric, Trigger Warnings, and the Work of Making Mental Illness Visible in the Writing Classroom," *Enculturation: A Journal of Rhetoric, Writing and Culture* (December 16, 2015).

20. Tomson Highway, *Kiss of the Fur Queen* (Norman: University of Oklahoma Press, 1998).

21. Orem and Simpkins, "Weepy Rhetoric."

22. Carter, "Teaching with Trauma."

23. Orem and Simpkins, "Weepy Rhetoric"; Carter, "Teaching with Trauma"; Maisha Z. Johnson, "How the Trigger Warning Debate Exposes Our F*cked Up Views on Mental Illness," *Everyday Feminism*, August 29, 2016, accessed September 15, 2016, http://everydayfeminism.com/author/mjohnson. Margaret Price, *Mad at School: Rhetorics of Mental Disability and Academic Life* (Ann Arbor: University of Michigan Press, 2001).

24. Orem and Simpkins, "Weepy Rhetoric."

25. Ibid.

26. Wyatt, "The Ethics of Trigger Warnings," 18.

27. Jordan B. Peterson, "Professor against Political Correctness: Part I," YouTube video, 57:42, posted September 27, 2016, https://www.youtube.com/watch?v=fvPgjg201w0.

28. Ibid.

29. Kimberly Dark, "What the Myth of 'Oversensitive Students' Gets Wrong about Trigger Warnings," *Everyday Feminism*, September 25, 2016, accessed October 3, 2016, http://everydayfeminism.com/2016/09/myth-of-oversensitive-students/.html.

30. 7 Humanitias Professors, "Trigger Warnings Are Flawed," *Inside Higher Ed*, May 29, 2014, accessed September 7, 2016, https://www.insidehighered.com/views/2014/05/29/essay-faculty-members-about-why-they-will-not-use-trigger-warnings.html; Jack Halberstam, "Trigger Happy: From Content Warning to Censorship," *Signs* 42, no. 2 (Winter 2017).

31. 7 Humanitias Professors, "Trigger Warnings Are Flawed."

32. Orem and Simpkins, "Weepy Rhetoric."

33. Ibid.

34. Ibid.
35. Wyatt, "The Ethics of Trigger Warnings."
36. 7 Humanitias Professors, "Trigger Warnings Are Flawed."
37. Wyatt, "The Ethics of Trigger Warnings."

Bibliography

Ahmed, Sara. "Against Students." *New Inquiry*, June 29, 2015.

The Berkshire Eagle, Pittsfield, MA "Our Opinion: 'Trigger Warnings' Ahead." June 3, 2014. Accessed September 12, 2016. http://www.berkshireeagle.com/stories/our-opinion-trigger-warnings-ahead, 371759.

Carter, Angela M. "Teaching with Trauma: Trigger Warnings, Feminism, and Disability Pedagogy." *Disability Studies Quarterly* 36, no. 4 (2016).

Dark, Kimberly. "What the Myth of 'Oversensitive Students' Gets Wrong about Trigger Warnings." *Everyday Feminism*, September 25, 2016. Accessed October 3, 2016. http://everydayfeminism.com/2016/09/myth-of-oversensitive-students/.html.

Gannon, Kevin. "UChicago's Anti-Safe Space Letter Isn't about Academic Freedom. It's about Power." *Vox*, August 26, 2016. Accessed September 15, 2016. http://www.vox.com/2016/8/26/12657684/chicago-safe-spaces-trigger-warnings-letter.html.

Halberstam, Jack. "Trigger Happy: From Content Warning to Censorship." *Signs* 42, no. 2 (Winter 2017). http://signsjournal.org/currents-trigger-warnings/halberstam/.

Hanlon, Aaron R. "How to Fix Our Toxic Debate about Political Correctness on Campus." *New Republic*, September 7, 2016. Accessed September 15, 2016. https://newrepublic.com/article/136600/fix-toxic-debate-political-correctness-campus.html.

Highway, Tomson. *Kiss of the Fur Queen*. Norman: University of Oklahoma Press, 1998.

Johnson, Maisha Z. "How the Trigger Warning Debate Exposes Our F*cked Up Views on Mental Illness." *Everyday Feminism*, August 29, 2016. Accessed September 15, 2016. http://everydayfeminism.com/author/mjohnson.

Loverin, Bailey. "Trigger Warnings Avert Trauma: Opposing View." *USA Today*, April 21, 2014. Accessed September 14, 2016, http://www.usatoday.com/story/opinion/2014/21/trigger-warnings-ptsd-bailey-loverin-editorials-debates/7985479/.

Orem, Sarah, and Neil Simpkins. "Weepy Rhetoric, Trigger Warnings, and the Work of Making Mental Illness Visible in the Writing Classroom." *Enculturation: A Journal of Rhetoric, Writing and Culture* (December 16, 2015).

Peterson, Jordan B. "Professor against Political Correctness: Part I." YouTube video, 57:42. Posted September 27, 2016. https://www.youtube.com/watch?v=fv Pgjg201w0.

Price, Margaret. *Mad at School: Rhetorics of Mental Disability and Academic Life.* Ann Arbor: University of Michigan Press, 2001.

7 Humanities Professors (Elizabeth Freeman, Brian Herrera, Nat Hurley, Homay King, Dana Luciano, Dana Seitler, and Patricia White). "Trigger Warnings Are Flawed." *Inside Higher Ed*, May 29, 2014. Accessed September 7, 2016. https://www.insidehighered.com/views/2014/05/29/essay -faculty-members-about-why-they-will-not-use-trigger-warnings.html.

Vivanco, Leonor, and Dawn Rhodes. "U. of C. Tells Incoming Freshmen It Does Not Support 'Trigger Warnings' or 'Safe Spaces.'" *Chicago Tribune*, August 25, 2016. Accessed October 3, 2016. http://www.chicagotribune .com/news/local/breaking/ct-university-of-chicago-safe-spaces-letter-met-20160825-story.html.

West, Lindy. "Trigger Warnings Don't Hinder Freedom of Expression; They Expand It." *The Guardian*, August 18, 2016. Accessed September 14, 2016. https://www.theguardian.com/education/commentisfree/2015/aug/18/trig ger-warnings-dont-hinder-freedom-expression.html.

Wyatt, Wendy. "The Ethics of Trigger Warnings." *Teaching Ethics* 16, no. 1 (2016): 17–35.

CHAPTER TEN

TRIGGER WARNINGS, PROTECTIONISM, AND THE FEMINIST STUDENT SUBJECT

Pinky Hota

How do trigger warnings, seen by some as tools of protectionist feminism and born from debates about the gendered body, sexual violence, and the body as a bearer of trauma, operate in the creation and disciplining of feminist student subjects? To answer this question, I turn to a discussion about how trigger warnings become implicated in reinforcing gendered stereotypes about female students. I attempt to show how trigger warnings might ultimately become tools through which a masculinist liberalism insistently invokes ideals of academic freedom and free speech to reinscribe female students as too sensitive to injury through intellectual debate. Amid larger debates about how liberal ideals of academic freedom and free speech are under siege in a climate of intolerance among an easily offended new generation of college students, I suggest that trigger warnings are becoming deployed as tools through which female students are reinscribed as vulnerable and coddled, thereby muffling their agentive intellectual and activist engagements. Though embedded within a larger political climate in which trauma has become almost fundamental to being recognized as a valuable political subject,[1] trigger warnings have become particularly indicted as creating and consolidating infantilized subjects who shy away from critical inquiry. This chapter does not attempt to argue against the role of trigger warnings in abetting increasing claims to trauma. Nor does it seek to make normative claims about their relationship to academic freedom and the devolution of critical inquiry on college campuses. Instead it asks: How and why does the dismissal of trauma and trigger warnings become entry points into the larger denial of substantive political issues? At what point do we stop insisting that trigger warnings can only be associated with infantile claims to trauma and thus should be wholly dismissed as lacking any political import whatsoever? And how does such an apoliticization of trigger warnings and debates about academic freedom become significant when they concern female students?

But first, because I'm an anthropologist, I must root these in particulars of historical time, institutional space, and sociocultural context. I teach at Smith College, where trigger warnings are not uncommon in the classroom space. Professors include them in lectures, students include them in presentations in class, and students employ the verb "triggered" in discussions of violent material, including film, poetry, and video games. In so doing, students attempt to demonstrate their understanding of speech as more than sound, as speech acts that do something in the world, including inflict violence. Through their use of trigger warnings, it could then be surmised that students at Smith attempt to grapple with a series of intellectually sophisticated claims that undergird an understanding of how images and speech can themselves do violence. The students also implicitly display a particular understanding of trigger warnings as feminist practice. Indeed, if uncurtailed speech assumes an unmarked masculine audience, trigger warnings remind us not only that bodies in the audience might be bearers of trauma but also that the forms of violence and trauma might be gendered, including domestic violence, rape, and sexual assault. How, then, did the use of trigger warnings become implicated in two incidents at Smith College where students' understanding became instead interpreted as acts of withdrawal from intellectual inquiry, and students' activism got interpreted as intolerance?

Free Speech and the Ignorance of Racial Injury

In 2014, Wendy Kaminer, a fierce advocate for free speech and a Smith alumna, participated in an off-campus panel for Smith College alumnae aimed at "challenging the ideological echo chamber." In her remarks, while discussing the teaching of an American classic such as Mark Twain's *Huckleberry Finn*, Kaminer described the term "the N word" as a euphemism and questioned its use. To underscore her point, Kaminer uttered the word in its entirety, and, according to some reports, she followed by saying that "nothing happened" after she had said the word, as if to reiterate that words in and of themselves, in fact, cause no harm. Kaminer insisted that her utterance be understood in the context of discussing "language, literature or prejudice" rather than as an epithet.[2] On campus, this incident led to outrage among some faculty and students, leading the president of the college, Kathleen McCartney, to issue an apology expressing regret that "some students and faculty were hurt" and made to "feel unsafe" by Kaminer's remarks.

Kaminer herself took issue to the fact that the panel was intended to be a discussion of free speech and it was in this context that she formulated her example. In an opinion piece following the incident, Kaminer expressed her regret that the panel's transcript had been printed in Smith's college newspaper, *The Sophian*, with the following "trigger/content warning": "Racism/racial slurs, ableist slurs, antisemitic language, anti-Muslim/Islamophobic language, anti-immigrant language, sexist/misogynistic slurs, references to race-based violence, references to antisemitic violence."

In her opinion piece, Kaminer self-identified as an equality or individual rights feminist and an early opponent of late twentieth-century "protectionist" feminism. She insisted that when "students talk about threats to their safety and demand access to 'safe spaces,' they're often talking about the threat of unwelcome speech and demanding protection from the emotional disturbances sparked by unsettling ideas."[3] Kaminer went on to make connections between trigger warnings and a larger embracing of censorship by progressives. Moreover, she indicted three big forces as key influences on the increasing use of trigger warnings—the feminist antiporn crusades, the pop-psychology recovery movement, and the emergence of multiculturalism on campuses. Kaminer insisted that the logic of protectionist feminism linked the censorship of pornography to trigger warnings, which, in her analysis, seemed merely two iterations of the same tendency to protect women from harm, thereby making them appear vulnerable rather than capable. Kaminer went on to further link the proliferation of trigger warnings to the increasing influence of the psychological language of trauma. Troublingly, she linked the supposed dilution of abuse to what she insisted were rising claims to oppression brought by historically marginalized groups who are increasingly present on college campuses. In this way, Kaminer linked protectionism to the weak feminine subject, thereby precisely reinscribing the feminist student as weak, vulnerable, and in need of special protections. Moreover, she also linked such protectionism of female subjects to the protection of minorities, not only implicitly feminizing minorities, but also reducing structural inequities and historical oppression to individualized claims of injury through the use of pseudo-psychology.

Kaminer's assertions illustrate two competing strands of feminist thought—a feminism that insists that women can only be equal to men without claiming "special" protections and accommodations, that the language of gender masks the sameness of political bodies, and another that acknowledges gender to be not just at the heart of bodily experience but of political subjectivities. These strands of feminist thought not only have differing vantage points on free speech and trigger warnings but also on what constitutes the ideal feminist student subject. Contrasting an interpretation of trigger warnings as born of feminist assertions about the body as a site of gendered violence, trauma, linguistic vulnerability, and the ability of words to injure, Kaminer's feminism believes precisely in a masculinist liberal ideal—of free speech at all costs, of creating "tough," even hawkish, feminists who can withstand injurious speech and are not seen as vulnerable or reluctant to participate in debate. At an event organized by faculty in the Africana Studies Department in the wake of Kaminer's remarks, faculty speakers asserted that Kaminer's use of "the N word" could never be explained as "doing nothing" or running no risk of injuring. In his remarks, Professor Kevin Quashie drew on Donna Haraway to urge students to think about the "non-innocence of the category woman" precisely to draw students' attention to the potential for aggressive liberal white feminism's complicity in injuring ethnic and racial minorities.[4] In so doing, Quashie drew attention to the fact that liberalism had always secured certain individuals' freedoms at the cost of marginalized others— and that both white liberal feminism and ideas of free speech must reckon with the historical circumstances out of which liberal ideals were birthed in order for feminism to account for the struggles of other marginalized groups marked by race, ethnicity, and class.

Kaminer's use of a racial slur as instrument is worth dwelling on, not just because she uses it to lament the new feminist students as soft, vulnerable, and overly protected. Literary scholars and gender theorists have already significantly rebutted Kaminer's insistence that words do nothing. Judith Butler, for example, has pointed out that theorists of hate speech have focused too much on comparisons between how words cause injury and the infliction of physical pain—her counterargument emphasizes that language can do injury because it is responsible for the social being of the body.[5] Per Butler, speech acts can be a threat precisely because they invoke the moment of social formation and because a person's social being is dependent on the address by the Other. Drawing on Louis Althusser, Butler argues that hate speech not only injures, but it also constructs one's social position through the process of social interpellation. The consequence of address is, therefore, that the addressee occupies that social/cultural position that is implied by this speech act.[6] Kaminer's use of "the N word," then, is an immediate harkening back to the historical relations within which the black subject was formed through/as epithet.

Moreover, Butler reminds us that language has agency independent of the speaker and that "an utterance performs meanings not precisely those that are stated or, indeed, capable of being stated at all."[7] Drawing on Foucault, she insists that power is diffused in language and subjects that constitute power.[8] Hence the danger of critical discourse about hate language: It, in a way, reproduces or at least invokes (in a classroom) "the sensibility of racism, the trauma and, for some, the excitement [of having power]."[9] Indeed, even as Kaminer insisted that her use of a racial epithet be understood in context of intellectual discussion, her invocation of such a charged and forbidden word precisely aimed to summon the immediate tense power that reverberated through its utterance and its ability to shock, provoke, and silence.

Christine Lagarde and Intellectual Intolerance

In 2014, the managing director of the International Monetary Fund (IMF), Christine Lagarde, was invited to deliver the 2014 commencement speech at Smith College. A week before she was due to speak, Lagarde withdrew as speaker due to faculty and student protests over the IMF's policies. President McCartney announced the decision less than a week before the commencement ceremony. According to McCartney, Lagarde wrote: "In the last few days, it has become evident that a number of students and faculty members would not welcome me as a commencement speaker. I respect their views, and I understand the vital importance of academic freedom. However, to preserve the celebratory spirit of commencement day, I believe it is best to withdraw my participation." Former

Smith College president, Ruth Simmons, instead went on to deliver the commencement address.

The *Washington Post* reported Lagarde's withdrawal as one of many similar incidents involving prominent speakers across college campuses.[10] It noted that Lagarde is one of the most accomplished and powerful women in the world, and the article detailed the several positions of power she had held—as the first female head of the IMF, the first female finance minister of a G8 nation, and the first female chairman of international law firm Baker & McKenzie. In this sense, the *Post* underscored Lagarde's undeniable qualifications as a speaker at a women's college that purports to have a tradition of cultivating young women to be leaders.

The furor that ensued echoed arguments that claimed academic freedom and free speech as dangerously compromised on American campuses. In an article in *The Atlantic*, Greg Lukianoff and Jonathan Haidt call this phenomenon "the coddling of the American mind."[11] The title of their essay is no doubt a nod to Allan Bloom's book *The Closing of the American Mind* that rued that by encouraging a climate of vulgar liberalism and an embracing of cultural relativism, higher education institutions were failing democracy and undermining critical thinking.[12] It is unclear if Lukianoff and Haidt agree with Bloom and locate the debates around academic freedom and free speech on the same continuum. However, they insist that the developments they describe on campuses in the present day are quite different from those earlier debates and revisions in the 1980s and 1990s that aimed at political correctness. Describing these earlier debates as necessary for greater inclusiveness, Lukianoff and Haidt contrast them with current developments on campuses as merely impulses of "vindictive protectiveness." The authors assert that, while the earlier movements toward greater political correctness sought to restrict speech (specifically hate speech aimed at marginalized groups), it also sought to challenge the literary, philosophical, and historical canon to include diverse perspectives. Dismissing the possibility that trigger warnings and the debates they engender could possibly bring about any critical reflection on liberal ideals or their influence on pedagogical cultures, Lukianoff and Haidt sharply contrast these earlier remediations with what they see as a current tendency to focus largely on emotional well-being rather than political issues. They insist that new protectionist measures presume an extraordinary fragility of the collegiate psyche, ultimately aiming only to protect students from psychological harm. Specifically invoking the Lagarde case, the authors ask why two prominent female speakers, the former U.S. Secretary of State Condoleezza Rice and the International Monetary Fund's managing director Christine Lagarde, were disinvited from speaking at college commencement events in 2014. The authors draw attention to their power as female role models occupying positions of power rarely held by women, writing:

> Rice was the first black female secretary of state; Lagarde was the first woman to become finance minister of a G8 country and the first female head of the IMF. Both speakers could have been seen as highly successful role models for female students, and Rice for minority students as well. But the critics, in effect, discounted any possibility of something positive coming from those speeches. Members of an academic community should of course be free to raise questions about Rice's role in the Iraq War or to look skeptically at the IMF's policies. But should dislike of *part* of a person's record disqualify her altogether from sharing her perspectives?[13]

Insisting that Rice and Lagarde's professional records should in no way be deterrents, Lukianoff and Haidt discuss the protesting students as intolerant of differing perspectives and unmindful of the women's powerful iconicity. Far from discussing the complicated nature of how a myopic focus on female leadership can whitewash the imperialist, hegemonic structures and institutions with which the leaders were associated, the authors instead paternalistically minimize the students' objections as ultimately detrimental to their own intellectual and professional progress.

Lukianoff and Haidt, like Kaminer, insist that psychological language has been instrumental in creating a fragile student who relies on the language of psychological trauma to shy away from intellectual engagement. Like Kaminer, they use the language of psychological trauma and psychopathology to insist that structural and political economic issues could not leave a trace on individual psyches. Others have echoed such a criticism of the rise of claims to trauma. Lauren Berlant has argued that the ubiquity of citizen claims to trauma has created a universal victimhood that turns national pain into a banality—a "crumbling archive of dead signs and tired plots."[14] But at the same time, Berlant has also been careful to parse out the neglected intimate and affective register in which politics unfolds and is experienced. This sharply contrasts dismissals such as those of Lukianoff and Haidt that insist that any politics located in psyches and bodies can only be spurious, ignoring the affective dimensions of political life and the public sphere and politics as embodied practice.

With this example I want to note another aspect of how arguments about academic freedom often muffle the agentive actions of feminist student activists. When students at Smith began protesting Christine Lagarde's invitation, they began to investigate the operations of the International Monetary Fund in the world's poorest, most debt-ridden economies to begin asking questions about the IMF's complicity in developed countries' control over less developed countries. Some students began to engage with how IMF policies were seen as antidevelopmental, how their policies led to losses of output and employment in economies where incomes were low and unemployment was high. Moreover, the students noted that the burden of the resultant deflation was disproportionately borne by the poor. Through their engagements, these students then began to consider the gap between macroeconomic policy as theoretical framework and the local economic conditions, cultures, and environments of countries to which policy reform is applied.

Yet even though students posed and thought through these sophisticated questions about the role of transnational aid organizations in perpetuating economic inequity which, one would agree, showed a deepening of intellectual inquiry and a serious consideration of forces structuring socioeconomic inequities in the world, these students were nonetheless described as "coddled" rather than as politically active and intellectually engaged. In the petition against Lagarde, Smith students asserted that the "IMF has been a primary culprit in the failed developmental policies implanted in some of the world's poorest countries. This has led directly to the strengthening of imperialist and patriarchal systems that oppress and abuse women worldwide." In so doing, they showed their understanding of the ways in which gender was embedded in larger questions of political economy. Far from the media's facile assertions that Lagarde, as a woman, was an appropriate role model for a feminist institution such as Smith, Smith students displayed a critical engagement with the forces that structure the inequality of women and thus inform their contemporary version of feminism. Moreover, at a time when youth are lamented as uninterested in politics, these students engaged in a form of protest politics that can be seen as vital for political and civic engagement. Yet once again, masculinist liberal ideals of free speech and academic freedom were invoked to reinscribe these students as coddled and intolerant, rather than as politically engaged.

These incidents at Smith College illustrate several recurrent refrains in discussions of trigger warnings, academic freedom, and free speech. A prominent one is commentators' insistence that the rise of the language of psychological injury is to be blamed for the increasing use of trigger warnings. It should be borne in mind that psychological and emotional work has long been associated with a feminine subject, and a duality between the rationally debating and the affective, emotive subject has frequently been used to draw lines between gendered ways of thinking. As a corollary, it appears that those most vociferous critiques of trigger warnings draw connections between affective, emotive language and the language of trauma and oppression, thereby attempting a pejorative feminization of minority speakers who dare lay claim to pasts marked by historical oppression and reducing structural and political injury to individual pathology. Moreover, these instances invite us to think about what, if anything, should be the aims of feminist pedagogy and their relationship to academic freedom and free speech? Should we aim to create students who can think, debate, and withstand masculinist liberal ideals? Or should we aim to decenter normative expectations of intellectual engagement to instead craft new feminist pedagogical practices? These are not questions that can be immediately answered but are worth considering.

Notes

1. Lauren Berlant, *The Queen of America Goes to Washington City: Essays on Sex and Citizenship* (Durham, NC: Duke University Press, 1997).

2. Wendy Kaminer, "The Progressive Ideas behind the Lack of Free Speech on Campus," *Washington Post*, February 20, 2015, https://www.washington post.com/opinions/the-progressive-ideas-behind-the-lack-of-free-speech-on -campus/2015/02/20/93086efe-b0e7-11e4-886b-c22184f27c35_story.html?utm _term=.3a8e380c02bb.

3. Ibid.

4. Donna Jeanne Haraway, "A Cyborg Manifesto: Science, Technology, and Socialist-Feminism in the Late Twentieth Century," in *Simians, Cyborgs, and Women: The Reinvention of Nature*, 149–82 (New York: Routledge, 1991).

5. Judith Butler, *Excitable Speech: A Politics of the Performative* (New York: Routledge, 1997).

6. Ibid., 19.

7. Ibid., 9–10.

8. Ibid., 36.

9. Ibid., 37.

10. Abby Phillip, "One of the Most Powerful Women in the World Won't Speak at Smith College after Protests," *Washington Post*, May 12, 2014, accessed December 13, 2016, https://www.washingtonpost.com/news/post-nation/wp/2014/05/12/one-of-the-most-powerful-women-in-the-world-wont-speak-at-smith-college-after-protests/.

11. Greg Lukianoff and Jonathan Haidt, "The Coddling of the American Mind," *The Atlantic*, September 2015, http://www.theatlantic.com/magazine/archive/2015/09/the-coddling-of-the-american-mind/399356/.

12. Allan Bloom, *The Closing of the American Mind: How Higher Education Has Failed Democracy and Impoverished the Souls of Today's Students* (New York: Simon & Schuster, 1987).

13. Lukianoff and Haidt, "The Coddling of the American Mind."

14. Berlant, *The Queen of America Goes to Washington City*, 2.

Bibliography

Berlant, Lauren. *The Queen of America Goes to Washington City: Essays on Sex and Citizenship*. Durham, NC: Duke University Press, 1997.

Bloom, Allan. *The Closing of the American Mind: How Higher Education Has Failed Democracy and Impoverished the Souls of Today's Students*. New York: Simon & Schuster, 1987.

Butler, Judith. *Excitable Speech: A Politics of the Performative*. New York: Routledge, 1997.

Haraway, Donna Jeanne. "A Cyborg Manifesto: Science, Technology, and Socialist-Feminism in the Late Twentieth Century." In *Simians, Cyborgs, and Women: The Reinvention of Nature*, 149–82. New York: Routledge, 1991.

Kaminer, Wendy. "The Progressive Ideas behind the Lack of Free Speech on Campus." *Washington Post*, February 20, 2015. https://www.washingtonpost.com/opinions/the-progressive-ideas-behind-the-lack-of-free-speech-on-campus/2015/02/20/93086efe-b0e7-11e4-886b-c22184f27c35_story.html?utm_term=.3a8e380c02bb.

Lukianoff, Greg, and Jonathan Haidt. "The Coddling of the American Mind." *The Atlantic*, September 2015. http://www.theatlantic.com/magazine/archive/2015/09/the-coddling-of-the-american-mind/399356/.

Phillip, Abby. "One of the Most Powerful Women in the World Won't Speak at Smith College after Protests." *Washington Post*, May 12, 2014. Accessed December 13, 2016. https://www.washingtonpost.com/news/post-nation/wp/2014/05/12/one-of-the-most-powerful-women-in-the-world-wont-speak-at-smith-college-after-protests/.

CHAPTER ELEVEN

BEYOND TRIGGER WARNINGS
Handling Traumatic Topics in
Classroom Discussion
Kari Storla

I began my teaching career at a time when concerns about trigger warnings in the college classroom were coming to a head. Equipped with the naive idealism of the new instructor, I wholeheartedly embraced trigger warnings, sure that this was the answer to fostering class discussions on difficult topics. I thought that by simply giving people enough time to prepare, they would be able to discuss topics such as racial and sexual discrimination, despite it still not being easy to do so. It should come as no surprise that my first class discussion focused on such a topic was, in many ways, disastrous—awkward silences, strident objections from a minority of students claiming that sexual assault was almost always falsely reported, and at least one student on the verge of tears. While that class period was by no means worthless, it, along with my own research on sexual assault and trauma, did make me realize that there was a problem with trigger warnings. Or, more specifically, that there was a problem with expecting trigger warnings to shoulder the entire burden of coping with trauma in the classroom.

The debate over trigger warnings is often presented as a choice between two options, academic liberty and free speech vs. caring responsibility and safe spaces. This dichotomy, however, is a false one; true academic freedom cannot exist outside of a safe space. In many ways, this relationship between academic freedom and safe spaces can be thought of as similar to one of the arguments for tenure: Just as academics might curtail their research without the safety offered by tenure, so too might students curb their speech without the security of a nonthreatening classroom environment. In neither the case of research nor of college classes, however, must this safety equal comfort.

Even those who do not see trigger warnings as inherently opposed to free speech may still hold reservations. Trigger warnings, in other words, can potentially create problems as well as solve them. While they have the ability to forewarn students of content that may evoke a psychological trauma and allow them to approach it in the way they find most suitable, it may also work to spotlight their trauma to others, making it an undesirably visible issue rather than relieving a relatively hidden one.[1]

What we need, then, is to figure out "how to strike that balance between fostering an atmosphere of openness and willingness to tackle difficult subjects while watching for the cues and signals that relate someone's discomfort and pain."[2] In other words, what we need is a trauma-informed pedagogical approach. While programs to implement such methods have been executed in primary and secondary schools,[3] considerably less attention has been paid to a more methodical application of trauma-informed pedagogy in higher education.[4]

In this chapter, I offer an overview of several techniques I have employed in my classroom that can be used *alongside*, not in place of, trigger warnings. While not a comprehensive guide to trauma-informed pedagogy in the college classroom, I do offer suggestions for how we as instructors can reflect on the role of trauma in our classrooms beyond whether or not to use trigger warnings. Trigger warnings alone cannot effectively manage the relationship between safety and freedom that is so often invoked as a struggle. Approaches to dealing with traumatic issues in the classroom are not a matter of either using trigger warnings or not but rather a matter of how traumatic topics are tackled. Trigger warnings may or may not be a part of that approach, but they should by no means comprise its entirety.

To be clear, I have never had a student directly ask me for trigger warnings. But there have been many times I have been unsure of whether or not I should bring something up in class. Likewise, I have often been concerned with my students' willingness to discuss sensitive issues—while they will engage in a lively debate on whether or not sandals are shoes as a class exercise on arguments by definition, I cannot imagine the same could be said if the question changed to whether or not a particular act qualifies as sexual assault. While some of this might be due to a degree of discomfort or uncertainty, for many students it could also be due to the fear of not only talking about a subject with

191

which with they have had a traumatic experience, but of not knowing what to expect during those conversations.

This is by no means an issue isolated to only a few students; the majority of college students have experienced a traumatic event,[5] and 9 percent of matriculating college students meet the criteria for PTSD.[6] Ignoring the problem of trauma in our classrooms means ignoring the needs of a significant portion of our students. Developing techniques to address trauma in our classrooms, therefore, is a necessary measure to engage our students.

Techniques for Addressing Trauma in the Classroom

Clearly, not everyone in college will have experienced the same types of trauma. Setting aside other difficulties with trigger warnings, it is therefore ridiculous to expect instructors to provide trigger warnings for every possible type of traumatic experience. To that end, I offer the following techniques that I have used in my own classroom to handle potentially traumatic topics. My goal is to focus on mutual understandings and expectations for class-room discussions, allowing awareness of the connection between theory and lived experience. By engaging students in frank discussions of what trauma is and how it can interact with what we are learning in the classroom, having students themselves debate whether or not trigger warnings should be used in the classroom, and establishing clear procedures for class discussions, I have worked to lay the groundwork for realizing the impact of traumatic experiences and the importance of discussing such topics.

Discussing Trauma in the Classroom

Before diving in to traumatic topics in my classroom, I first address the concept of trauma and trauma triggers. This serves several purposes. For those students who have experienced trauma and may be worried about the ways in which it could be addressed in class, it lets them know that I am aware of, if not their specific situation, at least the general idea. For those students who have not experienced trauma or who may not have ever thought about the ways in which it could interact with a classroom experience, it introduces them to the topic.

The content of this conversation can vary from semester to semester and from subject to subject. However, I have found it important to highlight both the interconnections between lived experience and theory, as well as the difference between discomfort and trauma. The former helps students to understand that what we talk about in the classroom is not separate from our everyday lives; they can expect their own lives and those of their classmates to impact the ways in which they each navigate class material. The latter works to differentiate between encounters with ideas that students disagree with and those that recall psychological distress.

This can be an especially fine distinction, given that what is uncomfortable for one student may be traumatic for another. Walking through several potential scenarios with students is helpful. For example, I relate to students how there are some things that I feel uncomfortable talking about in class, either due to a position of privilege (e.g., race, in my case), because they are controversial topics (e.g., gun control), or because they challenge some of my deeply held beliefs (e.g., certain discussions of gender). However, none of these are things that (re)traumatize me personally, and I make an effort to talk about all of them when appropriate because of how important those topics are. At the same time, such issues could very well be traumatic for others—while as a white person I have not had any traumatic experiences regarding race, people of color very well could have had. Pointing this out to students helps show that it is not a matter of some topics being too triggering or controversial for any and all class discussion but rather that such matters are context and person dependent.

Trigger Warning Classroom Debate

While such discussions of trauma in the classroom are useful, allowing students to themselves engage in a debate on the role of trigger warnings and trauma in the classroom can further help them parse through these issues. Such a debate can serve as an object lesson of the importance of considering multiple viewpoints. Particularly if students are assigned one perspective or another, it can help students to understand that thinking about a topic from a particular perspective, even if it is not one they agree with, is an important skill. Furthermore, having a debate allows students to further explore the issue, encouraging them to think about it as well as allowing them to express their own opinions.

Classroom Procedures

Of course, during all of these class discussions it is important to have a set of guidelines in place for how class interactions will be handled. I do this in two stages. First, I have students collaboratively write a set of class guidelines.[7] Second, I provide an overview of procedures and resources for what students can do in case something in class were to (re)traumatize them in some way. Together, these two measures work to give students an idea of what both the expectations are for typical class discussions and what the strategies are for contending with discourse that is in some way less typical. One common critique of trigger warnings, for example, is that they cannot possibly cover all circumstances—often topics may arise over the course of typical classroom conversations that were not planned and for which you cannot therefore warn. Accepting this fact and working to address it allows for a classroom environment open to the exploration of new ideas while still respecting individuals' experiences.

The first step is to develop class guidelines; students can then make a reasonable prediction for at least *how* things will be discussed, if not *what*, exactly, will be discussed. Having students set the norms for their own behavior strengthens the adoption of these standards as opposed to dictating rules; it also reinforces the idea that students' voices and experiences matter. The idea is not to police what students say or think but rather to encourage productive and critical conversations. Developing collective guidelines rather than dictating rules highlights, however subtly, the importance of students' freedom to speak, while maintaining a responsibility toward their community. In past semesters, my students have agreed upon guidelines ranging from ones that suggest an appropriate mind-set for approaching class discussion ("try to see different points of view" and "be aware that people have different backgrounds") to ensuring civility ("no personal attacks" and "argue against ideas not people") to those intended to foster trust and allow for openness ("don't repeat [someone else's] personal stories [outside of class]").

Such guidelines, of course, do not guarantee the absence of uncomfortable and/or traumatic discussions; no matter how respectful everyone in the classroom is of one another, people's views and experiences will inevitably conflict at some point. Walking students through what might happen in the event a classroom conversation evokes a traumatic experience for them furthers this balance between freedom and responsibility in class discussions. Not only does having this discussion reduce uncertainty, it also emphasizes the expectation that difficult conversations are not something we can—or even should—avoid. Instead, they are something that advanced preparation better equips us to handle and learn from.

I focus on three things when outlining these procedures. First, I make sure that students are aware of available resources, including student support and advocacy, campus counseling/mental health services, and centers both on and off campus that focus on specific groups or issues (e.g., el Centro Chicano or an LGBT resource center). As instructors, we cannot and should not be expected to be the sole source of support for our students, but we can point them in the right direction. Second, I let students know that just as they are free to exit the class to take care of their physical needs (e.g., using the bathroom), they can also get up and leave to take care of their psychological and emotional needs. While I encourage their engagement in class, I trust them to gauge their own abilities to effectively cope—or not—with the material at the time.

Finally, I offer a suggestion for how the class can handle discussions that do trigger people (having previously discussed the difference between being uncomfortable and being traumatized). Simply put, if class conversation veers in a direction that a student feels is distressing, they can say "yellow." Without having to explain why they felt the need to do so, this serves as a reminder to *everyone* that we need to consider how we speak, remembering that we are not discussing hypotheticals but things that may have affected us personally. The goal is not to curtail conversation but rather to make everyone think more critically about what they and others are saying. Saying "red" will stop the conversation, at least temporarily, with the goal being to allow everyone to take a step back and regroup before coming back to the discussion during the next class.

Use in the Classroom

The classroom procedures I outlined above may seem to offer students a convenient escape hatch, allowing them to circumvent discussing viewpoints with which they disagree. I have not found this to be the case; in the entire time I have been using these procedures, I have never once had students move to halt discussion. In fact, I have found the opposite to be true; establishing communal class guidelines, discussing trauma up front, and defining what students can do if they have such an issue concerning the class have actually led to richer learning experiences.

Such benefits are difficult to illustrate. Not only are they anecdotal, but the anecdotes themselves cannot be specific. I, too, after all, must honor class guidelines and not share personal stories with those outside of the classroom. Nevertheless, I can sketch the outlines of a discussion that took place in one of my classes to help illustrate the ways in which the techniques I have outlined can be effective.

During one class period, we were going to talk about gender and culture. I had informed my students the previous class that part of the discussion would be about gendered violence, essentially providing a trigger warning. While the rest of the class discussion went well, students were much more reticent when it came time to talk about gendered violence. Partway through the halting conversation, a student remarked that a male acquaintance had told the student, in effect, that all men would rape women if they could get away with it.

It was like a bomb going off in class; an air raid siren, not a trigger warning, would have been the commensurate advanced notice. Within a minute, almost everyone now had something to say; much of it was heated. There were expressions of anger, people nodding their heads in agreement, and at least one student looked shaken and upset.

I, too, was a bit thrown, but fell back on what we had already set in place: I paused and reminded everyone of our class guidelines and that they could leave the room or verbally indicate that the conversation needed to slow down a bit, and then let them talk. The students debated the matter among themselves, sharing their experiences, expressing frustration about the way sexual assault was discussed (or often not discussed) on campus, and relating what they were saying to earlier discussions and readings from class. Some students told incredibly personal stories, helping others to understand what they had not been able to when the information had been relayed to them as simple statements or statistics. By the end of class, we had run overtime by close to ten minutes. No one had even started packing up.

My students were able to have a critical, engaged dialogue about gendered violence. I give full credit to my students for their work in that conversation. However, I also acknowledge that regardless of someone's knowledge or experience, the interplay of subject and context can dampen conversation; I research sexual assault and even I can feel uncomfortable talking about it in the classroom. So while my students put in the effort, pedagogical techniques such as classroom guidelines helped provide the scaffolding to support them in their efforts.

Conclusion

Of course, I must acknowledge that the strategies I have described are by no means a perfect solution. Just as there have been times that I have shown a video in class and realized I forgot to preface it with a trigger warning I thought appropriate, so too have there been occasions where students refused to engage in debates over affirmative action or made remarks that were in some way offensive. As I continue to teach, however, I continue to develop ways to address trauma in the classroom beyond the trigger warnings upon which I initially relied. If there is a perfect way of handling controversial or traumatic topics in the classroom, I am not aware of it (though I would certainly like to hear of it).

The point of considering trauma in pedagogical practice is not to completely avoid mistakes but rather to acknowledge the lived experiences with our students, uncovering new ways of accessing and seeing both the class material and the world around us. As Janice Carello and Lisa Butler point out in their call for trauma-informed pedagogy in universities, "Trauma may be endemic to our present political, social, and private worlds, but marching it into the classroom to be prodded, provoked, and endured . . . is, we believe, not to transform trauma but to potentially recapitulate it."[8] Setting up class procedures for dealing with trauma in the classroom, discussing the idea of trauma with students, and allowing students to grapple with these ideas themselves are a few of the ways we can work to move beyond trigger warnings and engage in critical thinking with an attitude of caring. Students enter the classroom with a range of experiences that they cannot—and should not—be expected to abandon in the pursuit of academic knowledge. Instead, it is imperative to acknowledge the multiplicity of students' lives and work with them rather than discounting them and expecting students to separate the academic and the personal.

Notes

1. Ruxandra Looft, "How Do Trigger Warnings Fit into the Classroom Lesson Plan?" *Shakesville*, February 12, 2013, http://www.shakesville.com/2013/02/how-do-trigger-warnings-fit-into.html.

2. Ibid.

3. Diana L. Perry and Monica L. Daniels, "Implementing Trauma-Informed Practices in the School Setting: A Pilot Study," *School Mental Health* 8 (2016): 177–88, doi:10.1007/s12310-016-9182-3; Ann Morgan, Donna Pendergast, Raymond Brown, and Deborah Heck, "Relational Ways of Being an Educator: Trauma-Informed Practice Supporting Disenfranchised Young People," *International Journal of Inclusive Education* 19, no. 10 (2015): 1037–51, doi:10.1080/13 603116.2015.1035344.

4. Janice Carello and Lisa D. Butler, "Potentially Perilous Pedagogies: Teaching Trauma Is Not the Same as Trauma-Informed Teaching," *Journal of Trauma & Dissociation* 15, no. 2 (2014): 153–68, doi:10.1080/15299732.2014.867571.

5. Jennifer P. Read, Paige Ouimette, Jacquelyn White, Craig Colder, and Sherry Farrow, "Rates of *DSM-IV-TR* Trauma Exposure and Posttraumatic Stress Disorder among Newly Matriculated College Students," *Psychological Trauma: Theory, Research, Practice and Policy* 3, no. 2 (2011): 148–56, doi:10.1037/a0021260; Joshua M. Smyth, Jill R. Hockemeyer, Kristin E. Heron, Stephen A. Wonderlich, and James W. Pennebaker, "Prevalence, Type, Disclosure, and Severity of Adverse Life Events in College Students," *Journal of American College Health* 57, no. 1 (2008): 69–76, doi:10.3200/JACH.57.1.69-76.

6. Read et al., "Trauma Exposure."

7. I credit this idea to my colleague Leslie Berntsen, who introduced me to this technique.

8. Carello and Butler, "Potentially Perilous Pedagogies," 163.

Bibliography

Carello, Janice, and Lisa D. Butler. "Potentially Perilous Pedagogies: Teaching Trauma Is Not the Same as Trauma-Informed Teaching." *Journal of Trauma & Dissociation* 15, no. 2 (2014): 153–68. doi:10.1080/15299732.2014.867571.

Looft, Ruxandra. "How Do Trigger Warnings Fit into the Classroom Lesson Plan?" *Shakesville*, February 12, 2013. http://www.shakesville.com/2013/02/how-do-trigger-warnings-fit-into.html.

Morgan, Ann, Donna Pendergast, Raymond Brown, and Deborah Heck. "Relational Ways of Being an Educator: Trauma-Informed Practice Supporting

Disenfranchised Young People." *International Journal of Inclusive Education* 19, no. 10 (2015): 1037–51. doi:10.1080/13603116.2015.1035344.

Perry, Diana L., and Monica L. Daniels. "Implementing Trauma-Informed Practices in the School Setting: A Pilot Study." *School Mental Health* 8 (2016): 177–88. doi:10.1007/s12310-016-9182-3.

Read, Jennifer P., Paige Ouimette, Jacquelyn White, Craig Colder, and Sherry Farrow. "Rates of *DSM-IV-TR* Trauma Exposure and Posttraumatic Stress Disorder among Newly Matriculated College Students." *Psychological Trauma: Theory, Research, Practice and Policy* 3, no. 2 (2011): 148–56. doi:10.1037/a0021260.

Smyth, Joshua M., Jill R. Hockemeyer, Kristin E. Heron, Stephen A. Wonderlich, and James W. Pennebaker. "Prevalence, Type, Disclosure, and Severity of Adverse Life Events in College Students." *Journal of American College Health* 57, no. 1 (2008): 69–76. doi:10.3200/JACH.57.1.69-76.

CHAPTER TWELVE

ADAPTING TRIGGER WARNINGS IN THE INTRODUCTION TO WOMEN'S STUDIES COURSE

A Case Study

Elizabeth Tolman

While teaching a 100-level Introduction to Women's Studies course at a mid-sized midwestern university, I have used my own version of trigger warnings over the years without giving it much thought. The nature of the trigger warnings varies depending on the content covered in class. My students have never demanded the use of trigger warnings, and my use of them does not allow the student the option of skipping out of class or avoiding discussions, readings, or assignments. Rather, I frame the content prior to presenting it and also after the discussion. I am confident that students can "cope with" the content. In fact, on some level the use of trigger warnings is for my benefit as well. I do not offer trigger warnings every day of the course, but there are instances when they are appropriate. I started using trigger warnings in this course, as needed, without reflecting on what I was doing. The warnings were emerging in my classes when I was previewing examples and making links to course concepts. From my perspective as an instructor, topics such antipornography, human trafficking, and sexual assault in the military and on college campuses are difficult for me to cover. Previewing the type of content that will be covered in a class period or unit has value. Rather than avoiding topics so students do not feel uncomfortable, trigger warnings let them know the nature of the course content. As a result, I have found that the use of trigger warnings strengthens the quality of the course because they help to create a classroom climate that allows for discussion about dark topics.

In this chapter, I outline why providing brief trigger warnings prior to discussing and presenting course content is necessary. Note that students in the course are typically first-year students and are from a rural background. There is also an attendance requirement in the course. This chapter includes a chronological documentation of the course, discussion of the content, the nature of my trigger warnings, and my perceptions of how students respond. In many instances, I find myself affirming the students for their professionalism, maturity, and ability to discuss the course content. Other instructors will benefit from reading about the examples that were used in the course and why I found trigger warnings to be necessary, given the student population and the nature of the course content.

The use of trigger warnings is certainly controversial. Ingrid Sturgis notes that students have demanded explicit trigger warnings at universities across the country prior to content about racially offensive or sexually sensitive topics.[1] The American Association of University Professors' report about trigger warnings states that some discomfort within a college classroom is inevitable. The report also claims that a demand for trigger warnings can create a chilly climate for critical thinking. Furthermore, the statement asserts that the use of trigger warnings reduces students to "vulnerable victims rather than full participants in the intellectual process of education."[2] In addition, the statement claims that controversial topics that are typically associated with trigger warnings could be avoided by faculty members who fear complaints and because of academic freedom, institutions should not require or suggest the use of trigger warnings. I agree that students need to be exposed to new ideas, challenged, and taught to address ethical problems and also that this is an individual decision for each instructor. However, for those instructors, including myself, that do use trigger warnings, we know how our students respond to course content, how we feel presenting it, and how framing the content using a trigger warning has value. Certainly, I would not advocate for institutions requiring or suggesting trigger warnings, but I have found that trigger warnings can emerge spontaneously and instinctively.

In their 2015 much discussed article in the *The Atlantic*, Greg Lukianoff and Jonathan Haidt argue that the use of trigger warnings could potentially worsen mental health on campuses.[3] In response to their argument, Aaron Hanlon discusses why he uses trigger warnings, stating that trigger warnings prepare students for a discussion about the material. He does not see trigger warnings as a form of censorship.[4] I agree with Hanlon's claim that providing trigger warnings prior to teaching about the content frames the content and allows instructors not to avoid topics, and I do not see my students as overly sensitive.

Similar to Kate Manne's approach, I believe trigger warnings serve as "a quick heads-up" for students.[5] For example, trigger warnings let the students know that the upcoming readings include graphic depiction of sexual assault. The use of the warning allows students to prepare for their reactions and manage their reactions. Furthermore, she argues, "It's not about coddling anyone. It's about enabling everyone's rational engagement."[6] Trigger warnings in course syllabi allow students who are sensitive to these subjects to prepare themselves prior to the readings. For example, Manne points out that her use of trigger warnings acknowledges that at least some of her students have suffered some sort of trauma. In another example, a recent article in the *Chronicle of Higher Education*, Emma Pettit showcases three professors who use trigger warnings.[7] Patrick J. Keenan, a professor of law at the University of Illinois at Urbana-Champaign justifies his use of trigger warnings in international law courses by explaining that he tells his students that learning about sexual violence during war is difficult, but that students can sit quietly and listen. In order to more clearly demonstrate how trigger warnings can be integrated into the classroom, in the following section I present some of the topics covered in WMST 101: Introduction to Women's Studies, link to examples, and discuss how I approach this course content. Other instructors are welcome to use this content and consider my approach when teaching this course or similar courses.

Examples of Course Content

Topic 1: Research on Pornography by Gail Dines

Gail Dines, who serves as a professor of sociology and women's studies at Wheelock College in Boston, argues that we live in a porn culture and that these images have become commonplace in our society. Dines's analysis and her use of images highlight a dark side of our society, and students are not familiar with antipornography research prior to this course.[8] When covering this content in a college course, I preface the examples and discussions by telling the students that the content is difficult to discuss and that Dines makes a strong antipornography claim that may be counter to how they view pornography.

Based on my perceptions, the students in my courses are not familiar with antipornography research, specifically that conducted by Dines. From semester to semester, I have a few female students in class that share with this class that they are familiar with this antipornography research. For example, one student shared with the class that she owns a T-shirt that says "porn kills love." I use Julia Wood and Natalie Fixmer-Oraiz's definition of pornography in the lecture in order to differentiate pornography from erotica, which is defined as consensual and desired by all parties. They state that pornography is "material that favorably shows subordination and degradation of individuals by presenting sadistic behaviors as pleasurable, pain as enjoyable, and forced sex as positive."[9] I focus on how the examples that Dines uses match Wood and Fixmer-Oraiz's definition of pornography.

This research provides insight into inequity and female experiences. I find that this content is counter to their experiences because Dines presents the argument that violence is evident in mainstream pornography. Furthermore, her examples and analysis highlight physical or verbal abuse in the pornography. For example, at about the fifty-minute mark in Dines's lecture at the Nova Scotia Women's Summit the content becomes more graphic.[10]

In both her TEDx and the Summit lecture, Dines focuses on the implications of growing up in an image-based culture, as compared to a print culture. She argues that the culture is socializing young girls to be porn ready and provides examples of hypersexualized images. Furthermore, the culture changed because of the Internet, and pornography was now affordable, accessible, and anonymous. Dines blocked out some of the content in the images in her lecture; however, the audience could see how women were depicted as well as the abuse. Her analysis of the images is graphic.

When lecturing on the content and showing the Dines lectures, I focus on Dines's claim that based on her research, women work in the industry for three months and that their bodies are damaged and destroyed as a result. Providing a discussion or content warning about the nature of this content prior to showing the graphic lectures in class has value. This differentiates the content from other in-class material and discussions by highlighting the implications of Dines's claims and her points about the severity of how the women are treated. For those students unfamiliar with antipornography claims, viewing the graphic images and learning about

Dines's research could run contrary to their initial perceptions about pornography prior to the course, for example, when students are unfamiliar with the difference between pornography and erotica.

Topic 2: Sexual Assault in the Military: *The Invisible War*

I also show the 2012 documentary film *The Invisible War* in this course. Film critic Kate Taylor describes the film as exposing "the sexual assault of soldiers by other soldiers, and the failure of the military to give survivors the care and justice they deserve."[11] She also notes that "the Department of Defense estimates over 19,000 sexual assaults occurred in the military in 2010 alone. A conservative estimate states over 20 percent of women in the military will be sexually assaulted."[12] The film shows a military that refuses to take action and silences survivors. However, as Taylor points out, the film is not antimilitary nor is it anti-men. In fact, in the film, military husbands and fathers break "down sobbing discussing the ways the military failed the people they cared about the most."[13]

I have shown this film in class for three years, and yet I still have an emotional response as a viewer. Prior to showing the film in class, I explain that when I have screened the film in prior semesters the students report that they did not know about rape in the military. By focusing on several issues, including how sexual assault cases are handled in the U.S. military, military policy, professional retaliation, victim blaming, and the implications of this closed system, the film provides insight into human experiences and inequity. The filmmakers focus on several female veterans and show that they are currently affected by sexual assault and how the assaults they experienced affected both their military careers and their day-to-day lives. Students have stated in discussion and in exams that the film was a turning point in the course and viewing it allowed them to see inequity and injustice in both the military and society as a whole.

Topic 3: Rape and Human Trafficking: Elizabeth Smart

In this ten-minute TEDx Talk, Elizabeth Smart recounts being kidnapped from her home at knifepoint, raped, and held captive for nine months.[14] For me, warning the students about her case prior to the TEDx Talk is important because I want to frame the content prior to Smart recounting being kidnapped and raped at age fourteen. Because Smart's abduction occurred in 2002, most students are unfamiliar with the case. Smart begins by recalling the fourteen-year-old girl she was at the time. She states, "Nothing stood out about me," and says that she may not have been the most forward-thinking fourteen-year-old. She recounts how she felt after being raped the night she was kidnapped and that she felt that she was "beyond hope" after the rape and that she was not worth saving. During the second half of the TEDx Talk, Smart focuses on her life after she was rescued and what her mother told her. She focuses on the positive outcomes and her work to date. Even though the presentation is powerful in terms of the work that Elizabeth Smart has done bringing attention to survival, acknowledging that she will recount details about her rape is appropriate and necessary prior to viewing the TEDx.

Previewing the nature of her presentation and how it relates to course content and readings allows students to more fully understand her lived experiences as a fourteen-year-old girl living in an upper-middle-class home in Salt Lake City. Discussing Smart's story and providing a trigger warning allows me to alert students to her painful experience while also connecting to the rest of the course content and prompting students to consider girls' experiences in the United States.

Topic 4: Rape on Campus: *The Hunting Ground* and Baylor University

I use these examples when lecturing about sexual assault and rape on college campuses. The documentary film *The Hunting Ground* highlights rape on college campuses.[15] In an article on the film, Tim Goral states it is "sparking calls for reform on campuses across the country for humanizing a topic that is too often conveyed in the media as a set of statistics."[16] In an interview, filmmaker Amy Ziering states:

> We were not planning on making this film at all. We've never made two films in the same arena back to back. Kirby and I had actually started working on a very different project after *The Invisible War*, but in the course of going around to campuses screening that film, each time someone would invariably come up to us and say, "This happened to me here. There are a lot of similarities between what you pointed out going on in the military and what I experienced here at my school." We both were completely blindsided by this. . . . We really sort of felt an obligation to do so."[17]

The Hunting Ground and Baylor University examples and clips provide examples about Title IX, how administrators at Baylor University responded in these cases, and individual experiences. The clips and examples focus on these cases, and others focus on female experiences. More specifically, the examples highlight institutional responses to sexual assault allegations, how administrators responded, the potential implications of athletes being accused of sexual assault, and accusations of cover-ups. Framing the topic of sexual assault on college campuses prior to the examples and discussions has value because it addresses the nature of the course content. Accusations and claims about how university administrators and coaches responded are unsettling and run contrary to our expectations for those in power within higher education.

For me, trigger warnings emerge as needed within the college classroom. As instructors, we work to gauge our students' level of comfort, prior knowledge on the topics, and interest in discussing the course content. Trigger warnings provide an opportunity to frame the content prior to a lecture, example, or discussion. I need to transition from one dark topic to another and trigger warnings allow me to do this. Trigger warnings help to create a classroom climate that allows for discussions about these topics. Students are not allowed to skip course content or class because of the examples and discussion. Rather, the use of trigger warnings sets the content apart from other course topics by acknowledging that the content will not be discussed casually.

Notes

1. Ingrid Sturgis, "Warning: This Lesson May Upset You," *Diverse: Issues in Higher Education* 33, no. 3 (2016): 33–35.
2. American Association of University Professors, "On Trigger Warnings," last modified 2014, https://www.aaup.org/report/trigger-warnings.
3. Greg Lukianoff and Jonathan Haidt, "The Coddling of the American Mind," *The Atlantic*, September 2015, 42–52.
4. Aaron R. Hanlon, "The Trigger Warning Myth," *New Republic*, August 14, 2015, 52–55.
5. Kate Manne, "Why I Use Trigger Warnings," *New York Times*, September 19, 2015, 5.

6. Ibid.

7. Emma Pettit, "How 3 Professors Actually Use Trigger Warnings," *Chronicle of Higher Education*, September 16, 2016, A8.

8. Gail Dines, *PornLand: How Porn Has Hijacked Our Sexuality* (Boston: Beacon Press, 2010).

9. Julia T. Wood and Natalie Fixmer-Oraiz, *Gendered Lives: Communication, Gender, and Culture* (Boston: Cengage Learning, 2017).

10. See: https://www.youtube.com/watch?v=-Z5iANEfQUU, Dr. Gail Dines, published November 16, 2012.

11. Kate Taylor, "The Military's 'Invisible War': A Call to Action to Stop Sexual Assaults," *Forbes*, June 21, 2012, 73.

12. Ibid.

13. Ibid.

14. See: https://www.youtube.com/watch?v=h0C2LPXaEW4, *My Story*, Elizabeth Smart, TED-University of Nevada, published January 31, 2014.

15. See: http://thehuntinggroundfilm.com/ and Rape at Baylor, https://www.youtube.com/watch?v=kFAw0s4zbXY.

16. Tim Goral, "Documentary Highlights Survivors' Search for Justice," *University Business* 18 (2015): 17.

17. Gary Crowdus, "Transforming Trauma into Political Activism," *Cineaste* 40, no. 3 (2015): 44–49.

Bibliography

American Association of University Professors. "On Trigger Warnings." Last modified 2014. https://www.aaup.org/report/trigger-warnings.

Crowdus, Gary. "Transforming Trauma into Political Activism." *Cineaste* 40, no. 3 (2015): 44–49.

Dines, Gail. *PornLand: How Porn Has Hijacked Our Sexuality*. Boston: Beacon Press, 2010.

Goral, Tim. "Documentary Highlights Survivors' Search for Justice." *University Business* 18 (2015): 17.

Hanlon, Aaron R. "The Trigger Warning Myth." *New Republic*, August 14, 2015, 52–55.

Lukianoff, Greg, and Jonathan Haidt. "The Coddling of the American Mind." *The Atlantic*, September 2015, 42–52.

Manne, Kate. "Why I Use Trigger Warnings." *New York Times*, September 19, 2015, 5.

Pettit, Emma. "How 3 Professors Actually Use Trigger Warnings." *Chronicle of Higher Education*, September 16, 2016, A8.

Sturgis, Ingrid. "Warning: This Lesson May Upset You." *Diverse: Issues in Higher Education* 33, no. 3 (2016): 33–35.

Taylor, Kate. "The Military's 'Invisible War': A Call to Action to Stop Sexual Assaults." *Forbes*, June 21, 2012, 73.

Wood, Julia T., and Natalie Fixmer-Oraiz. *Gendered Lives: Communication, Gender, and Culture*. Boston: Cengage Learning, 2017.

CHAPTER THIRTEEN
TRIGGER WARNING EXPECTATIONS
Potential Ripples and Ramifications
Susan Stearns

This chapter discusses potential ripples and ramifications of placing constraints on classroom communication in relation to trigger
warnings. Of concern is how a positive desire to assist students
could eventually evolve into a "triggers-required-norm" ultimately negatively impacting teaching effectiveness. This discussion will occur through
a case study of a senior capstone on stigma.[1] I conduct this course via a
modified version of a graduate-level seminar—that is, no lectures, but
rather a large-group, face-to-face discussion format facilitated by me. We
meet two days a week in a group discussion and one day a week online for
large-group discussion. Additionally, the teaching strategy consistently
encourages students to bridge the gap between stigma theory and the
stigmas they, their families, and friends face in everyday life.

Of significance to this discussion is the very pedagogy used for the
course: (1) the choice of topic, stigma, can become a multitude of triggers;
(2) that trigger warnings encourage, or possibly presuppose, a particular
teaching style—that is, lecture—because with the lecture style the instructor can structure the information and choose the questions to be answered
in the classroom, and so on, thereby deflecting potential triggers; and (3)
the choice of learning goals, in this case encouraging students toward integration, bridging the gap between theory and their lives, and personalizing
stigma theory to make the concepts presented more relatable and thereby
more prone to triggering a past event. As I bring forward each of these
three topics, I will (1) give an overview of the higher education research,
(2) show anonymous student comments from my teaching evaluations
illustrating how discussing and labeling life events has helped students

grow rather than causing harmful triggers (Eastern Washington University's institutional review board approved the use of these comments), and (3) discuss/ponder how further constraints on classroom teaching methods may encourage a narrower range of choices for instructors that could result in less student engagement and learning. I also discuss the one time a student talked with me about a potential anticipated trigger: her concerns, my responses, and how we worked through this situation together. And finally, I conclude by suggesting ways in which we may compassionately care for our students without further constraining classroom communication and climate.

Choice of Topic

Many college courses examine concepts that inherently have potential triggers embedded in them: racism, domestic violence, rape, pornography, war, drunken driving, sexism, and others. I have heard each of these topics touched upon in one class, in one term, while teaching public speaking. These were my students' choices, their speech topics. So when we talk choice, let it be clear that I mean not only the instructor's choices could be dramatically constrained but also students' choices.

Trigger warnings could take these choices away; a course like the senior capstone on stigma could become nonexistent. For example, from our class text, stigma is defined as an attribute that reduces a person

> in our minds from a whole and usual person to a tainted, discounted one. Such an attribute is a stigma, especially when its discrediting effect is very extensive; sometimes it is also called a failing, a shortcoming, a handicap. . . . The term stigma, then, will be used to refer to an attribute that is deeply discrediting.[2]

Thus, to discuss stigma means to discuss people who are treated as less than fully human—that is, when their sense of humanity is discounted. We specifically discuss sexism; racism; classism; and stigmas toward the physically maimed, disfigured, or disabled, along with religion; mental competence; and disability. These stigmas are those Erving Goffman examined, but they only reflect his era, the later fifties to early sixties, so as a class we bring the content up to current times with topics such as homosexuality, gender identity, HIV status, bisexuality, and others. As you can see, the topic of stigma is rampant with potential triggers. This means that the entirety of the course, including the readings, would necessitate a trigger warning. And if trigger warnings come to be expected, instructors may choose to cease offering courses like this.

Yet stigma is a relevant topic; its complexity and potential for emotional impact and insight do not make it worthy of dismissal but rather of exploration. Individuals deal with stigma on a daily basis, and a course such as this opens students' eyes to what is occurring around them, alerts students to their own implicit and explicit participation, and offers students opportunities to create communicative strategies by which to attempt to alter the discourse of stigma. These are the types of courses needed in higher education.

Erving Goffman is one of the premier sociologists of the twentieth century.[3] So in this capstone we have the complexity of a phenomenal theoretician's work applied to our everyday lives. In addition, I consider myself an expert on Goffman, in particular his work on stigma, so as the instructor I bring my expertise and enthusiasm to our discussions. Noel Entwistle and Paul Walker state, "Such expressions of feeling, both of enthusiasm and empathy, make an important contribution to inducing deep approaches to learning."[4] My enthusiasm does not guarantee deeper learning for the students, but it may be one of the many variables that assist students' deeper learning. This enthusiasm is readily apparent in students' anonymous teacher evaluation comments from this course. [Italicized quotes throughout this chapter are student evaluation comments.] *"I really appreciated the fact that she was a very enthusiastic teacher and was excited about the course content"* (Spring 2014), and *"Dr. Sue, your attitude and energy really worked for me. It helped me stay engaged and wanting to learn more. When someone is excited about the course material, it makes me want to know why, which engages me in the course even more"* (Spring 2014). At issue is that a focus on student triggers may constrain instructors from offering their best student-learning strategies: Instructors may choose not to offer particular topics regardless of their own expertise and enthusiasm for a topic.

Our discussions are weighty as we ponder that stigma is not the label—that is, it is not obesity, low education levels, or being a liar; rather, stigma is society's or our individual relationship, or attitude, to that label.[5] If stigma were in the label, then (1) all cultures would stigmatize the same labels, and (2) society would consistently treat individuals with these stigma labels the same over time—whether it was 1950 or 2015. In response, students put forward stigma labels that vary by culture—for example, being a single adult female in America, Saudi Arabia, or India—and stigma labels that have changed over time, such as interracial marriages in America in the 1930s compared to 2015, as they verbally express their cognitive grappling. And these are only our discussions in week two of the course; we delve cognitively deeper into stigma as we discuss why communication scholars should find this important: How do we communicate stigma? How do we deal with individuals communicating stigma to us? How do we counter stigmas being communicated to us? Are there times it is good to stigmatize? What would you encourage society to stigmatize?

It is not possible for an instructor to offer specific trigger warnings because it is not possible to fathom the plethora of instances wherein students' minds will relate stigma in their personal lives and to know the possible emotional impact of these thoughts on each student in the class. Instead, I opt for student choice. Classroom and online discussion offers a fundamental rule that each student willingly chooses their input; no student is forced to disclose personal stigma issues. For example, in an online discussion, the initial prompt might read like this:

> Focusing on the beginning of chapter 2, pages 41–47 on *Social Information*, choose a quote that most interests, puzzles, intrigues, or in some other way catches your interest (it could be that you totally disagree with it).
>
> 1. Type out the quote to share with your colleagues.
>
> 2. Explain why this quote captured your attention and give a current up-to-date example (personal, observed happening to someone else, saw on TV, etc.) of what this quote is talking about.

Note the openness of the invitation: (1) each student chooses the quote to focus upon, and (2) each student chooses whether to share a personal experience or to distance this example from the self thereby limiting their self-disclosure. But also note that there is no control over what individual students offer, nor is there a way in which to know the potential triggers that might occur from each individual student's offering.

We examine academically complex and societally sensitive questions that place high demand upon the students: *"Very tough and demanding course but definitely informative and fun"* (Spring 2015). And yet, students have taken delight in this topic. Students' responses run counter to what trigger warning enthusiasts suggest. The potential harm this unsafe topic might bring to bear upon students did not occur. Over a span of seven years and fourteen classes, not one student mentioned being triggered. Instead, students expressed keen appreciation for the course content: *"This class was very enlightening. It is such an eye opener to people & their perceptions. I feel that it should be a class that everyone should take"* (Spring 2013); *"I loved the content & thought the material was very thought provoking"* (Fall 2012); and *"Was a great course and the material was very interesting. Made me look at society as a whole reconsider stigmatizing people"* (Spring 2014). One student went so far as to say, *"Really enjoyed this course—very eye opening. Wish that more classes along these lines were offered"* (Spring 2015).

When we ponder the incorporation of trigger warnings in academe, we need to consider the potential consequences: loss of choice for both students and faculty. And this is merely the initial ripple, because as their choices are constrained, instructors' enthusiasm in teaching and students' enjoyment in learning may decrease. An expectation of trigger warnings may compel instructors to offer less than their best options for student learning.

Choice of Teaching Method

This section is a discussion of best practices in the classroom. At issue is that the goal of an instructor should be to offer the best teaching methods for student learning, not the best teaching methods for student learning when constrained by further concerns such as triggers. Faculty should not be limited in their choices for offering the best to their students. The issues in this section examine the interaction between triggers and pedagogical concerns.

Upon reviewing the education literature, Muhammad Asif Bhalli, Abdul Sattar, and Midhat Asif argue:

> In recent years, a great paradigm shift has been observed in the field of education in general. . . . Traditional teacher centered approach is

gradually being replaced by a student centered learning. Teachers who conceive teaching as simple transmission of knowledge use content/ teacher centered approaches, and teachers who take teaching as facilitating learning use learner centered approaches.[6]

A "simple transmission of knowledge" is a reference to the lecture method that is instructor centered, not student centered. Two major benefits of the lecture method are that it allows instructors to cover a larger quantity of "educational content" and there is less likelihood of losing control of the classroom interaction.[7] The relative ease of controlling the classroom is why the lecture method becomes the preferred teaching method when contemplating trigger warnings: Instructors can control whether they ask any questions to students, what questions they ask, which students they allow to respond, and when to interrupt and stop a student's response. This strict control is not a part of a student-centered classroom, particularly in a large-group discussion format with approximately twenty to twenty-five students: conversation flows quickly, new topics are introduced unexpectedly by anyone in the group, students challenge each other for further clarification, all students are encouraged to participate, what is covered on a given day cannot be predicted, and so on. And when these same twenty to twenty-five students interact in online discussions, it is even more student centered because I remove myself from the discussion so that they, as college seniors, develop the ability to effectively resolve differences of fact and opinion. Instructor-centered techniques may offer a safer classroom for known trigger issues, but the research is clear that students learn more effectively in student-centered classrooms.

Current learning theories encourage student-centered frameworks: Student engagement and active learning are effective evidence-based teaching strategies.[8] Andrea Revell and Emma Wainright discuss active learning by explicitly tying student engagement into the process: Students are "*actively engaged* in the learning process" which involves "discussion, problem-solving, presentations, group work . . . anything that gets students interacting with each other and engaging with the lecture material" [my emphasis].[9] The discussion method, face-to-face and online, currently used in the capstone course is quite effective in achieving both student engagement and active learning as frequently exhibited by student comments. Two particular students address both concepts: "*I really like sitting in a circle during class it was a lot easier to stay focused and more interactive*" (Spring 2010), and "*Loved the class! Very relational & I was always engaged & thinking! I also enjoyed class/ on-line discussions & relating communication to life*" (Winter 2014). Even students who usually remain quiet, talked: "*Although I prefer to observe & listen, I found her discussions moving & informative. It takes the class material & makes it real tangible*" (Fall 2012). And many students mentioned their sheer enjoyment of learning through discussion: "*I really enjoy being able to have so much discussion in class. It really helped me be able to understand the material*" (Fall 2013); "*Loved the discussion aspect of the class, it made learning easier for me, and also made the class less boring*" (Fall 2013); and "*This is my favorite class I've ever had, the discussion structure was wonderful*" (Spring 2013).

The encouragement of trigger warnings may impede the use of particular teaching methods, student-centered methods. If trigger warnings become expected, then pedagogies wherein faculty cannot provide *specific* trigger warnings may become extinct; in student-centered classes, the most that can be offered is a *generic general* trigger warning about the entire course. Thus, the choices we make regarding trigger warning expectations ripple into instructors' decisions regarding teaching methods, and, as previously discussed, the topics instructors and students choose. This can create a constrained teaching environment where the best classroom teaching methods for student learning may no longer be offered.

Choice of Learning Goal

"Learning thus works best when students are encouraged to be actors as well as observers, *to interact and experience as well as to apply abstract reasoning and theoretical constructs to issues*" [my emphasis].[10] Integration, the concept referred to in the italicized part of this quote, is an excellent learning goal whenever theory is an aspect of the course content. Integration encourages students' deep learning as they integrate their knowledge of theory to life.[11] Furthermore, Alison Cook-Sather and Alia Luz say, "Recent research suggests that students will work hard and engage deeply when they experience learning as personally meaningful."[12] And yet stigma presents highly sensitive topics that may make students more vulnerable to triggers once they personalize the theory. For instance, I offer students the opportunity to examine any stigma issue they would like for their final paper and inform me if they want to keep the topic private so that I don't mention it in class. I've had students discuss deeply personal issues that they tell me they never mention to other people; for example, bisexuality, shame about being hirsute, childhood memories of living with a parent with bipolar issues. These students reported deep learning and appreciation for the opportunity to explore these concepts.

If integration of theory with their personal lives were a problem for the many students who have taken the course, it would be reflected in their comments. Instead, students speak positively of successful integration: "*I enjoyed applying Goffman to real life scenarios*" (Spring 2011); "*It was a great class, I learned a lot & loved having the students get involved w/ their personal experiences & examples*" (Winter 2014); "*Wow, that's the best way to describe this course. Sue allowed me to see a whole another perspective to society. It relates to our daily life so much and it allows us to communicate with society*" (Spring 2014); and "*I thought the course was really valuable to real life*" (Spring 2015). Deep learning, in this case via integration, also encourages greater retention.[13] One student mentioned retention directly: "*I felt that this class was awesome . . . learned tons from it, and I actually feel like I am going to remember much of this information for years to come as opposed to many of my other classes where it's memorized then lost*" (Spring 2011). And others mentioned an expectation of keeping this course in mind as they move into their future: "*I liked how relatable this course was and how I learned material I can use in the future as well*" (Spring 2015), and "*Stigma has become a part of my life. Thanks*" (Spring 2013). Not one student has expressed any negative concerns regarding integrating theory into their personal lives; instead students mention the depth and predicted long-term duration of their learning.

Yet, as with the other choices mentioned above, a focus on trigger warnings might discourage integration as a learning goal when teaching theories of a sensitive nature. Once again, effective evidence-based course design might be harmed. Trigger warnings might constrain the effective choices instructors make to design courses that foster enhanced student learning.

Concerned about a Potential Trigger

A few years ago, a concerned student, Lindsey (a pseudonym to protect her identity), approached me about a potential trigger. Lindsey's concern was an upcoming required viewing of a *Law & Order: Criminal Intent* episode in the classroom. She alerted me that violence could trigger her. She asked for an alternative assignment and I said I would think about it. This was my first experience with triggers and I truly wanted to assist Lindsey. I require students to watch "The Silencer" (*Law & Order: Criminal Intent*, Season 6, Episode 18) and write an essay choosing three concepts from chapter 3 of Goffman's *Stigma*. This particular *Criminal Intent* episode investigates a murder and attempted murder at a college for the deaf during which time the writers display Goffman's concepts on how society will stigmatize groups of individuals while members of a stigmatized group may combat the societal viewpoint by creating perceptions of themselves in which they are equal to or better than individuals in the overall society. I had four or five days to find an alternative assignment for Lindsey, but it became an impossible task. There was no alternative. I did watch the *Criminal Intent* episode again, trying to view it through Lindsey's eyes. I told her my dilemma and added that I did notice music plays right before any violence. After our discussion, Lindsey decided to give it a try by averting her eyes whenever the music played and knowing she could get up and leave at any point. She did fine, and she wrote an excellent essay.

This experience with Lindsey opened my eyes in many ways. While the music in the episode could be considered a trigger warning, I realize that is not the most important element I learned from this experience. I believe the more critical issue is that I was oblivious to placing a trigger warning on the original assignment. It would not occur to me to place a trigger warning on a television episode from a major network, a show that had presumably passed numerous industry censors prior to broadcast. So I discovered I could offer Lindsey my care and compassion but it made me question if the deep understanding of any potential trigger is an instructor's responsibility.

Discussion

An expectation for trigger warnings comes from a legitimate concern for students' well-being. Yet, as explained above, there is the potential to limit effective teaching choices via the ripples and ramifications of creating trigger warnings as normative expectations. Additionally, trigger warning expectations contain at least three assumptions: (1) that trigger warnings can be successfully predicted by instructors, (2) that this issue is a classroom issue, and (3) that trigger warnings actually are for the students' best interest. First, earlier in this chapter, I referenced the lecture model as being the preferred teaching method for "known" triggers. But how are all the triggers to be known? This assumes instructors are proficient in knowing every aspect of what could be a trigger to each and every individual in their class. Second, classroom trigger warnings assume this is a classroom issue. Instead, I suggest the unit of analysis is the individual and not the group—that is, the classroom. And, the third assumption is that protecting these students from their triggers is actually in their best interest. This highly controversial third point, I leave to the rest of the authors in this book; I merely note that this is an assumption and not research based. Two of these assumptions fall more appropriately within the purview of a psychologist/counselor than an instructor: the first, the knowledge to label, know, and predict potential triggers, and the third, the ability to know when an individual is at a stage where handling a potential trigger offers them potential growth or damage as an individual. Trained counselors available at many college campuses can best deal with these needs; this is their professional training. And the second assumption, treating these psychological needs at the classroom level, as a group phenomenon, is ill-suited. Each student needs individualized attention; specific triggers are particular to an individual.

Though triggers are very different from learning disabilities, we can learn from the way we assist students with learning disabilities: (1) learning disabled students are diagnosed by professionals, and (2) these students approach individual faculty to express their needs—for example, extra exam time or other such accommodations—backed up by professional evaluations and the institution's support. An individualized route such as this honors the student's needs, the professional training of counselors, and professional training of instructors while simultaneously not infringing on the instructors' and students' teaching and learning options.

Notes

1. Erving Goffman, *Stigma: Notes on the Management of Spoiled Identity* (New York: Simon & Schuster, 1986) [1963].
2. Goffman, *Stigma*, 3.

3. Gary Allen Fine and Philip Manning, "Erving Goffman," in *The Blackwell Companion to Major Contemporary Social Theorists*, edited by G. Ritzer, 34 (Malden, MA: Blackwell, 2003).

4. Noel Entwistle and Paul Walker, "Strategic Alertness and Expanded Awareness within Sophisticated Conceptions of Teaching," *Instructional Science* 28, no. 5 (2000): 356, doi:10.1023/A:1026579005505.

5. Goffman, *Stigma*, 3.

6. Muhammad Asif Bhalli, Abdul Sattar, and Midhat Asif, "Teaching Strategies: Perception of Medical Students, Used in Basic Science Years," *Professional Medical Journal* 23, no. 5 (2016): 614, http://www.theprofesional.com/article/vol-23-no-05/prof-3206.pdf.

7. Ibid., 614–15.

8. Ömer Delialioğlu, "Student Engagement in Blended Learning Environments with Lecture-Based and Problem-Based Instructional Approaches," *Journal of Educational Technology & Society* 15, no. 3 (2012): 310; Evelien Opdecam, Patricia Everaert, Hilde Van Keer, and Fanny Buysschaert, "Preferences for Team Learning and Lecture-Based Learning among First-Year Undergraduate Accounting Students," *Research in Higher Education* 55, no. 4 (2014): 401, doi:10.1007/s11162-013-9315-6.

9. Andrea Revell and Emma Wainwright, "What Makes Lectures 'Unmissable'? Insights into Teaching Excellence and Active Learning," *Journal of Geography in Higher Education* 33, no. 2 (2009): 209, doi:10.1080/03098260802276771.

10. Ibid., 221.

11. Tracy R. Frame, Stephanie M. Cailor, Rebecca J. Gryka, Aleda M. Chen, Mary E. Kiersma, and Lorin Sheppard, "Student Perceptions of Team-Based Learning vs Traditional Lecture-Based Learning," *American Journal of Pharmaceutical Education* 79, no. 4 (2015): 1, doi:10.5688/ajpe79451; Noel Entwistle, "Styles of Learning and Approaches to Studying in Higher Education," *Kybernetes* 30, nos. 5–6 (2001): 593–603, doi:10.1108/03684920110391823.

12. Alison Cook-Sather and Alia Luz, "Greater Engagement in and Responsibility for Learning: What Happens When Students Cross the Threshold of Student-Faculty Partnership," *Higher Education Research & Development* 34, no. 6 (2015): 1097, doi:10.1080/07294360.2014.911263.

13. Frame et al., "Student Perceptions of Team-Based Learning," 1.

Bibliography

Bhalli, Muhammad Asif, Abdul Sattar, and Midhat Asif. "Teaching Strategies: Perception of Medical Students, Used in Basic Science Years." *Professional*

Medical Journal 23, no. 5 (2016): 614–19, http://www.theprofesional.com/article/vol-23-no-05/prof-3206.pdf.

Cook-Sather, Alison, and Alia Luz. "Greater Engagement in and Responsibility for Learning: What Happens When Students Cross the Threshold of Student-Faculty Partnership." *Higher Education Research & Development* 34, no. 6 (2015): 1097–1109. doi:10.1080/07294360.2014.911263.

Delialioğlu, Ömer. "Student Engagement in Blended Learning Environments with Lecture-Based and Problem-Based Instructional Approaches." *Journal of Educational Technology & Society* 15, no. 3 (2012): 310–22.

Entwistle, Noel. "Styles of Learning and Approaches to Studying in Higher Education." *Kybernetes* 30, nos. 5–6 (2001): 593–603. doi: 10.1108/03684920110391823.

Entwistle, Noel, and Paul Walker. "Strategic Alertness and Expanded Awareness within Sophisticated Conceptions of Teaching." *Instructional Science* 28, no. 5 (2000): 335–61. doi: 10.1023/A: 1026579005505.

Fine, Gary Allen, and Philip Manning. "Erving Goffman." In *The Blackwell Companion to Major Contemporary Social Theorists*, edited by G. Ritzer, 34–62. Malden, MA: Blackwell, 2003.

Frame, Tracy R., Stephanie M. Cailor, Rebecca J. Gryka, Aleda M. Chen, Mary E. Kiersma, and Lorin Sheppard. "Student Perceptions of Team-Based Learning vs Traditional Lecture-Based Learning." *American Journal of Pharmaceutical Education* 79, no. 4 (2015): 1–11. doi: 10.5688/ajpe79451.

Goffman, Erving. *Stigma: Notes on the Management of Spoiled Identity.* New York: Simon & Schuster, 1986 [1963].

Opdecam, Evelien, Patricia Everaert, Hilde Van Keer, and Fanny Buysschaert. "Preferences for Team Learning and Lecture-Based Learning among First-Year Undergraduate Accounting Students." *Research in Higher Education* 55, no. 4 (2014): 400–432. doi: 10.1007/s11162-013-9315-6.

Revell, Andrea, and Emma Wainwright. "What Makes Lectures 'Unmissable'? Insights into Teaching Excellence and Active Learning." *Journal of Geography in Higher Education* 33, no. 2 (2009): 209–23. doi: 10.1080/03098260802276771.

CHAPTER FOURTEEN

LIVED EXPERIENCES OF MILITARY VETERANS IN THE COLLEGE ENGLISH CLASSROOM
A Case Study

Gretchen Oltman and Kristine Leibhart

M ilitary veterans are one of the primary student groups involved in the debate about the appropriate use of trigger warnings on today's college campuses. Because many military veterans have experienced traumatic events or suffer posttraumatic stress disorder (PTSD) after retiring from service, college instructors are left wondering if veterans should be warned about potentially disruptive course content with military themes or ties. Today's colleges provide a wealth of opportunities for learning, growth, and development for many former military members seeking to pursue or finish a degree. The National Conference of State Legislatures reported nearly one million veterans and families of veterans are utilizing education benefits through the Post 9/11 GI Bill.[1] This veteran population in college includes a large group of adults transitioning from one life to another. While veterans enter the college classroom older and with more life and work experiences than traditional students, transitioning from military ranks to the classroom can host its own set of challenges, including the residual effects of combat, physical or mental challenges, and academic struggles within a multigenerational classroom.

It is within the college classroom that this exploration and consideration of trigger warnings takes place. The college English classroom is a place for exploration, discovery, and investigation of literature and writing. It can be an emotionally charged experience as students unravel the meaning of words by Hemingway or tell their own stories through narrative composition. As college faculty and trained English educators, we clearly appreciate the value of discourse and dialogue within the English classroom. It is a unique setting much different than the black and white "right and wrong" feature of an accounting classroom or a history exam. Jim Burke has called the English classroom "a crucial forum for discussions about values, ethics, and morality."[2] His work promoted the notion that literature forces the discussion of closely held dispositions and stories: How can one read *The Adventures of Huckleberry Finn* without exploring the significant role of race in society? How can one delve into Hemingway's *A Farewell to Arms* without exploring the role of war? The discussion surrounding literature is vibrant; personal; and if done properly, perplexing. Thus, utilization of trigger warnings within the college English classroom becomes even more troublesome when seeking to work with a student population that enters with real-life wartime experiences—that is, if the purpose of the content of a class is to wrestle with meaningful, ugly, detailed, life-reflecting content, how should students be "warned" of the content, and more importantly, why?

As college instructors, we are grateful for the military service performed by some of our students. In our experience, military students provide some interesting lived experiences and a cultural understanding that is atypical of the traditional, younger college student. In addition, as instructors, we are cognizant of meeting and accommodating student needs. While we have no specific military experience ourselves, we do have the lived experience of teaching a wide range of learners, from high school freshmen to graduate-level college students. The experiences we share here reflect situations that cause us to step back and wonder if trigger warnings might readily assist the learning of military veterans within the English classroom, and if so, the potential cost of doing so. As we worked through our shared experiences with military veterans in the English classroom, several themes emerged—the gap of shared experiences between veterans and their traditional college classmates, the personal nature of writing the self-story, the impact of war themes within literature, and the mystery of the unseen scars around which we attempt to navigate our teaching.

The Gap of Shared Experiences

Carter was an older veteran who had spent time in the early 1990s in Desert Strom. He readily displayed his physical scars to any willing audience.

While Carter was a decent student, he was also an absent student, and any presence in class was multiplied by double the absences. He was also known across campus for having an unpredictable anger problem. When Carter was present, his classmates viewed him as obnoxious and overbearing. When he was absent, it was typically due to his various appointments with military agencies. When challenged on the number of absences, he was appalled that anyone would question his military service. He was simply a difficult person with whom to relate to on any level.

Carter's personality was less than engaging to his literature circle classmates. While he had a mortgage, a daughter the same age as his classmates, and was working on his second marriage, his classmates had recently graduated from high school and were mostly receiving financial support from their parents. Typically in a literature circle, differences can be overcome and the literature can be the foundation of the relationship. This was not the case with Carter. His military experiences—living overseas, doing some mundane tasks while in service, attending the funeral of his closest military friend—were unique to the group. He was defensive that his own lived experiences were more important or more meaningful than those of his classmates. He outwardly shared his dissatisfaction with being older and more "life-experienced" than others. As young adult college students, they simply could not relate, and this was magnified by Carter's obstinacy toward those with much less life experience than he. The response of the group, including those working with Carter in administrative capacities, was to not confront Carter with his reality. It was best to remain at surface level in nearly every conversation, from discussing grades to current events to the literature being studied in class. It left most students in the class nervous. Not that they believed Carter was dangerous, but more in the attempt to find a way to connect that would not lead to hard feelings. So, rather than dive into discussions about the constructs of loyalty or the metaphor within a story, students would sit back, listen, and often let Carter's comments in class go uncontested.

While Carter could have used this as a growth experience, one in which he understood the innocence of youth or the immaturity that comes with most first-time college students, he simply could not. He grew angrier and angrier as time went by. Their lack of insight into his experiences became a chasm of misunderstanding. Discussions over innocuous texts led to raised voices and silenced students. The group as a whole complained about Carter. Individually, some expressed fear at his abrasive and explosive nature. Carter noted he was simply trying to be understood by kids who had no idea what life was really like. Eventually, Carter stopped attending class. The sudden disappearance of Carter was unexplained and very well may have been completely unrelated to class, but as faculty, we were left pondering the what-ifs of the situation—what if Carter had found a way to constructively participate? Would that have brought him back? Would it have been better to address some of the group dynamics with the class as a whole rather than maintaining a glaring chasm of silence around an issue most knew was present? Was there some way to address this from the beginning to help foster better communication from all students rather than to simply expect it?

The Personal Narrative: Writing from within Traumatic Events

In order to become better writers, the common practice in college English classrooms is to do just that: practice writing. In order to do so, students are tasked with writing personal narratives or stories from their own memories or past that can then be illustrated with sensory details and descriptive events.

Another of our students, whom we shall call Cory, had a difficult time with this practice. So much so, he struggled to put any words on paper. One of the assignments was to write about a memory. Some students wrote about childhood events—vacations to Disney World or breaking a leg. Cory wrote about the first time he shot someone during his military service. During a collaborative share in class one evening, Cory shared his story to his small group of fellow students, all younger and much less experienced in life than he. Silence took over the group. No one commented on the story except to say "good job." The group progressed to a much easier topic in the next student's writing.

Cory shared his frustration through his writing, not only of his military experiences, but also about the lack of understanding found within the college setting. Cory's pain from military service was apparent, yet the structure of the classroom was not one where much support could be found. Over time, he revealed that he had written similar pieces in other English classrooms only to receive C-level grades. He said that he felt judged by instructors that may not have supported his military service or who may have judged the specificity in which he recalled the death of someone at his hands. The task of writing, which was aimed at drawing on personal experiences, then became one of self-censorship and wondering if one's own life experiences were suitable for publication even within the confines of class. As we discussed the possibility of trigger warnings within college-level English classes, it became clear that no warning could protect students from their own lived experiences. In addition, it is counterproductive, when teaching writing, to limit the topics about which students can write, particularly when the task itself is to write about a personal event. Attempting to limit student writings to only the "happiest" discourages students from writing about very personal issues, some of which can be impressively constructed and described through word. Why, then, would we as instructors attempt to mitigate someone else's reality?

Depictions of War within Literature

The fact that the story began with the sentence "This is true" did nothing to warn one student. "How to Tell a True War Story" by Tim O'Brien alluded to a fellow soldier being killed, danger, reconnaissance missions, and night patrols. But none of this short introduction to the essay was enough to make Chris, a veteran turned college student, get up and leave the room before the really painful, really mind-blistering portion of the story happened. That part resected what little he had left of his heart and he would show up to class only one more time.

Chris was a young, clean-cut student. He appeared to be in his late twenties and carried a different look than the rest of the young class. He wore a military haircut. He wore no telltale shirts advertising a branch of the U.S. military, although there was a noticeable tattoo peeking out of his shirtsleeve near one bicep. These were elusive clues that Chris may have spent time in the military. At the beginning of the semester, the class spent time getting to know one another through the traditional icebreakers and introductions. Chris did not choose to mention any details about his history in the military or his time spent in Afghanistan. He was a conscientious student who participated in class, interacted in a friendly manner with his classmates, handed in B-quality work, and had perfect attendance. Until Tim O'Brien's essay.

One evening during a class discussion about "How to Tell a True War Story," Chris suddenly began to exhibit signs of distress. This essay had been assigned for several weeks. It was listed in the syllabus. Chris, it appeared, had not read the essay prior to coming to class that evening. As discussion began, he grew still and pale. When called on to add details or opinion, Chris said he had nothing to say. He remained in class the entire evening, however, but said nothing.

The next week, Chris came to class intoxicated. He brought a Starbucks coffee, but his eyes could not focus and he swayed back and forth when he tried to stand still. When he was called on a few times he produced only a few slurred responses. He was not disruptive and he seemed to sober up as the class continued. Yet this was his last class. He never returned.

Six months later, long after Chris had gone missing from class, word came down that he was requesting a retroactive withdrawal from the course, citing personal issues. As it turned out, he had committed himself to an inpatient alcohol rehab center the night of the last class he attended. Evidently this had been a problem in his past. He had been suffering from severe PTSD because of his experiences in Afghanistan.

While the O'Brien story was one of many read throughout the semester, it did not go unnoticed that this particular story, a descriptive tale of war and military experience, could certainly cause one to relive similar events. Was the syllabus notation of the story enough to warn Chris of where the class would venture? And even with a warning, would it have made a difference?

Unseen Scars

Classroom experiences have shown us that within the world of working with veterans, there is more that we do not know about the veteran's experience than what we actually do. We are not veterans and have no relative experience to relate to serving in the military so some of our attempts to understand or connect with our students are without success. As students enter the classroom, there are numerous unknowns—the extent of mental illness, the lived experiences of conflict, or the lasting effects of separation from family and friends.

Patrick exhibited physical scars of war that were much more visible than with other student veterans. One did not have to ask him if he had been a combat vet—it was obvious just from looking at him. At about twenty-three years old, he walked with a cane due to his leg injury. He had stepped on an improvised explosive devise in Iraq and suffered from severe hearing loss and wore hearing aids all of the time.

Patrick was extremely withdrawn. Because he was enrolled in a lower-level writing class, he was one of many that needed a lot of remedial instruction. A few of the students were severely sight impaired, and it seemed that Patrick wanted to separate himself from any kind of disability identification or stereotype. He did introduce himself quietly to the class as an army veteran, but he did not outwardly speak of his experiences.

Patrick did not smile, most likely due to his apparent depression. It took a while to get to know him, layer after layer. He was willing to write about his experiences and build relationships, and he was personable and invested in class. While he was a decent student, probably only in the introductory writing class due to a low entrance score, he appeared bright and talented. Patrick suffered from the administrative nightmare of being a student veteran. He missed a lot of class, mostly due to appointments with various veterans' agencies and administrations, all of which he was unable to reschedule without running the risk of remaining on a month-long waiting list.

The pronounced need for counseling and other interventions are common denominators of the many student veterans we encounter. As instructors, we lack counseling backgrounds and are certainly unqualified to diagnose or treat anyone. However, student veterans in the English classroom, like all students, are asked to draw on their lived experiences to relate to the readings and to create the writings involved in becoming a college student. Student veterans have demonstrated evidence of depression and anxiety, along with posttraumatic stress disorder. Some students have indicated a potential PTSD trigger could be something as simple as a slamming door, a book dropping, or a car outside the classroom backfiring. This means that the scope of potential triggers of mental illness or traumatic stress is simply unknown and unpredictable to us as instructors.

Just when Patrick was demonstrating an investment in the writing process, touching gently on the edges of his experiences in Iraq, he left school. He packed up his dorm room and vanished without indicating where he was going. He dropped out of all of his classes and never returned to campus. We were left wondering if a trigger warning or some sort of indication about the content of the literature we discuss would have made any difference at all. Perhaps having the time to mentally prepare to confront military stories within our literature would have helped. Or perhaps it would have led him to never come to class at all.

Reflections on Trigger Warnings in Relation to Military Students

These vignettes demonstrate some of the issues brought forth in the college English classroom related to teaching military veterans. While certainly not representative of all veterans, our experiences have led to serious consideration of trigger warnings as a means of assisting these students, specifically in regard to the unique nature of the college English classroom and the importance of personal discourse and literature based on real-life experiences. While some of the troubling experiences had by military veterans in our classrooms, like group dynamics, cannot be avoided, perhaps a statement about the purpose and function of the English classroom would suffice—that is, noting that the study of English, literature, and writing is best done when one can personally invest in the process and in that process of self-investigation and discovery, one will be called upon to relate meaningful life experiences. In addition, the experience of being a student in the English classroom is more than a passive activity; one must read, write, and discuss in order to be engaged. The trigger warning, therefore, must be broader than "We will read military-themed work"; it should be more like "We will delve into life itself within the pages of what we read and what we write, and some of it will be very ugly." In addition, students will be expected to relate to others throughout this experience in order to make it meaningful. While a trigger warning would certainly prime a student about military-related content, it could also prepare the student for the atmosphere of the English classroom. However, it seems impossible to capture the nature of the English classroom in a few syllabi-appropriate sentences. Perhaps the onus should lie on the instructor, the one who guides the classroom and can best help students study literature and writing. Rather than warn students about the discomfort that any student might feel when reading a novel or writing an essay, we should entrust the instructors to make the best decision regarding the students sitting within the classroom. If colleges are built with strong support systems outside the classroom, we should be able to believe that the instructional leaders will do their best within the classroom.

As we reflected on our shared experiences, one reality was clear—that many of our students who were former military members would drop out or disappear completely from campus without warning. While this cannot readily be attributed to our experiences with these students, and is not representative of all military students we have taught, we do think it is symptomatic of a larger problem in which these students simply could not find a way to fit into the mold of the college setting serving mostly traditional students. Perhaps the students were facing economic or health challenges that made attending classes impossible. Or maybe the red tape of tuition reimbursement or veterans benefits caused too much of a hurdle to proceed. However, as English teachers, we value diversity and particularly the diversity of experience. These students are valuable to our classrooms in that they bring perspective and life experiences that can teach others. When they disappear from campus, whether due to job demands, mental illness, or other issues, we struggle with their sudden absence.

As instructors, we advocate and appreciate academic freedom, but working with veterans who have served in the military has demonstrated that we are ill prepared to handle some of the traumatic experiences had by some of these students. While we do not want to discourage them from entering the English classroom through the broad use of trigger warnings to serve as deterrents, we do think it might be fair to provide a philosophical statement about how an English classroom differs from that of a math or science class and to openly share and invite the experiences of military students into the fray. The tone of the class should be one that values personal experience, including traumatic or deeply private events, in a safe and nurturing environment. In addition, it can help prepare non-military students to understand that the classroom is shared not by just others like them but also others who come from different walks of life, whose experience is to be shared and appreciated. One facet we reflect on often is not only our lack of preparation to deal with unexpected issues brought forth by military students but also their frustration with the lack of services available within the "system." Perhaps the teaching philosophy we share should also be paired with the available campus resources, should a student need those. Instead of the end result being credit hours earned or time spent in seats, it is important to value the investment of these students in literary processes that draw on highly personal events. If students are likely to quit school because we could not provide a supportive environment, have we really succeeded at teaching literature and writing? We are a piece of that puzzle and we can only hope that the English classroom provides not only a learning environment that is respectful of their service but also one that fosters personal growth and development. Our hope is that the invitation to participate in the English classroom will be accompanied by supportive classmates and a well-prepared instructor so that any student can confront issues within literature and writing in meaningful and constructive ways. Trigger warnings undermine the culture we are creating, but we can proactively describe the focus and processes of the English classroom in a way that supports student investment and participation.

Notes

1. National Conference of State Legislatures, "State and Community Roles in Supporting College Completion for Veterans," accessed September 12, 2016, http://www.ncsl.org/research/education/veterans-and-college.aspx.
2. Jim Burke, *The English Teacher's Companion: A Complete Guide to Classroom, Curriculum, and the Profession* (Portsmouth, NH: Heinemann, 2003), 390.

Bibliography

Burke, Jim. *The English Teacher's Companion: A Complete Guide to Classroom, Curriculum, and the Profession*. Portsmouth, NH: Heinemann, 2003.
National Conference of State Legislatures. "State and Community Roles in Supporting College Completion for Veterans." Accessed September 12, 2016. http://www.ncsl.org/research/education/veterans-and-college.aspx.

CHAPTER FIFTEEN

TRIGGER WARNINGS TO PROTECT LEARNING

A Case Study in Public Speaking

Kristina Ruiz-Mesa, Julie Matos, and Gregory Langner

In a public speaking course, student speeches can address a myriad of complex, troubling, and traumatic topics, such as homelessness, gang violence, sexual assault, and poverty. Public speaking students blend empirical research and personal experiences to inform or persuade an audience on a subject. When speaking to an audience, whether as an instructor or as a student, one must consider who an audience is and how a topic may impact audience members. With more than twenty million students currently enrolled in U.S. colleges and universities,[1] educators are faced with the challenge of training effective and ethical speakers from around the globe.

With the diversity of campus audiences, it is important to recognize the struggles, experiences, and resiliency of many in the student population. For example, within the California State University (CSU) educational system, many students have experienced high rates of poverty. An estimated 10 percent of students in the CSU system have been homeless and more than 20 percent are food insecure.[2] High rates of poverty, food insecurity, and mental illness, in addition to national sexual assault statistics where one in five women and one in sixteen men have experienced sexual assault while in college,[3] lead to classroom environments where many students have experienced trauma.

To help inoculate students against future trauma caused by exposure to violent images or recounting of painful experiences, trigger warnings are advisable in public speaking courses. Trigger warnings do not impede learning; rather, they provide an opportunity for students to protect their mental health and their ability to focus and learn in class.[4] By informing audience members about a speech topic before vivid details and images are shared by a speaker, audience members can brace themselves for potential trauma or choose to remove themselves from the audience. The following case study addresses how a trigger warning protected audience members and enhanced the learning of the student speaker who offered the trigger warning.

Case Study: Trigger Warnings and Guns

The following case study centers on a California university's general education public speaking course where students are required to present both an informative and persuasive speech. In preparation for both speeches, students are encouraged to pick speech topics that they have experience in and a passion for, and they are given freedom in their topic selection. While this freedom creates a classroom rich with diverse perspectives, it can also, at times, mean that students may want to speak on a subject that could (re)ignite trauma for other students in the class. In this case study, a trigger warning paired with instructor guidance allowed a student speaker to present a topic that he was passionate about while also ensuring that he remained sensitive to the audience's previous experiences and trauma that may impede both his message and audience learning.

In the weeks leading up to the informative speech, students were required to submit rough drafts of their outlines to the instructor for feedback on logic, organization, and grammar, as well as guidance in important areas of effective public speaking, such as audience analysis and ethical language. One student, who was also a U.S. military veteran, chose to inform the class about different types of firearms, including assault rifles. Upon review of the first draft of the speech outline, the instructor spoke to the student and expressed concern that the tone of the speech seemed to glorify guns and firearm usage. While the subject of firearms met the class requirement of being a topic that the student was passionate about and had experience with (through military service), the topic also had the potential of violating the safe public speaking space of the classroom.

Maintaining a safe and comfortable space for public speaking classrooms is vital to combating the fear of public speaking and communication apprehension students may experience in a public speaking course. For the university where this class took place, many in the student population reside in neighborhoods that have experienced gun violence and where students may have been a witness to and/or personally impacted by gun violence. Additionally, the institution has a large student population of U.S. military veterans and veteran dependents. The student population's potential experience with firearms and gun violence paired with the news of mass-shootings on U.S. college campuses caused the instructor some apprehension about the topic. It was the instructor's belief that presenting a speech on firearms in the way that the student had proposed in his first draft could prove problematic given the experiences of this particular student body and the current climate of gun violence on college campuses.

After reviewing the draft of the speech outline, the instructor asked the student to come to office hours to discuss the topic and ways of framing and presenting the speech. At the first meeting during office hours, the instructor commended the student for a well-researched and organized speech. The instructor and student spent time discussing the student's military background and how his military experience influenced his choice of topic and content. Additionally, the student and instructor discussed how assault rifles, and guns generally, might be negatively perceived by the student population as well as the larger campus community. The instructor posed open-ended questions to guide the student through the reflexive process of how this speech topic might impact his peers and audience members. Some of the questions asked by the instructor to the student during the office hours meeting included:

- What sparked your interest in this topic?

- What experiences do you think audience members may have had with guns?

- How do you think the audience will respond to this speech about guns?

- Do you think this speech might impact your ethos and/or credibility with the audience?

- How could this speech be modified to still focus on this topic that you have passion for and experience with but also consider the audience and their experiences with guns?

Time was spent reviewing key public speaking elements such as rhetorical sensitivity, being mindful and aware of audience perspectives and experiences, and how speakers can approach topics in ethical and responsible ways. Through thoughtful discussion and reflection with the instructor, the student demonstrated his care and respect for the class and his peers by modifying the speech.

Stemming from the student's care and concern for his classmates, the student speaker decided that the speech would be amended and would now focus on how to properly handle and respect firearms. This reframing of the speech allowed the class audience to focus on a subject that was important to the student speaker while also taking into consideration the current national climate and debates about gun ownership, assault rifles, incidents of mass shootings, and the possible negative experiences students in the class may have had with firearms and gun violence. The revised second draft of the speech maintained much of the same information about guns, but now focused on how firearms are used, misused, and how the student was taught, through his military experience, to handle firearms in combat situations. Upon review of the new draft, the instructor and student discussed incorporating a trigger warning at the beginning of the speech.

Adding a trigger warning was recommended by the instructor as a way to prepare students to learn about the topic or, if needed, to exit the classroom in a respectful way prior to the beginning of the speech. The trigger warning was incorporated into the attention getter in the opening of the speech. The speaker began the speech by sharing a personal story about his time in the military. He then let the audience know that his speech was going to focus on guns and gun usage, which could prove to be a traumatic topic for some audience members. He finished the trigger warning by issuing the following statement: "If this topic brings up trauma for you, please know that you may leave the room at this time. If after the speech you are experiencing distress about this topic, please visit the counseling and psychological services on campus located here or by calling this number." The student then projected a presentation slide with the location and phone number of the university's student health center. By issuing this trigger warning, the student speaker could gain goodwill with the audience by demonstrating concern for peers and by providing audience members with the opportunity to brace or remove themselves from the potential trigger. The opportunity for an audience member to leave the classroom prior to the speech prevents a situation where a student relives a traumatic experience and, thus, disrupts student learning. Further, because the instructor and student had spent time discussing the potential traumatic nature of guns for some students, the speaker continually acknowledged the audience's potential feelings toward guns and demonstrated an understanding of differing views on the topic, gaining a more favorable audience.

On the day of the speech, the student used the trigger warning and presented a solid, well-organized, and ethical speech on firearms. The speech received positive feedback from both the audience and the instructor. The use of a trigger warning paired with instructor guidance to consider audience experience and ethical language choices meant that this difficult topic did not need to be censored from the classroom. Instead, by acknowledging potentially traumatic experiences related to the topic, the student speaker was able to preserve the classroom environment where students and their experiences were engaged and valued.

Reflecting on Trigger Warnings and Censorship in Public Speaking Courses

In this case study, the student speaker presented on a controversial topic while maintaining a positive learning environment for all students. Unlike *censorship*, where students are restricted from speaking on controversial topics, *trigger warnings* are a pedagogical tool to facilitate discussions and presentations on difficult and complex subjects without damaging student learning. The use of trigger warnings in public speaking classrooms provides educators with an opportunity to teach students how to effectively engage an audience and respond to a speaking situation. By training speakers to reflect on their own social positions and experiences while considering the diverse experiences and perspectives of audience members about a topic, speakers can be better prepared to present a logical, organized, and ethical speech.

For instructors concerned with issues of voice, inclusion, and social justice, trigger warnings are a useful practice in public speaking classrooms. Seasoned public speaking educators have experienced moments where a student audience member bursts into tears, has an anxiety attack, and/or runs out of the classroom because of a graphic image or vivid description that dredges up a traumatic experience. In other classrooms, students may have felt unable to respond or retreat and were left harboring a reignited trauma that they carry with them. Negative classroom experiences where trauma is reignited are damaging to the learning environment, distract students, and can be emotionally taxing to both students and teachers. By discussing and implementing trigger warnings in public speaking courses, educators can model productive communication where ideas are expressed in a manner that is respectful of different experiences and that provides a space for dialogue.

The recent public rejection of trigger warnings and safe spaces by institutions such as the University of Chicago[5] suggest that academic freedom is jeopardized by the creation of classroom and campus environments where students have an indication of a potentially traumatic topic and the agency to leave a discussion or presentation where they feel unsafe. Educators committed to teaching effective public speaking where arguments and positions are researched, organized, and presented in strategically engaging, informative, and persuasive ways feel that the objective of trigger warnings is not to threaten academic freedom or to censor controversial topics, but rather to create a space where such topics can be discussed without reinjuring a student who has suffered a trauma related to the topic. Much like a content warning for nudity, profanity, or graphic images before a new blockbuster film does not change the story line or the enjoyment of the film, a trigger warning before a speech does not prohibit a student from speaking on a topic; it merely enhances the message by showing care for the audience so that all who are involved in the discussion are able to participate without the psychological noise stemming from fear of trauma.

Our primary job as educators is to create classroom learning environments where ideas can be shared, debated, and discussed in an arena where all experiences and identities are acknowledged and where differences are recognized and valued. Trigger warnings are a tool for educators to protect learning in the classroom and to respect that college students, as adults, have the right to remove themselves from situations that will cause them mental or emotional harm and that may impede their ability to learn. Using warnings about potential triggers for harm because of traumatic experience prepares students to be empathetic and reflexive communicators who have considered the potential experiences of their audience. The rights of the speaker to share ideas, the rights of the audience to listen to ideas, and the rights of the students to learn ideas are emblematic of freedom and agency and are best facilitated in learning environments free from fear and trauma.

Notes

1. National Center for Education Statistics, *Fast Facts*, report, 2015, accessed September 29, 2016, http://nces.ed.gov/fastfacts/display.asp?id=372.

2. Rashida Crutchfield, Keesha Clark, Sara Gamez, Aaron Green, Deidre Munson, and Hanna Stribling, *Serving Displaced and Food Insecure Students in the CSU*, California State University, Long Beach, January 2016, accessed September 29, 2016, https://presspage-production-content.s3.amazonaws.com/uploads/1487/cohomelessstudy.pdf?10000.

3. National Sexual Violence Resource Center, *Media Packet: Statistics about Sexual Violence*, 2015, accessed September 29, 2016, http://www.nsvrc.org/publications/nsvrc-publications-fact-sheets/media-packet-statistics-about-sexual-violence.

4. Kate Manne, "Why I Use Trigger Warnings," *New York Times*, September 19, 2015, accessed September 29, 2016, http://www.nytimes.com/2015/09/20/opinion/sunday/why-i-use-trigger-warnings.html?_r=0.

5. Richard Pérez-Peña, Mitch Smith, and Stephanie Saul, "University of Chicago Strikes Back against Campus Political Correctness," *New York Times*, August 26, 2016, accessed September 29, 2016, http://www.nytimes.com/2016/08/27/us/university-of-chicago-strikes-back-against-campus-political-correctness.html.

Bibliography

California State University. *Analytic Studies Reports*. Long Beach: California State University, July 21, 2016. Accessed September 29, 2016. http://www.calstate.edu/as/.

Crutchfield, Rashida, Keesha Clark, Sara Gamez, Aaron Green, Deidre Munson, and Hanna Stribling. *Serving Displaced and Food Insecure Students in the CSU*. Long Beach: California State University, January 2016. Accessed September 29, 2016. https://presspage-production-content.s3.amazonaws.com/uploads/1487/cohomelessstudy.pdf?10000.

Manne, Kate. "Why I Use Trigger Warnings." *New York Times*, September 19, 2015. Accessed September 29, 2016. http://www.nytimes.com/2015/09/20/opinion/sunday/why-i-use-trigger-warnings.html?_r=0.

National Center for Education Statistics. *Fast Facts*. Washington, DC: NCES, 2015. Accessed September 29, 2016. http://nces.ed.gov/fastfacts/display.asp?id=372.

National Sexual Violence Resource Center. *Media Packet: Statistics about Sexual Violence*. Enola, PA: NSVRC, 2015. Accessed September 29, 2016. http://www.nsvrc.org/publications/nsvrc-publications-fact-sheets/media-packet-statistics-about-sexual-violence.

Pérez-Peña, Richard, Mitch Smith, and Stephanie Saul. "University of Chicago Strikes Back against Campus Political Correctness." *New York Times*, August 26, 2016. Accessed September 29, 2016. http://www.nytimes.com/2016/08/27/us/university-of-chicago-strikes-back-against-campus-political-correctness.html.

CHAPTER SIXTEEN

TEACHING DISRUPTIVE LITERATURE IN PRECARIOUS TIMES

A Case Study from Library and Information Science

Davin L. Helkenberg

The text connects with the target reader in a manner which is provocative and enabling—perhaps even empowering. Although the experiences of the primary characters are more often than not intensified, dangerous, and magnified versions of the average teen reader's life, there is nonetheless a sense in which the knowledge acquired by the reader's vicarious experience becomes the source for transgressive and transformative possibilities.[1]

As advocates for reading, library and information science (LIS) researchers often frame the transformative and affective dimensions of reading within a positive framework: Stories can remind us of happy memories, they are fodder for our identities, they support us in times of need, and they help us to understand the world and our place in it in such a way that we become better, more complete individuals. But what happens when reading reminds us of our trauma? Are these relationships we have to a text and the influences they have after we close the cover any less powerful than their positive counterparts? This case study is based on my experiences teaching students about young adult (YA) literature during my tenure as a doctoral student at the University of Western Ontario, an institution where political economic tensions have been especially high in the last few years. Specifically, I draw upon a lesson I taught on "Mermaid in a Jar," a short story from critically acclaimed Toronto author Sheila Heti's first book *The Middle Stories*. This fantastical story, about a young girl[2] who keeps a mermaid as a pet, is a disquieting confrontation with intense emotional turmoil. Through this experience, this case study identifies and examines a unique scenario in regard to trigger warnings: where the rejection of trigger warnings can be justified when they have the potential to interfere with the pursuit of intellectual freedom—a core value of LIS—but the need to inform students of potentially re-traumatizing topics is overtly apparent when teaching on emotionally charged materials. This need cannot be ignored by instructors, but it is still necessary to critically examine the implications of and motivations for using warnings such as trigger warnings. To that end, this case study also considers how the current political economic climate of postsecondary institutions, especially the precarious positions of graduate students and adjunct faculty like myself, has contributed to a culture of fear, paranoia, and censorship that has obscured our understanding of the intended use of trigger warnings in our classrooms.

Disruptive Literature in Precarious Times

Young Adults, Disruptive Literature, and Emotion

I used "Mermaid in a Jar" as part of an introductory lesson on YA literature with a group of graduate LIS students.[3] As an introduction, the lesson I had planned was meant to disrupt any preconceived notions that many have about the behavior, identities, and interests of young adults. The lesson included a lecture component centered on the questions "What is a young adult?" and "What is young adult literature?" This introduced the students to the idea of young adulthood, or adolescence, as a culturally constructed concept[4] and built up young adults as mature, autonomous, dynamic beings that are often marginalized and pigeonholed based on limitations of age and stereotypes. While planning for this lesson, I thought about the first time I read "Mermaid in a Jar." I was new to studying YA literature and most of what I had read during my youth had been the quintessential formulaic YA stories of hearts and flowers, which left with me with the impression that YA literature was artless and weak. This is what I was reminded of when I read the first line of Sheila Heti's story: "I have a mermaid in a jar that Quilty bought me at a garage sale for twenty-five cents."[5] I was expecting it to be an easy, childish story about a pet mermaid, but immediately after the first line Heti writes, "The mermaid's all, 'I hate you I hate you I hate you,' but she's in a jar, and unless I loosen the top she's not coming out to kill me."[6] This sudden twist caught my excitement in a way I was not expecting, and as I continued to read I was increasingly struck by the rawness and intensity of the writing. It was dark and horrible, but I loved it. By the time I finished the story, totaling all of one page, my mind had a completely different conceptualization of what the boundaries of YA literature were.

Heti's story is a natural example to use as a gateway into questioning how we understand who young adults are and what YA literature is. Ideologically, Heti's story challenges dominant understandings of childhood by contrasting classic childhood fantasies and friendships with the harsh emotional realities of violent inner turmoil. The protagonist of the story lives in a magical feminine world, one where mermaids actually exist and she has her friends in for sleepovers at which they make prank calls and do séances. This could almost be a setting for a *Sweet Valley High* novel. But the images of the girl's pet mermaid show us a more horrifying reality, the mermaid is trapped in the jar and "swimming in the murky little pool of her own shit and vomit."[7] The girl will not let the mermaid out, and the violent relationship that ensues between them, a metaphor for the relationship the girl has with herself, is a powerful juxtaposition to what we have come to expect from stories about childhood fantasies. Heti's story is also an example of genuine suffering. Mary Hilton and Maria Nikolajeva note that, problematically, young adults are often portrayed as "lolling in front of televisions, behaving rowdily in public places, sulking in bedrooms, challenging parental and educational authority, appearing difficult, recalcitrant, contradictory, alienated, and troublesome."[8] However, "Mermaid in a Jar" goes beyond stereotypical teenage angst and is a candid reflection of a young girl's struggle with depression and self-loathing.

As an example of YA literature,[9] Heti's use of disturbing images and graphic language also challenges the boundaries of what is considered appropriate for young readers.

Since early examples of YA literature began to appear in the mid-twentieth century, the genre has risen to become one of the most controversial and contested bodies of literature in the history of library practice.[10] As Deborah Caldwell-Stone, the deputy director of the American Library Association's Office for Intellectual Freedom, has stated:

> The young adult section, in particular, is becoming a flashpoint in many local libraries. . . . This inclination to treat young adults as 5-year-olds

who are not capable of handling materials that are more sophisticated is a real problem we are seeing in many communities.[11]

Concerned parents, conservative groups, and even library staff have challenged what is considered (in)appropriate for young readers, resulting in restricted access to materials for youth on an institutional level.[12] This is in direct opposition to library advocacy for, and policy on, intellectual freedom. These groups are concerned with protecting the innocence and purity of children and youth from becoming tainted by "filth": profanity, violence, and sexual acts.[13] As educators Alleen Pace Nilsen and Kenneth Donelson explain in their book *Literature for Today's Young Adults*, "Censors often have a simplistic belief that there is an easily established and absolute relationship between books and deeds. A bad book, however defined, produces bad actions. What one reads, one immediately imitates."[14] Heti's story, at once awesomely beautiful and fitting the description of "filth" on a multitude of levels, has the power to disrupt narratives of young adults as naive and corruptible. For this reason, it was a valuable story to present to students as an introduction to YA literature.

In this context, it would be counterintuitive to teach a piece of controversial literature such as "Mermaid in a Jar" prefaced with a warning. As a pragmatic researcher, I believe that education for YA librarians requires a considerable amount of radical intervention, not only through teaching the long and continuing history of censorship but also by attempting to broaden the boundaries of what is considered culturally acceptable content for young adults. In light of this, I believe that trigger warnings, or any kind of warnings, targeting controversial themes have the potential to interfere with the core values of intellectual freedom upheld by my discipline. Even if it is not the intended purpose, trigger warnings can act to reinforce and exacerbate taboo subjects. This is mainly due to the fact that there is no clear consensus, even at the highest level of administration of universities,[15] about what trigger warnings are intended to accomplish. In general, the function of trigger warnings seems to have been debased to a point where they are now acting as content warnings in disguise. When acting more like content warnings, trigger warnings become directly linked to the issues, debates, and tensions surrounding censorship, the struggle to find consensus on where the line for a legitimate need to protect people from harm ends and unnecessary censorship begins. For instructors and librarians, this tension can be major source of fear and paranoia because they are the ones being asked to take on the responsibility of choosing to use/not use trigger warnings or to censor/not censor materials. They may then face the bulk of the reprimand when someone is affected or offended by their choices. These are the conditions under which self-censorship begins to manifest. For these reasons, I deliberately chose not to use trigger warnings in my classroom when teaching on YA literature. I wanted to start off on a strong note regarding intellectual freedom. My line of thought: How can you effectively normalize taboo subjects or empower future YA librarians to value and promote controversial literature if it comes prepackaged with a warning that labels it as potentially harmful?

In spite of my consideration of these factors, when I put the lesson on "Mermaid in a Jar" into practice it became clear to me that my effort to maintain my professional integrity regarding censorship and intellectual freedom proved to be too rigid when dealing with literature on sensitive topics. Research on reading tells us that it can be a highly affective process and often incites emotions directly related to past personal experiences.[16] Raymond Mar and colleagues have sought to review the multiple stages of emotion experienced when reading:

> Once having chosen a book, the narrative itself acts to evoke and transform emotions, both directly through the events and characters depicted and through the cueing of emotionally valenced memories. Once evoked by the story, these emotions can in turn influence a person's experience of the narrative. Lastly, emotions experienced during reading may have consequences after closing the covers of a book.[17]

In the name of promoting and valuing reading, reading studies usually focus on the positive emotional relationship we have to books: They entice us to relive happy memories, transformative moments, and meaningful relationships with others. But reading undoubtedly has the potential to elicit the negative memories, moments, and relationships in our lives as well.[18] In Bob Usherwood and Jackie Toyne's study of the impact of fiction on its readers, one participant demonstrates how deeply a reader can interact with a text: "I just get completely absorbed and I'm there and I'm involved and I'm feeling all of the emotions and everything else."[19]

DAVIN L. HELKENBERG

There are many different kinds of emotional responses readers can have to literature, and they include the *relived* and *remembered emotions*[20] that manifest from a reader's own life experiences. Responses such as these can be directly associated with the process of re-traumatization. What all of these reading studies reveal is that it is not the book alone that gives power to emotions, but the relationship between the book and the reader's life experiences. Janice Radway describes this as the interaction between text and context; reading is an *event* where readers construct the meaning of a text from "within a particular context and on the basis of a specific constellation of attitudes and beliefs."[21]

Some of the students that participated in the lesson where I taught "Mermaid in a Jar" seemed shocked or upset to a degree that I had not anticipated.[22] As we began to discuss the story, the students expressed a general distaste for it, the violence being a particular concern, and it was suggested to me that I could have provided a warning beforehand. My intent in using this story was not to excessively shock the students, but because the story was meant to be disruptive I had predicted a certain amount of pushback. I was confident that any unease about the graphic nature of the story could be settled through discussion. On that day, we used Aidan Chambers's "Critical Blueprint"[23] to structure the discussion in both understanding the story and evaluating it as a reading material for young adults. What was apparent by the end of the discussion was that although the students could recognize the value of the text in a disinterested way, they had very little personal tolerance for the violence and tone of the story.

Since no one came forward after the lesson, there is no way for me to know how deeply the students were affected by the story. Some of them may simply have been disenchanted, as I had expected. For others, particularity those with a history of violence or suicide in their lives, it may have affected them on a deeper level. Many of them may not even remember the story or the discussion now, but as a green and very replaceable instructor, the outcome of the lesson threw me into a state of panic. The request for an explicit warning is what concerned me the most. I became paranoid that I had inadvertently hurt someone by not introducing the content of the story with emotional well-being in mind. I feared that I had ruined my rapport with the students. This forced me to consider a potential use of trigger warnings in my future lessons to help avoid what

I perceived as a disaster. Facing this setback at such an early stage of my teaching career, I felt as though I should take a step back from rocking the boat and focus more on developing good relationships with students.

Precarious Times

For a new instructor like me, failed lessons, dissatisfied students, and the threat of negative evaluations are a frightening prospect in the current economic climate of higher education. My institution, the University of Western Ontario, can serve as an excellent microcosm for one of the major underlying sources of this anxiety, the corporatization and neoliberalization of the university. For the past few years, associations, unions, and student governments on campus have been taking action to counteract the effects of austerity measures that are in place at our university. These struggles came to a head simultaneously to when I started teaching lessons on YA literature. During this time, the Province of Ontario released their annual "Sunshine List,"[24] which disclosed that our university president, Dr. Amit Chakma, had made nearly $1,000,000 in 2014.[25] What ensued was campus-wide upheaval, generating outrage across faculty, staff, and students (dubbed #chakmagate). This extraordinary example of income disparity, and at a time when departments were being forced to make cutbacks, was what the president of the faculty association, Alison Hearn, labeled as "a slap in the face."[26] It called into question the priorities of our leadership and their dedication to the democratic principles that are supposed to be upheld by universities. Protests erupted across campus.

Graduate students were central figures in these protests. Student poverty is especially prevalent among graduate students and is only exacerbated by economic factors such as cutbacks on travel/conference funds, nonexistent overtime pay for teaching assistants, required payment of ancillary fees, lack of funding beyond fourth year, and fierce competition for external funding. I consider myself lucky to belong to the faculty of Information and Media Studies, a notoriously left-leaning faculty, that had a strong presence in the debates and protests during #chakmagate. However, economic challenges are especially salient in the humanities and social sciences and, even with the candid efforts of faculty like those in my department, very little headway has been made in improving these conditions. Part of this is because the money needed to support these programs, such as from major Canadian government grants, is often directed toward more impactful and marketable fields.[27] Nonetheless, despite this direction of funds to faculties such as science and engineering, all departments at this time are suffering from financial hardships on a day-to-day basis.[28] The pay scandal involving our university president was a tipping point for many, and through the events that continued over the following months it not only became clear just how unjust the system is but also that we appear to be nearly powerless against it.

Beyond the current struggles, what is now occupying the minds of graduate students is the routine reminder that all we have to look forward to is a future of precarious labor. Pessimism about job prospects is incredibly high among adjunct faculty in the province of Ontario[29] and this bleak hiring situation has trickled pessimism down into the thoughts of graduate students as well. Many PhD students have given up on the idea of a career in academia completely and the word *alt-ac*[30] has been floating down from the administration like a desperate promise. For instructors like me, keeping students happy seems now, more than ever, essential to our careers. For new PhDs dedicated to staying in academia, and the adjunct faculty already doomed to the rotation of four-month contracts year after year after year, "evidence of effective teaching" is required if one wants to dare to dream of tenure. For the most part, this refers to the quantitative portions of student evaluations. Incidentally, new research has found there is little evidence that students learn more from instructors with high(er) evaluation scores.[31] What this means is that student evaluations are basically meaningless customer-service instruments, and Bob Uttl, Carmela White, and Daniela Gonzalez have suggested that universities may want to drop student evaluations as evidence of effective teaching altogether.[32] Nevertheless, student complaints have considerable power over us, to the point where instructors may feel the need to act more like customer-service minions than experts on teaching and research. For example, I have often observed class averages and grade ranges being based on how many informal/formal grade appeals one can avoid instead of departmental policy. Until this customer-service attitude changes, many instructors are at the mercy of their students and how they rate them on a scale of likeability, not necessarily effective teaching. Which leads me to the question: What are we pandering to when we offer up "trigger warnings" for everything and anything that could be upsetting or offending to students—likeability or effective teaching?

Teaching under Uncertainty

All of these heated issues were at the forefront of my mind as I continued to teach lessons on young adult literature and to some degree they modified my instruction, politics, and interpersonal relationships with students. Around this time, I read the controversial *Vox* article entitled "I'm a Liberal Professor, and My Liberal Students Terrify Me"[33] written by Edward Schlosser,[34] which was one of the first in-writing accounts of a nontenured faculty member admitting to being afraid to challenge, and inadvertently upset, students because even just one complaint could get one fired. I also began to see a general trend in how closely (trigger) warnings were (are) being linked to student satisfaction and therefore directly related to career success. Combined with the negative experience I had teaching "Mermaid in a Jar," and the request that I use warnings, this put me in a further state of paranoid concern about my success as an instructor. As a new instructor not looking for any problems, it seemed considerably safer to modify my plans for future lessons than to risk a score of complaints from students if I upset them again.

These avoidance tactics are not unique to me alone. As Schlosser wrote in his article, "In this type of environment, boat-rocking isn't just dangerous, it's suicidal, and so teachers limit their lessons to things they know won't upset anybody."[35] Even experienced instructors and researchers well versed on the dangers of censorship can fall into this trap. I have seen an instructor censor sensitive, but nowhere near graphic, photographs from lecture slides because they might be "too much" for students to handle. I can understand why this happened. When you are catering to the satisfaction of what seems like increasingly entitled students, what may start off as a legitimate concern for students' welfare can easily become warped into paranoid concern. The big problem with this is that it undoubtedly has negative effects on teaching. As Alice Dreger, renowned scholar on academic freedom, has stated:

> Universities in which the majority of the faculty feel unsafe in terms of job security become places where *no one* feels safe to do anything that might risk upsetting someone. And that's a recipe for generally useless research as well as impoverished teaching.[36]

Anecdotally, a few weeks after the lesson on "Mermaid in a Jar" I taught another lesson on two short stories from Kathy Stinson's *101 Ways to Dance.*[37] This book was a significant part of my own introduction to YA literature and my understanding of the changing attitudes toward sexually explicit content written for young adults. I had originally planned to use only one story, which was about a young girl who questions her sexual orientation after she masturbates to the lesbian romance novel that is being passed from girl to girl at the Catholic high school she attends. As someone who studies sexuality, I am normally desensitized to the squeamishness that might come along with this kind of content. However, shortly before the lesson I became incredibly concerned that the content might offend the students. I could not bring myself to censor the story out of the lesson, but to protect myself from any backlash, I added another story from the book that was considerably less sexual but also less interesting and effective in the lesson. I then allowed the students to choose between them. When I presented the stories to them, I warned the students about the highly sexual content of the first story.

This was a disappointing moment for me as a researcher and instructor. I was well aware that by allowing the students to opt-out of a story that was neither violent nor emotionally intense I was bowing under fear. Moreover, the fact that I had given the students a *content warning* about the story was undermining my progressive, liberal librarian politics. To the credit of the students, most of them chose the story I had described to them as being highly sexual. They obviously did not care about the sexual content in the story, and I had the feeling the rest of the students chose the other story for the sake of variety. In this moment, I realized that I had been acting more in my own defense than through a concern for student well-being. I was then prompted to further consider in which situations it is necessary to provide students with a warning, trigger or otherwise. My use of Sheila Heti's "Mermaid in a Jar" was justifiable and valuable to future librarians, but based on the level of disturbing violence in the story I could have taken steps to reduce the potential for any re-traumatization. In this case, a trigger warning could be an appropriate step to take if the instructor feels it is necessary to inform students of the nature of the story. On the other hand, when I used the story from Kathy Stinson's book, none of the literature we discussed that day had enough violent or upsetting content that would reasonably justify a trigger warning. This particular story about female masturbation and homosexuality may have made some students feel uncomfortable or offended, but taking action to avoid these kinds of reactions was never the purpose or motivation behind trigger warnings.

Moving Forward with Trigger Warnings

Trigger warnings are put in place to prevent the re-traumatization of students who have experienced emotional trauma. They are not provided to prevent what Schlosser identifies as "a hint of discomfort"[38] for sensitive and paranoid students. Trigger warnings signify an empathetic relationship between instructor and student, where the instructor has considered the affective nature of the course content. What I think is important here is not the use of trigger warnings specifically but the empathetic relationship between instructor and student. I do not think a general attitude of care in the classroom is objectionable to most instructors, except for maybe philosopher Slavoj Žižek, who once said in an interview about students' personal issues: "I don't care. Kill yourself. It's not my problem."[39] Whether this is our problem or not needs to be made clear by informed policy, but because this decision is still largely made by instructors on an ad hoc basis I think it is best to suggest here that it is our problem. After my experience teaching sensitive topics and observing how affected students can be by literature, I see a need to consider my students and how they may respond to the content of the materials I choose to teach. However, I have not forgotten the need to maintain the integrity of my core values in tandem.

Moving forward, I think it is vital for there to be a greater emphasis placed on a *shared* responsibility between faculty and students in preventing instances of re-traumatization. Trigger warnings are a quick and easy way to communicate with students, but I do not think they should be required, and alternatives are possible. A simple alternative would be a blanket statement on a syllabus that: (1) informs students that some of the content of the course may deal with potentially re-traumatizing topics, (2) encourages students who have experienced emotional trauma to apply for accommodations through official channels, and (3) lets students know that the instructor is open to making accommodations. This would avoid targeting specific books and, if required on all syllabi at the institution, would avoid targeting whole courses as well. In addition, it would let every student on campus know the policy and procedures surrounding concerns for their mental well-being in regard to course content.

DAVIN L. HELKENBERG

Undoubtedly, many students already do take these types of precautions, but to take preventative action they need instructors to be explicit about the materials used in the course. Instructors should provide students with an exhaustive list of course topics, readings, and materials on the syllabus to allow students the time to review the course content privately and determine if there may be any issues. I have seen syllabi with no reading list, and as in the case of "Mermaid in a Jar," I used this story without the students' prior awareness that it would appear in the lesson. It is no wonder that in these types of situations students act defensively. Lastly, special arrangements can and should be made for students who have legitimate concerns about their mental well-being. This can no longer be done on an ad hoc basis; administrative support is imperative in assessing the legitimacy of mental health concerns and to what reasonable extent students can be accommodated.

Conclusion

It is an empathetic relationship between instructors and students—not necessarily trigger warnings—that is needed to create safe, inclusive, reciprocal classrooms. If used as intended, trigger warnings can be an effective practice toward fostering this environment. At the same time, instructors have a duty to protect intellectual freedom by questioning new pedagogies that appear to be censorial. It never hurts to remind students, and ourselves, that radical literature is meant to be challenging, not just on a political level but also on an emotional level. How better to make a text relevant than to draw upon our emotions? As Louise Rosenblatt similarly asks in *The Experience of Reading*, "Will the history of the Depression impress [the student] as much as will Steinbeck's *The Grapes of Wrath*?"[40] We should be openly acknowledging, and embracing, that powerful texts can be deeply affective. But in doing so we also need to carefully consider the experiences of others and what they bring to the reading of a text, the experiences that make reading a highly individual and unpredictable *event*.

On an ending note, I would like to emphasize that the current political economic climate affecting North American universities is a major underlying source of the anxiety and paranoia that is fueling contentions with trigger warnings. These battles are just beginning. The outcome of protests at the University of Western Ontario was disheartening to say the least. A year after #chakmagate, the university named "Hungry" Jack Cowin, fast-food mogul of Australia, as chancellor and the ceremonial figurehead of our institution. This action all but confirmed a blatant disregard for the heavy-hearted concerns both faculty and students have when considering the effects of the corporatization of universities. Alice Dreger raised a scary point in regard to the direction universities are taking when hiring faculty: "A workforce without job security is obedient and cheaper."[41] Universities need faculty willing to be whistleblowers, to teach controversial topics, and to entice radical change, but it is difficult to be bold, to be political, and to make change when you feel unsupported and entirely replaceable.

Notes

1. Georgie Horrell, "Transgression and Transition," in *Contemporary Adolescent Literature and Culture: The Emergent Adult*, edited by Mary Hilton and Maria Nikolajeva, 47 (Surrey, UK: Ashgate, 2012).

2. Presumed to be female but the gender is never disclosed.

3. I would like to acknowledge my supervisor Dr. Paulette Rothbauer's contribution to my lesson plan, as her teaching materials informed aspects of this module, including the use of this story.

4. Nancy Lesko, *Act Your Age: A Cultural Construction of Adolescence* (New York: Routledge, 2012); Mary Louise Adams, *The Trouble with Normal: Postwar Youth and the Making of Heterosexuality* (Toronto: University of Toronto Press, 1997).

5. Sheila Heti, "Mermaid in a Jar," in *The Middle Stories* (Toronto: Anansi, 2001), 19.

6. Heti, "Mermaid in a Jar," 19.

7. Ibid.

8. Mary Hilton and Maria Nikolajeva, introduction to *Contemporary Adolescent Literature and Culture: The Emergent Adult*, edited by Mary Hilton and Maria Nikolajeva, 1 (Surrey, UK: Ashgate, 2012).

9. *The Middle Stories* is not marketed as Young Adult but is considered a "cross-over" based on the relevance of themes, content, and characters to young adult readers.

10. American Library Association, "Top 100 Banned/Challenged Books: 2000–2009," accessed December 16, 2016, http://www.ala.org/bbooks/top-100-bannedchallenged-books-2000-2009; Alleen Pace Nilsen and Kenneth L. Donelson, *Literature for Today's Young Adults* (Boston: Pearson, 2009).

11. Anne-Marie Dorning, "Library Book Riles Small Wisconsin Town," *ABC News*, June 19, 2009, http://abcnews.go.com/US/story?id=7874866, quoted in Loretta M. Gaffney, "No Longer Safe: West Bend, Young Adult Literature, and Conservative Library Activism," *Library Trends* 62, no. 4 (2014): 731.

12. Anne Curry, "Where Is Judy Blume? Controversial Fiction for Older Young Adults," *Journal of Youth Services in Libraries* 14, no. 3 (2001): 28–37; Nilsen and Donelson, *Literature*; Gaffney, "No Longer Safe"; Emily Knox, *Book Banning in 21st-Century America* (Lanham, MD: Rowman & Littlefield, 2015).

13. American Library Association, "Statistics," accessed December 16, 2016, http://www.ala.org/bbooks/frequentlychallengedbooks/statistics.

14. Nilsen and Donelson, *Literature*, 396.

15. See, for example, the recent University of Chicago letter on trigger warnings: David Schaper, "University of Chicago Tells Freshman It Does Not Support 'Trigger Warnings,'" *NPR*, August 26, 2016, http://www.npr .org/2016/08/26/491531869/university-of-chicago-tells-freshmen-it-does-not -support-trigger-warnings.

16. Catherine S. Ross, "Finding without Seeking: The Information Encounter in the Context of Reading for Pleasure," *Information Processing & Management* 35, no. 6 (1999): 783–99; Bob Usherwood and Jackie Toyne, "The Value and Impact of Reading Imaginative Literature," *Journal of Librarianship and Information Science* 34, no. 1 (2002): 33–41; Lynne E. F. McKechnie, Catherine S. Ross, and Paulette Rothbauer, "Affective Dimensions of Information Seeking in the Context of Reading," in *Information and Emotion: The Emergent Affective Paradigm in Information Behaviour Research and Theory*, edited by Diane Nahl and Dania Bilal, 187–96 (Medford, NJ: Information Today, 2007); Raymond A. Mar, Keith Oatley, Maja Djikic, and Justin Mullin, "Emotion and Narrative Fiction: Interactive Influences before, during, and after Reading," *Cognition and Emotion* 25, no. 5 (2011): 818–33.

17. Mar et al., "Emotion and Narrative Fiction," 818.

18. Ibid., 819–20.

19. Usherwood and Toyne, "Value and Impact of Reading," 36.

20. Mar et al., "Emotion and Narrative Fiction," 824–25.

21. Janice Radway, "Women Read the Romance: The Interaction of Text and Context," *Feminist Studies* 9, no. 1 (1983): 55.

22. To protect the identity of individual students, comments reflect the general attitudes of the class.

23. Aidan Chambers, *Introducing Books to Children* (Boston: The Horn Book, 1983), 174–93.

24. The Ontario public sector salary disclosure that releases names, positions, and salaries of public sector employees that make more than $100,000 in a given tax year.

25. Ontario Government, "Public Sector Salary Disclosure Act: Disclosure 2014," accessed December 16, 2016, https://www.ontario.ca/page/public-sector -salary-disclosure-act-disclosures-2014.

26. *Canadian Association of University Teachers Bulletin*, "Western Pay Scandal Sparks Demands for Governance Changes," April 15, 2015, https://www. caut.ca/bulletin/articles/2015/04/western-pay-scandal-sparks-demands-for-gov ernance-changes.

27. Paul Barrett, "None of the Nearly 1 Billion Just Allocated by Canada First Research Excellence Fund Is Going to the Humanities. Why?" *TVO*, September 19, 2016, http://tvo.org/article/current-affairs/shared-values/none -of-the-nearly-1-billion-just-allocated-by-canadas-first-research-excellence-fund -is-going-to-the-humanities-why.

28. Paul Wells, "Canada's Everyday Researchers Still Starved for Funds," *Toronto Star*, September 7, 2016, https://www.thestar.com/news/canada/2016/ 09/07/canadas-everyday-science-researchers-still-starved-for-funds-paul-wells .html.

29. Cynthia C. Field and Glen A. Jones, *A Survey of Sessional Faculty in Ontario Publicly-Funded Universities*, report to the Ontario Ministry of Advanced Education and Skills Development, Toronto: University of Toronto, https:// www.oise.utoronto.ca/hec/UserFiles/File/Sessional_Faculty_-_OHCRIF_ Final_Report_-_July_2016.pdf.

30. Meaning alternative-academic, jobs that utilize the same skill sets gained during graduate studies but are not tenure-track research positions.

31. Bob Uttl, Carmela A. White, and Daniela W. Gonzalez, "Meta-Analysis of Faculty's Teaching Effectiveness: Student Evaluation of Teaching Ratings and Student Learning Are Not Related," *Studies in Educational Evaluation*, published electronically September 16, 2016, http://dx.doi.org.proxy1.lib.uwo .ca/10.1016/j.stueduc.2016.08.007.

32. Ibid., 19.

33. Edward Schlosser, "I'm a Liberal Professor, and My Liberal Students Terrify Me," *Vox*, June 3, 2015, http://www.vox.com/2015/6/3/8706323/college -professor-afraid.

34. A pseudonym used in the article to protect the author.

35. Schlosser, "I'm a Liberal Professor."

36. Alice Dreger, "Without Tenure, Professors Become Terrified Sheep," *Aeon*, September 27, 2016, https://aeon.co/ideas/without-tenure-academics-are -becoming-terrified-sheep.

37. Kathy Stinson, *101 Ways to Dance* (Toronto: Second Story Press, 2001).

38. Schlosser, "I'm a Liberal Professor."

39. Slavoj Žižek, "Interview with Slavoj Žižek—or Why He Hates Snow and Office Hours," YouTube video, 10:16, posted by *Global Art & Ideas Nexus*, May 17, 2014, https://www.youtube.com/watch?v=4rcG5mX6nB4.

40. Louise Michelle Rosenblatt, *The Experience of Reading* (Portsmouth, NH: Boynton/Cook, 1991), quoted in Usherwood and Toyne, "Value and Impact of Reading," 38.

41. Dreger, "Without Tenure."

Bibliography

Adams, Mary Louise. *The Trouble with Normal: Postwar Youth and the Making of Heterosexuality*. Toronto: University of Toronto Press, 1997.

American Library Association. "Statistics." Accessed December 16, 2016. http://www.ala.org/bbooks/frequentlychallengedbooks/statistics.

———. "Top 100 Banned/Challenged Books: 2000–2009." Accessed December 16, 2016. http://www.ala.org/bbooks/top-100-bannedchallenged-books-2000-2009.

Barrett, Paul. "None of the Nearly 1 Billion Just Allocated by Canada First Research Excellence Fund Is Going to the Humanities. Why?" *TVO*, September 19, 2016. http://tvo.org/article/current-affairs/shared-values/none-of-the-nearly-1-billion-just-allocated-by-canadas-first-research-excellence-fund-is-going-to-the-humanities-why.

Canadian Association of University Teachers Bulletin. "Western Pay Scandal Sparks Demands for Governance Changes." April 15, 2015. https://www.caut.ca/bulletin/articles/2015/04/western-pay-scandal-sparks-demands-for-governance-changes.

Chambers, Aidan. *Introducing Books to Children*. Boston: The Horn Book, 1983.

Curry, Anne. "Where Is Judy Blume? Controversial Fiction for Older Young Adults." *Journal of Youth Services in Libraries* 14, no. 3 (2001): 28–37.

Dorning, Anne-Marie, "Library Book Riles Small Wisconsin Town." *ABC News*, June 19, 2009. http://abcnews.go.com/US/story?id=7874866.

Dreger, Alice. "Without Tenure, Professors Become Terrified Sheep." *Aeon*, September 27, 2016. https://aeon.co/ideas/without-tenure-academics-are-becoming-terrified-sheep.

Field, Cynthia C., and Glen A. Jones. *A Survey of Sessional Faculty in Ontario Publicly-Funded Universities*. Report to the Ontario Ministry of Advanced Education and Skills Development. Toronto: University of Toronto, 2016. https://www.oise.utoronto.ca/hec/UserFiles/File/Sessional_Faculty_-_OHCRIF_Final_Report_-_July_2016.pdf.

Gaffney, Loretta M. "No Longer Safe: West Bend, Young Adult Literature, and Conservative Library Activism." *Library Trends* 62, no. 4 (2014): 730–39. http://muse.jhu.edu.proxy1.lib.uwo.ca/article/552024.

Heti, Sheila. "Mermaid in a Jar." In *The Middle Stories*. Toronto: Anansi, 2001.

Hilton, Mary, and Maria Nikolajeva. Introduction to *Contemporary Adolescent Literature and Culture: The Emergent Adult*, edited by Mary Hilton and Maria Nikolajeva, 1–16. Surrey, UK: Ashgate, 2012.

Horrell, Georgie. "Transgression and Transition." In *Contemporary Adolescent Literature and Culture: The Emergent Adult*, edited by Mary Hilton and Maria Nikolajeva, 47–60. Surrey, UK: Ashgate, 2012.

Knox, Emily. *Book Banning in 21st-Century America*. Lanham, MD: Rowman & Littlefield, 2015.

Lesko, Nancy. *Act Your Age: A Cultural Construction of Adolescence*. New York: Routledge, 2012.

Mar, Raymond A., Keith Oatley, Maja Djikic, and Justin Mullin. "Emotion and Narrative Fiction: Interactive Influences before, during, and after Reading." *Cognition and Emotion* 25, no. 5 (2011): 818–33.

McKechnie, Lynne E. F., Catherine S. Ross, and Paulette Rothbauer. "Affective Dimensions of Information Seeking in the Context of Reading." In *Information and Emotion: The Emergent Affective Paradigm in Information Behaviour Research and Theory*, edited by Diane Nahl and Dania Bilal, 187–96. Medford, NJ: Information Today, 2007.

Nilsen, Alleen Pace, and Kenneth L. Donelson. *Literature for Today's Young Adults*. Boston: Pearson, 2009.

Ontario Government. "Public Sector Salary Disclosure Act: Disclosure 2014." Accessed on December 16, 2016. https://www.ontario.ca/page/public-sector-salary-disclosure-act-disclosures-2014.

Radway, Janice A. "Women Read the Romance: The Interaction of Text and Context." *Feminist Studies* 9, no. 1 (1983): 53–78.

Rosenblatt, Louise Michelle. *The Experience of Reading*. Portsmouth, NH: Boynton/Cook, 1991.

Ross, Catherine S. "Finding without Seeking: The Information Encounter in the Context of Reading for Pleasure." *Information Processing & Management* 35, no. 6 (1999): 783–99.

Schaper, David. "University of Chicago Tells Freshman It Does Not Support 'Trigger Warnings.'" *NPR*, August 26, 2016. http://www.npr.org/2016/08/26/491531869/university-of-chicago-tells-freshmen-it-does-not-support-trigger-warnings.

Schlosser, Edward. "I'm a Liberal Professor, and My Liberal Students Terrify Me." *Vox*, June 3, 2015. http://www.vox.com/2015/6/3/8706323/college-professor-afraid.

Stinson, Kathy. *101 Ways to Dance.* Toronto: Second Story Press, 2006.

Usherwood, Bob, and Jackie Toyne. "The Value and Impact of Reading Imaginative Literature." *Journal of Librarianship and Information Science* 34, no. 1 (2002): 33–41.

Uttl, Bob, Carmela A. White, and Daniela W. Gonzalez. "Meta-Analysis of Faculty's Teaching Effectiveness: Student Evaluation of Teaching Ratings and Student Learning Are Not Related." *Studies in Educational Evaluation*, published electronically September 16, 2016. http://dx.doi.org.proxy1.lib.uwo.ca/10.1016/j.stueduc.2016.08.007.

Wells, Paul. "Canada's Everyday Researchers Still Starved for Funds." *Toronto Star*, September 7, 2016. https://www.thestar.com/news/canada/2016/09/07/canadas-everyday-science-researchers-still-starved-for-funds-paul-wells.html.

Žižek, Slavoj. "Interview with Slavoj Žižek—or Why He Hates Snow and Office Hours." YouTube video, 10:16. Posted by *Global Art & Ideas Nexus*, May 17, 2014. https://www.youtube.com/watch?v=4rcG5mX6nB4.

INDEX

AAUP. *See* American Association of University Professors

academia: Canadian, 73; First Amendment and, 62, 66; safe spaces in, 190; trigger warnings in, 12–13, 22, 56–58, 67n1, 80–81, 153–55, 161–62

academic freedom, 154

accessibility: accommodations and, 61, 169–70; PTSD and, 22, 33; trigger warnings in, 88–89, 92, 169–70

accommodations: accessibility and, 61, 169–70; for disabilities, 60–61; First Amendment and, 62–63; for gender, 62; harm and, 89; trigger warnings as, 61–63, 65–66, 97–98; women and, 63

ACRL. *See* Association of College and Research Libraries

activism: of feminists, 186; trigger warnings as, 93

ADA. *See* Americans with Disabilities Act

addiction model, for eating disorders, 41

The Aetiology of Hysteria, 8–9

Ahmed, Sara, 107

ALA. *See* American Library Association

American Association of University Professors (AAUP), 74, 81; on sexual assault, 134–36; on Title IX, 129; on trigger warnings, 123–24, 128–32, 134–39, 142–46, 154, 201

American Library Association (ALA), 132–33, 136–38

American Psychological Association, 7

Americans with Disabilities Act (ADA), 60–61, 95, 142; PTSD in, 128, 136

anorexia, 37, 43, 46, 57

anti-pornography research, 202–4

anxiety disorder, 170–73

Ao3, 11

Asif, Midhat, 213–14

Association of College and Research Libraries (ACRL), 124, 132, 135, 137, 142

avoidance, trigger warnings and, 30–31

Barbed Wire Disease, 5

Battiste, Marie, 76–77

Baylor University, 206

University of California at Berkeley, 126
University of Chicago, 13, 123, 154
University of Halifax, 82
University of Illinois at Urbana-Champaign, 142
University of Kentucky, 156–60
Usherwood, Bob, 243
Uttl, Bob, 246

veterans: PTSD of, 130, 221, 226–27; as students, 221–28; trigger warnings and, 221–22, 225–30; of Vietnam War, 6–7
Veterans Administration, 130
Veterans Affairs, 6
victimization: mental health and, 24–25; of survivors, 83; trauma and, 23–26; of women, 24
Vietnam War, 6–7
vindictive protectiveness, 38
Vingiano, Ali, 10–11
violence, 196; speech and, 180, 182–83; structural, 89, 103–4; students and, 167–68; symbolic, 93; systemic, 168–69, 171, 175. *See also* sexual violence
violent crimes, 24–26; trauma of, 28. *See also* sexual violence
vulnerability, 106–7

Wainwright, Emma, 214
Walker, Paul, 211
war, in literature, 225
Warner, Michael, 102
war neurosis, 4
Wasted (Hornbacher), 43
West, Lindy, 15

"We've Gone Too Far with 'Trigger Warnings'" (Filipovic), 75
White, Carmela A., 246
Williams, Wendy, 54–55, 58, 60, 63–67
Wolgast, Elizabeth, 54–55, 60–62, 66–67
women, 9–10; accommodations and, 63; black, 107; in culture/society, 63–65; Equal Protection Clause and, 58–59, 64; indigenous, 24, 72, 74, 79; PTSD in, 8–10; sexual violence and, 28–29, 82–83; transgender, 58; trauma and, 27, 55, 58, 66; trigger warnings for, 54–55, 57–58, 63, 66–67; victimization of, 24. *See also* feminism
women's liberation movement, 9
women's studies, 200–202
Wood, Julia T., 203
Woolf, Naomi, 45
World Health Organization, 10
World War I, 6
writers, 102–4
writing, 224–25
Wyatt, Wendy, 166–67, 170, 172, 174

YA. *See* young adult literature
Yergeau, Melanie, 103
young adult literature (YA), 239–41, 246–48; trigger warnings, 242–45

Ziering, Amy, 205
Zimmer, Robert, 154
zines, 109n3
Žižek, Slavoj, 249

ABOUT THE EDITOR AND CONTRIBUTORS

Emily J. M. Knox is an assistant professor in the School of Information Sciences at the University of Illinois at Urbana-Champaign. Her research interests include information access, intellectual freedom and censorship, information ethics, information policy, and the intersection of print culture and reading practices. Emily's book, *Book Banning in 21st-Century America*, was published by Rowman & Littlefield in 2015. It is the first monograph in the Beta Phi Mu Scholars Series. She received her PhD from the doctoral program at the Rutgers University School of Communication and Information. Her master's in library and information science is from the iSchool at Illinois. She also holds a BA in religious studies from Smith College and an AM in the same field from the University of Chicago Divinity School.

* * *

Sarah Colbert graduated in May 2016 with a master's degree in library and information science from the University of Missouri. She is interested in issues of intellectual freedom in both academia and public library settings, youth services, fandoms, and how to incorporate all of those things into librarianship. Sarah received a bachelor's degree in social science education in 2008, taught high school English in rural Missouri for five years, and worked as a barista at a global coffee chain for several months prior to pursuing her master's degree. When she is not studying or working, Sarah enjoys reading, crafting, and traveling.

* * *

Jordan Doll, a native of Cleveland, Ohio, graduated from Oberlin College with high honors in political science. Her academic interests include the U.S. Constitution's First and Fourteenth Amendment, gender under the law, and what has been called the hyper-political-correctness in modern higher education. In her free time, she likes writing creatively, playing Dragon Age Inquisition, and cooking. She lives in Chicago with her cat, Irene.

* * *

Brandi N. Frisby (PhD, 2010, West Virginia University) is an associate professor of instructional communication at the University of Kentucky. She studies faculty-student relationships and student learning and has published her work in *Communication Education, Computers and Education*, and the *Journal of Online Learning and Teaching*, among others.

* * *

Jane Gavin-Hebert, MA, MSW, works as a trauma therapist at Avalon Sexual Assault Centre and sessional faculty at the Dalhousie University School of Social Work. She holds graduate degrees in women and gender studies and social work. Jane lives in Halifax, Nova Scotia, with her daughter, Kayla, and dog, Lucy.

* * *

Stephanie Houston Grey is an associate professor of communication studies at Louisiana State University, Baton Rouge. Her scholarship explores the intersections of science, society, and culture, with emphases on food politics and environmentalism and the impacts of accelerating consumption on vulnerable populations and bodies. Her coauthored book *Rooted Resistance: The Rhetorical Struggle for Agrarian Place in Modern American Culture* is under contract with University of Arkansas Press, and her single-authored book *Live from the Sacrifice Zone: Citizen Resistance in Petro-Colonial Louisiana* is under contract with West Virginia University Press. Her chapter on eating disorder triggers extends a line of research that has included work on the pro-ana movement and its critics, as well as portrayals of eating disorders and obesity in popular culture. She is the editor of *Louisiana Speaks*, the journal of the Louisiana Communication Association and, as a local environmental activist, has written for Greenpeace and appeared frequently in the media. She is a resident of Covington, Louisiana.

* * *

Davin L. Helkenberg is a PhD candidate in the library and information science program at the University of Western Ontario. Her doctoral research examines fictional narratives of sexuality in young adult literature and explores, through in-depth interviews, how these narratives have informed the sexual lives of young women readers. Her research is also concerned with the role public libraries can play, as authoritative community sites, in supporting unfettered access to sexually explicit materials for youth—intended for both educational and recreational purposes. Davin's broader interests include research methodology for sensitive topics, creative writing, and the political economy of independent book publishing. She is originally from Surrey, British Columbia.

* * *

Pinky Hota is an assistant professor of anthropology and affiliated faculty with the Study of Women and Gender and the South Asia Concentration at Smith College. Her research and teaching focuses on minority politics, Indigenous recognition, and conservative politics in South Asia.

* * *

Barbara M. Jones devoted her career to academic librarianship, serving as director of four: Fashion Institute of Technology (State University of New York) in New York City; University of Northern Iowa in Cedar Falls; Union College in Schenectady, New York; and Wesleyan University in Middletown, Connecticut. She has published, written, spoken, and conducted workshops on freedom of expression around the world. Her last position was director of the Office for Intellectual Freedom and executive director of the Freedom to Read Foundation in Chicago. She was a James Scholar and received her BA with high honors and Phi Beta Kappa from the University of Illinois at Urbana-Champaign, her MLS with high honors at Columbia

University in New York, and her PhD in history from the University of Minnesota/Twin Cities. She continues to serve as a liaison/advisor to the FAIFE Committee of IFLA (Free Access to Information and Freedom of Expression of the International Federation of Library Associations). She is currently coauthoring a book on the topic of "information poverty" and serves on the library board of the Urbana (IL) Free Library.

* * *

Gregory Langner is the former assistant basic course director of oral communication for the Department of Communication Studies at California State University, Los Angeles. Cal State LA is also where he earned his master's in communication studies and bachelor's in theatre arts and dance. Langner is currently a PhD student in communication and performance studies at Louisiana State University. His research spans from critical pedagogy to popular media to religious rhetoric, each intersecting with identity performance. He has experience in curriculum building, implementation, and redesign and continues to develop practical classroom applications for pedagogical scholarship.

* * *

Kristine Leibhart, MA, is a member of the English department faculty at Mid-Plains Community College in North Platte, Nebraska. She has spent nearly two decades teaching high school and college-level English courses. At Mid-Plains, she specializes in teaching developmental and adult-level foundational English classes that help prepare today's students and nontraditional students, particularly those who have recently been active in the U.S. military.

* * *

Joe C. Martin is a faculty lecturer in instructional communication and research at the University of Kentucky. He earned his MDiv (2010) and his ThM (2012) from the Southern Baptist Theological Seminary and is currently pursuing a PhD in instructional communication at the University of Kentucky. His research interests include instructional communication, instructional technology, and the biology of human communication.

* * *

Julie Matos is the assistant basic course director of oral communication and a lecturer in the Communication Studies Department at California State University, Los Angeles. Matos received her BA and MA in communication studies from Cal State LA. Her research focuses primarily on the intersections of communication, gender, and women's rights. Outside of higher education, she has taught English as a second language in China and leadership and communication classes at charter schools in the Los Angeles area. At Cal State LA, Matos has worked closely with the basic course director to redesign the basic public speaking course, developed new learning materials and curricula, and served on the managing editing team for a custom public speaking textbook designed specifically for the student body at Cal State LA.

* * *

Jami McFarland is currently a second-year PhD student in the department of women's studies and feminist research at the University of Western Ontario. McFarland's PhD research focuses on representations of sexuality in later life, with a specific focus on the intersection of discourses on age, gender, sexuality, and ability. McFarland received her MA in women's studies at the University of Ottawa and her BA in English studies from Nipissing University. She has published articles on issues of sexuality, identity, and young adult fiction in the *Journal of Dracula Studies* and *Journal of Popular Romance Studies*. McFarland has broad-ranging research interests in queer representation, sexuality studies, media studies, feminist theory, critical disability studies, and fat studies.

* * *

Gretchen Oltman, JD, PhD, is an assistant professor of interdisciplinary studies at Creighton University in Omaha, Nebraska. She is a licensed attorney and certified English teacher with more than two decades of experience in education, including roles in teaching and administration. She is the author of *Violence in Student Writing: A Guide for School Administrators* and coauthor of *Law Meets Literature: A Novel Approach to the English Classroom*.

* * *

Kristina Ruiz-Mesa (PhD, University of Colorado, Boulder) is an assistant professor of communication studies and the basic course director of oral communication at California State University, Los Angeles. Prior to joining the Cal State LA faculty, Ruiz-Mesa, a New Jersey native, worked in diversity and retention at her alma mater, Villanova University in Pennsylvania. At Villanova, Ruiz-Mesa founded the St. Thomas of Villanova Scholars (STOVS) program, a residential academic bridge program designed to prepare underrepresented students for college success. Her previous research on the academic impact of experiencing racial microaggressions in higher education has been used to create programming and to improve support services for underrepresented students in programs around the United States. Currently, Ruiz-Mesa's research involves critical communication pedagogy, identity formation, and improving communicative practices for diversity, retention, and inclusion in U.S. institutions of higher education.

* * *

Susan Stearns is a professor of communication studies at Eastern Washington University. Her research interests include instructional design with a particular interest in increasing student learning by encouraging students' responsibility for their own learning. An unexpected and pleasant outcome of this research is the discovery that these instructional techniques have fostered student confidence and pride in their own educational development. Further areas of research include Erving Goffman's work on presentation of self—that is, impression management, conversational ploys and deception, and the concept of stigma.

* * *

Kari Storla is a PhD candidate in communication at the University of Southern California, where she teaches courses on public speaking and argumentation and advocacy. Her research focuses on the intersection of rhetoric, gender, social movements, and trauma. Specifically, she examines the shifting interactions between gender ideologies and anti-sexual-assault movements since the late nineteenth century. As one of the Teaching Assistant Fellows at the USC Center for Excellence in Teaching, Kari has trained new teaching assistants and designed workshops on a variety of pedagogical issues. She recently received USC's Award for Excellence in Teaching.

* * *

Holly Taylor is a feminist activist and scholar currently living in London, Ontario. She holds a master of arts degree in women's studies and feminist research from Western University and a bachelor of arts degree in political science and women's studies from Saint Mary's University. Her contribution to this book was inspired by experiences teaching and learning in university classrooms and working through nonprofit and grassroots advocacy with marginalized communities impacted by violence and trauma. Her academic interests include feminism, reproductive justice, sexuality studies, queer theory, sex work, and intersectionality.

* * *

Elizabeth Tolman is a professor in the Department of Communication Studies and Theatre at South Dakota State University. She teaches a variety of communication courses including interpersonal communication, communication theory, and communication and gender. She also serves as the women's and gender studies coordinator and enjoys organizing events and teaching introduction to women's studies. Her interests include service learning, online instruction, and communication and gender.

* * *

Bonnie Washick is a postdoctoral research associate in the Political Science and Gender and Women's Studies Departments at the University of Illinois. Her scholarly interests lie at the intersection of contemporary political theory, feminist thought and activism, and digital media studies. Her research explores how public speech practices affirm or challenge the ideal of an individuated, independent, sovereign democratic subject. She is particularly interested in the ways in which public speech addresses structural violence and vulnerability.